Teaching Writing with Latino/a Students

Teaching Writing with Latino/a Students

Lessons Learned at Hispanic-Serving Institutions

EDITED BY

Cristina Kirklighter,
Diana Cárdenas, and
Susan Wolff Murphy

Foreword by
Michelle Hall Kells

State University of New York Press

Published by
State University of New York Press, Albany

Printed in the United States of America

For information, contact State University of New York Press, Albany, NY
www.sunypress.edu

Production by Diane Ganeles
Marketing by Anne M. Valentine

Library of Congress Cataloging-in-Publication Data

Teaching writing with Latino/a students : lessons learned at Hispanic- serving
institutions / edited by Cristina Kirklighter, Diana Cárdenas, Susan Wolff Murphy.
p. cm.
Includes bibliographical references and index.
ISBN: 978-0-7914-7193-7 (alk. paper) — ISBN 978-0-7914-7194-4 (pbk. : alk. paper)
1. Hispanic American children—Education. 2. English language—Composition and
exercises—Study and teaching—United States. 3. Language arts—United States.
4. Education, Bilingual—United States. I. Kirklighter, Cristina. II. Cárdenas, Diana.
III. Murphy, Susan Wolff.

LC2672.4.T43 2007
808'.042071—dc22

2006037451

10 9 8 7 6 5 4 3 2 1

CONTENTS

FOREWORD: LESSONS LEARNED AT HISPANIC-SERVING INSTITUTIONS

Michelle Hall Kells

In the past ten years, composition studies has seen the growing representation of "frontline" teachers as well as nationally recognized scholars interrogating notions of academic discourse and approaches to writing instruction as these relate to historically unrepresented student groups. We have seen these changes taking place in various areas of research: basic writing (e.g., McNenny 2001); U.S. college composition and second-language writing (e.g., Horner and Trimbur 2002; Matsuda et al. 2006; Canagarajah 2006b); and global Englishes and nonstandard language varieties (e.g., Canagarajah 2002, 2006a; Nero 2006; Smitherman and Villanueva 2003). As a field, we have questioned the qualities of the academic discourses we value and wish to promote in undergraduate as well as graduate education (e.g., Schroeder et al. 2002). We have gained a growing recognition within composition studies as well as in affiliated areas, such as WAC (e.g., McLeod et al. 2001; Russell 2002; Thaiss and Zawacki 2006) and computer-mediated writing instruction (e.g., Selfe and Hawisher 2004; Hawisher and Selfe 2006), that literacy education for college students of the new millennium involves a broad range of discourses and engagement with diverse communities of practice—in and beyond English studies and in and beyond the university.

These realizations have complicated the scope of writing instruction and challenge us to enhance our visibility as literacy advocates in our communities. Doug Hesse asked in his 2005 CCCC keynote address, "Who owns writing?" (Hesse 2005). Clearly, we compositionists cannot stake exclusive claim to the domain of literacy education. Current intellectual shifts within the field help us resist intellectual provincialism and forge alliances across subareas (e.g., service learning, WAC, writing centers,

English as a second language (ESL), bilingual education, professional and technical writing) and across disciplines. Moreover, these changes bring into focus the valorization of essayist literacy, the myth of linguistic homogeneity, and the instability of alphabetic text, inviting us to consider a range of genres, linguistic codes, and symbol systems in print and digitized forms as appropriate avenues for intellectual work. Socially and politically, these shifts are beginning to destabilize intellectual elitism within the field and the entrenchment of a three-tier profession that privileges the point of view of research-university scholars over the perspectives of regional and two-year college professors. The changes in our profession also highlight the ever-expanding tertiary labor force comprised of lecturers, part-time instructors, and graduate teaching assistants who are doing the frontline work of literacy education in colleges and universities across the nation.

What appears disturbingly resistant to change is an enduring pattern of Latina and Latino underrepresentation in the front rows of higher education and professional leadership. In their introductions to *Rhetoric, the Polis, and the Global Village: Selected Papers from the 1998 Thirtieth Anniversary Rhetoric Society of America Conference*, C. Jan Swearingen and Jaime Mejía called attention to the gap in scholarship, and they openly called for more research in Latino/a rhetoric and writing (Swearingen and Pruett 1999). Nearly ten years later, we claim only a handful of voices focusing on Latino/a issues in the field of rhetoric and composition. Moreover, Hispanic-Serving Institutions (HSIs) are among the most underserved and underrecognized sites for teaching, research, and educational activism. While Hispanic populations represent the largest and fastest-growing minority group in the nation, the professional visibility and national prestige of HSIs have failed to keep pace. Nearly ten years ago, Valerie Balester, Victor Villanueva, and I responded to that gap by inviting front-row scholars to engage with regional college teachers in the examination of college writing instruction and "historically excluded" student populations (Kells and Balester 1999; Kells, Balester, and Villanueva 2004). It was a beginning. This volume represents another beginning.

What lessons have I learned teaching at HSIs? Since the first day I walked into the classroom at Texas A&M University-Kingsville[1] in 1993, I have come to understand the social practice Juan Guerra calls transcultural repositioning, "a rhetorical practice that mainstream dwellers who rarely venture outside the matrices of their own safe houses are not as likely to cultivate." Guerra describes transcultural repositioning as the communicative repertoire that members of a community "enact intuitively but must learn to self-consciously regulate, if they hope to move back and forth more productively between and among different languages and dialects, different social classes, different cultural and artistic forms, different ways of seeing and thinking about the increasingly fluid and hybridized world emerging around us" (Guerra 2004). Alacrity is everything.

After nearly fourteen years of shuttling between the diverse sociolinguistic contexts of HSIs, I have learned a number of life-changing lessons. Five are particularly relevant to this volume. First lesson: Our students arrive already embedded in complex discourse communities; their membership in different discourse communities is a dynamic (ever expanding and receding) process as students shift between the communities to which they already belong and those to which they seek to belong. Second lesson: Students bring an array of discursive resources and literacy practices variably conditioned by the cultural and intellectual communities of the academy. Agency in language does not begin and should not end in the college classroom. Third lesson: Writing programs, WAC, and writing centers should serve as advocates of literacy and language awareness for speakers of English as well as members of other ethnolinguistic communities present on and around campus. As literacy educators, we need to actively resist the multiple permutations of linguistic hegemony enacted within formal educational contexts. Fourth lesson: Teachers in WAC programs, writing classrooms, and writing centers serve an important role as cultural mediators between the academy, students, and their home languages as well as their target academic and professional discourse communities. We need to acknowledge, affirm, and apply the range of rhetorical resources available to Latino/a student writers through the use of different genres, media, linguistic codes, and audiences in our classrooms. Learning written American English for academic contexts should be an additive process, not subtractive. Fifth lesson: As a field, we should be establishing effective mentoring programs for Latino/a students in order to promote new scholars into PhD programs, job placements, publication opportunities, and tenured positions. Seeding a new generation of Latino/a scholars will demand nationwide MA and PhD program reform that pushes the boundaries of rhetoric and composition and builds partnerships with related disciplines such as history, sociology, linguistics, bilingual education, Spanish, and law, as well as border, urban, race, and ethnic studies. We need graduate programs reimagined and revisioned for the kind of work we are doing in HSIs.

It is all about belonging. South Texas Mexican American civil rights reformer, Dr. Héctor P. García, once reflected:

> Psychologically we Mexican Americans want to belong. In other words, I say this: we always want to end our days in somebody's arms. Is it our mother's arms, is it our wife's arms, is it our priest's or minister's arms,

> is it our children's arms, we want to be loved and to [be] taken in by someone. We Mexican Americans up to the time of 1960 were dejected people because we were rejected by everyone. In Mexico we were never accepted by the Mexicans, and here we were not accepted by the Texans. So since 1960 is the first instance that we feel that we are Americans. (Kells 2006)

García saw the presidential administrations of John F. Kennedy and Lyndon B. Johnson as critical historical moments for Latino/a populations, political shifts García ardently promoted through the mobilization of Spanish-speaking voters. What eventually evolved out of the mobilization of the Hispanic electorate in the 1960s was the institutionalization of a number of important federal initiatives: bilingual education, affirmative action, school desegregation, the Voting Rights Act, fair housing legislation, and the first national summit on Hispanic issues in 1967 at the historic El Paso Hearings. Forty years later, commercial marketing gurus and political campaign organizers recognize the collective economic and political power of Latino/a populations. And forty years later, we are witnessing pernicious political backlash through the reversal of many of the advances for which García so ardently rallied.

The current wave of immigration protests across the nation again reminds us that social criticism and change begin in the personal and collective acts of naming, articulating a condition, and reality. The rallies of over 1 million demonstrators in cities coalescing throughout the United States, asserting "*Somos América*" (we are America) and "*Si se puede*" (yes, we can), challenge us as educators to recognize and engage the discursive currents shaping this nation. The Americas (of which the United States is only one geopolitical facet) are and will continue to be deeply Latino/a identified. Declaring English the official national language will not erase that reality. Sealing the southern border will not erase that reality. Ignoring history will not erase that reality. *Latinidad* of the Americas is historically integral and culturally intrinsic to our New World identities, shaping our immigrant legacy for over 500 years.

Teaching in HSIs has made me conscious of two potent exigencies: first, the enduring impact of our colonial history (a durable source of oppression), played out in language attitudes and educational placement systems; and second, the dynamic heterogeneity within Latino/a communities, politically, economically, culturally, linguistically, and nationally (a dynamic source of generativity). Linguistic racism, not linguistic diversity, is the disabling fiction that inflects the process of learning to write in English classrooms (Kells 2002). Linguistic terrorism insidiously silences students in the classroom, workers in the field, and voters at the polls. The rich rhetorical and linguistic resources of Latino/a students too often remain unrecognized and unaffirmed, eluding the notice and appreciation of many English monolingual teachers and administrators preoccupied with the myth of a "monoglot standard" (Silverstein 1996). Literacy education is more than reading and writing a set of texts. It is a process of cultivating authority within and across social worlds.

When I was a new teaching assistant (TA) in Kingsville of developmental writing, one of my students, Javier, wrote a story "Life in the Barrio." It was a poignant description of growing up in the inner city of San Antonio. I told Javier that if he revised his essay for a public audience, I would FedEx it to Henry Cisneros in Washington, D.C. Cisneros was no longer mayor of San Antonio at the time but the newly appointed commissioner of the Department of Housing and Urban Development (HUD) in the Clinton administration. Javier did revise his essay. Three weeks later, the Department of English secretary came running down the hall with a phone message for me as I was on my way to class: the office of Henry Cisneros called to thank Javier for his essay. I passed the message to Javier and his eyes welled up with tears as the class applauded him. We all celebrated the possibilities of rhetorical action. Like the contributors in this collection who work with Latino/a students on a consistent basis and witness similar poignant breakthroughs in their writing classroom, I realized that teaching is, first and foremost, an exercise in advocacy.

I have been asked many times in the past fourteen years why I am such a strong advocate for Mexican American issues. One Aggie undergraduate once asked me in front of my General Linguistics lecture class of 130 students: "Why do you like Mexicans so much?" How does one answer a question like that? How does one defend the invisible threads of cultural identification? Several key moments in my past certainly shaped my politics and passions—growing up in the 1960s in the Sacramento and San Joaquin valleys during César Chávez's farm worker protests certainly impacted me. Perhaps it goes back even farther. My paternal grandparents lived in Mexico City when my father was a young man attending *universidad* in the late 1940s. He spoke fluent Spanish—an unusual trait for an Anglo man from California. I still wear my grandmother's luscious burgundy-red *rebozo*, a gift from *la senora*, a cherished neighbor from those early days in Mexico. Perhaps it has to do with love. When I was a child, my favorite uncle was Steve González. He was married to my blonde, blue-eyed aunt, my mother's baby sister. I spent my summers with them and their four children, coming to understand firsthand their poverty and ostracism from my huge Irish Catholic family. I learned that racism and hereditary privilege begin close to home. When I was a young woman, I named my son Jacob after Steve's father. And Spanish became my language of intimacy. Certainly my family history impacted me. But the lessons learned by my students at Texas A&M-Kingsville claimed and named me.[2] *Maestra.* They changed me and made me a teacher and a scholar. This is home for me.

This volume describes the intellectual contours and social texture shaping the academic "homes" of diverse teachers and their students. They describe and name their realities as teachers, scholars, and researchers from every corner of the United States—East Coast, West Coast, and both shores of the Gulf of Mexico. A number of their educational sites are two-year colleges, where these teachers carry a 4–4 or 5–5 course load in addition to engaging in an active research program. Most pursue their work without travel allowances, course releases, research leave, or tenure. Their homes have been homogeneously labeled "Hispanic-Serving Institutions," or HSIs (one more acronym to add to our list of labels parsing up students according to elusive categories of race and ethnolinguistic identity).

What this label disguises is the tremendous heterogeneity within these educational contexts. Some of their students speak Spanish. Many probably do not. Some vote Democrat, and many vote Republican. Many were raised Catholic, but not all. A number of them may have religious roots that extend to Judaism and Islam. Their racial/ethnic backgrounds are no less complex, often blending *un mestizaje* of indigenous, African, European, Caribbean, and Asian/Pacific Islander histories. Many sustain enduring transnational affiliations with family systems rooted in the Dominican Republic, Mexico, El Salvador, and other places. Some of these students call themselves Chicano, Chicana, Latino, Latina, Hispano, or Hispana, or perhaps Mexican American, Puerto Rican, or Cubano, Cubana. The convenient official cover term since the 1980s is "Hispanic." What this label risks is essentializing students who share a few historical traits: a linguistic connection to Spanish (past or present), a sociocultural link to Spain (recent or from generations long ago), and the legacy of colonization (as colonizer or colonized). What this term elides is even more elusive. The unifying bond we are privileged to share as teachers and students in HSIs is the intangible social fabric called *la cultura*, the connective tissue that identifies a people and defines the soul of belonging. It is transmitted by language, song, dance, food, story, art, architecture, medicine, religion—by some or all of these, but always by *el corazón.*

Teaching in HSIs reaffirms the need to protect open-access, open-admission education. In our corporatized, increasingly segregated social world—where trust fund babies go to Stanford, Cornell, and Columbia, while the less well-off take on a lifetime of debt for a chance to go to Texas A&M University-Kingsville, El Paso Community College, and the University of New Mexico—the democratization of higher education remains our greatest challenge. Education should not be a commodity, a vestige of hereditary privilege, but a gift we keep circulating.

Notes

1. Texas A&I University in Kingsville was established in 1925 and claims a long legacy of serving first-generation Mexican American college students. This institution established the first doctoral program in bilingual education in the nation and was a rich site for Chicano mobilization through the 1960s and 1970s. Texas A&I was adopted into the Texas A&M University system in 1989. Its official name became Texas A&M University-Kingsville in September 1993.

2. I extend my deepest appreciation to Juan Guerra, who has generously shared his research. Guerra's understanding of the cultural and social significance of the role of *maestro* and *maestra* in the *mexicano* home, as depicted in *Close to Home: Oral and Literate Practices in a Transnational Mexicano Community* (Guerra 1998), reminds us to keep sacred the bond of trust and respect between teacher and student. His encouragement and insight have inspired much of my work, including this foreword.

Works Cited

Canagarajah, A. Suresh. 2002. *Geopolitics of Academic Writing.* Pittsburgh: University of Pittsburgh Press.

———. 2006a. "The Place of World Englishes in Composition: Pluralization Continued." *CCC* 57:4 (June): 589–619.

———. 2006b. "Toward a Writing Pedagogy of Shuttling between Languages: Learning from Multilingual Writers." *College English* 68:6 (July): 589–603.

Guerra, Juan C. 1998. *Close to Home: Oral and Literate Practices in a Transnational Mexicano Community.* New York: Teachers College Press.

———. 2004. "Putting Literacy in Its Place: Nomadic Consciousness and the Practice of Transcultural Repositioning." In *Rebellious Reading: The Dynamics of Chicano/a Literacy,* ed. Carl Gutierrez-Jones, 19–37. Center for Chicana/o Studies, University of California at Santa Barbara.

Hawisher, Gail E., and Cynthia L. Selfe, with Yi-Huey Guo and Lu Liu. 2006. "Globalization and Agency: Designing and Redesigning the Literacies of Cyberspace." *College English* 68:6 (July): 619–36.

Hesse, Doug. 2005. "2005 CCCC Chair's Address: Who Owns Writing?" *CCC* 57:2 (December): 335–57.

Horner, Bruce, and John Trimbur. 2002. "English Only and U.S. College Composition." *CCC* 53:4 (June): 594–630.

Kells, Michelle Hall. 2002. "Linguistic Contact Zones in the College Writing Classroom: An Examination of Ethnolinguistic Identity and Language Attitudes." *Written Communication* 9:1 (January): 5–43.

———. 2006. *Héctor P. García: Everyday Rhetoric and Mexican American Civil Rights.* Carbondale: Southern Illinois University Press.

Kells, Michelle Hall, and Valerie Balester. 1999. *Attending to the Margins: Writing, Researching, and Teaching on the Front Lines.* Portsmouth, NH: Heinemann-Boynton/Cook.

Kells, Michelle Hall, Valerie Balester, and Victor Villanueva. 2004. *Latino/a Discourses: On Language, Literacy, and Identity*. Portsmouth, NH: Heinemann-Boynton/Cook.

Matsuda, Paul Kei. 2006a. "The Myth of Linguistic Homogeneity in U.S. College Composition." *College English* 68:6 (July): 637–50.

——— et al. 2006b. *Second-Language Writing in the Composition Classroom: A Critical Sourcebook*. Urbana, IL: National Council of Teachers of English.

McLeod, Susan, et al. 2001. *WAC for the New Millennium: Strategies for Continuing Writing-Across-the Curriculum Programs*. Urbana, IL: National Council of Teachers of English.

McNenny, Gerri, ed. 2001. *Mainstreaming Basic Writers: Politics and Pedagogies of Access*. Mahwah, NJ: Lawrence Erlbaum.

Nero, Shondel J., ed. 2006. *Dialects, Englishes, Creoles, and Education*. Mahwah, NJ: Lawrence Erlbaum.

Russell, David. 2002. *Writing in Academic Disciplines: A Curricular History*. 2nd ed. Carbondale: Southern Illinois University Press.

Schroeder, Christopher, Helen Fox, and Patricia Bizzell, eds. 2002. *ALT DIS: Alternative Discourses and the Academy*. Portsmouth, NH: Heinemann-Boynton/Cook.

Selfe, Cynthia, and Gail E. Hawisher, eds. 2004. *Literate Lives in the Information Age: Narratives on Literacy from the United States*. Mahwah, NJ: Lawrence Erlbaum.

Silverstein, Michael. 1996. "Monoglot 'Standard' in America: Standardization and Metaphors of Linguistic Hegemony." In *The Matrix of Language: Contemporary Linguistic Anthropology*, ed. Donald Brennis and Ronald K. S. Macaulay, 284–305. Boulder, CO: Westview Press.

Smitherman, Geneva, and Victor Villanueva, eds. 2003. *Language Diversity in the Classroom: From Intention to Practice*. Carbondale: Southern Illinois University Press.

Swearingen, C. Jan, and Dave Pruett, eds. 1999. *Rhetoric, the Polis, and the Global Village: Selected Papers from the 1998 Thirtieth Anniversary Rhetoric Society of America Conference*. Mahwah, NJ: Lawrence Erlbaum.

Thaiss, Chris, and Terry Myers Zawacki. 2006. *Engaged Writers and Dynamic Disciplines: Research on the Academic Writing Life*. Portsmouth, NH: Heinemann-Boynton/Cook.

ACKNOWLEDGMENTS

Many individuals helped make this book a reality, and we owe them a debt of gratitude. We first thank Larin McLaughlin, James Peltz, Diane Ganeles, and others at State University of New York Press for their strong endorsement of our project. We are proud to work with a press that has wholeheartedly supported research addressing racial and cultural issues in rhetoric and composition. We also acknowledge our colleague, Susan Loudermilk Garza, for the time and effort she put forth in the early and middle stages of this project. Her insights proved invaluable to us and the contributors. Our wonderful and dedicated Hispanic-Serving Institution contributors cannot go unnoticed—their meaningful chapter contributions and their patience and perseverance throughout these last three years have bolstered us. Throughout this process, we have made enduring friendships and collaborated on other scholarly endeavors.

We thank our university for funding our research assistants for two years through the Faculty Research Enhancement Grants. A special thank-you goes to Butch Cárdenas, our recent research assistant, for his help in researching, marketing, and editing the manuscript. We also thank our previous research assistants, Tito Cárdenas and Becky Andrews, for their assistance in the early stages of this manuscript. Our colleague, Sharon Talley, gave us a fresh set of editorial eyes when we needed it as we reviewed our writings.

Lastly, and most importantly, we pay tribute to our *familias* and dear friends. Cristina Kirklighter lovingly expresses her thanks to her daughter Madeline, who offered her help with our household during her mother's stressful days working on this project. She also thanks Andrew Piker for lending an ear during this process. Susan Wolff Murphy thanks her family, Tom, Sophia, Anna, and Elanor, for their sacrifices of time and attention. Diana Cárdenas thanks her brother Orlando and her sister Terry, who shared the responsibilities of caring for our father, Raul Torres.

INTRODUCTION

Cristina Kirklighter, Susan Wolff Murphy, and Diana Cárdenas

> *Students, and their professors, are going ahead and developing new ways of writing in the academy that make use of "their own" languages as well as the still-valuable resources of traditional academics.* (Schroeder, Fox, and Bizzell 2002, ix)

> *Rather than merely transplant theories into this space, we need to alter both our practice and theories using our students' particular cultural space as our mediator. In this new space we can try to avoid choosing either to teach academic discourse or value individual difference.* (Ramírez-Dhoore and Jones 2007, 2)

Times of demographic shift in our nation have created cultural challenges connected to identity and language. As sites of "cultural positioning," writing classrooms and, by extension, the programs and institutions that house those classrooms are microcosms that make visible these challenges. As Schroeder, Fox, and Bizzell (2002) and Ramírez-Dhoore and Jones (2007) point out, students and teachers, the inhabitants of these microcosms, must find ways to transform that space to adjust for difference, to change the culture more broadly. If these changes are not made, if these new languages, literacies, rhetorics, and ways of knowing and being are not embraced, then the writing classroom, as Horner (2006) has so astutely pointed out, remains complicit in the "tacit policy of monolingualism" that has scarred its history (569); more broadly, the writing classroom will remain ideologically, socially, culturally, and rhetorically "Standard American Edited English-Only"—no additions allowed.

A Brief History

By definition, Hispanic-Serving Institutions (HSIs) occupy a site of difference and educational activism. Deborah A. Santiago, Vice President for

Policy and Research at *Excelencia* in Education, presents a history of HSIs that reflects this claim. At a congressional hearing in 1983, Latino/a institutional leaders testified that Latino/a students faced the following challenges: (1) access to higher education, (2) completion of their degrees, and (3) attendance at institutions with limited funds (Santiago 2006, 6). After gathering evidence from these hearings, "Congressman Paul Simon introduced legislation" that advocated measures to recognize these challenges and address them (ibid.). The bill failed in 1984. However, institutional leaders from Texas and New Mexico decided that an academic organization was necessary to represent Latinos/as in higher education. The Hispanic Association of Colleges and Universities (HACU) formed in 1986, and "the term 'Hispanic-Serving Institution' was coined at the first HACU conference" (ibid.). In response to Texas community leaders who recognized these inequities in South Texas and border areas, the League of United Latin American Citizens (LULAC) sued the state of Texas in 1987, and the Mexican-American Legal Defense Education Fund (MALDEF) argued the case. Although it lost the lawsuit, it called attention to the state's neglect of its Latino/a residents by failing to furnish a first-class college system in South Texas. In 1989, Texas legislators created the South Texas Border Initiative, providing over $880 million to predominantly Latino/a institutions in Texas (2006, 7). Some of the contributors to this collection, including the editors, work or have worked at these predominantly Latino/a student-based Texas community colleges and universities. We are part of the history of HSIs, and our brief telling of this history pays homage to those who made it possible for us to effectively teach at HSIs in our region. Concerns regarding Latino/a students reached a national audience in 1989 when Representative Albert Bustamante (D-TX) introduced a bill to financially benefit HSIs across the nation. In 1994, President Clinton signed the executive order, Educational Excellence for Hispanic Americans, under the reauthorization of the Higher Education Act. This act officially recognized the government designation of HSIs. HSIs are "accredited, degree granting, public or private, non-profit colleges or universities with 25% or more total undergraduate full-time equivalent (FTE) Hispanic enrollment" (Laden 2004, 186).

Hispanic-Serving Institutions Today

In the United States and Puerto Rico there are 236 HSIs (Santiago 2006).[1] This number represents an increase since the period 1995–1996, when there were 131 institutions (Santiago 2006, 10). Over half of all Latinos/as are enrolled in California and Texas institutions alone, and almost 75 percent of Latinos/as are enrolled in five states: California, Texas, New York, Florida, and Illinois. Fifty percent of Latino/a students in higher education attend HSIs. Enrollment increased at HSIs by 14 percent from 1990 to 1999, and graduate student enrollment grew by 24 percent. Estimates of population growth reveal that the Latino/a population in this country will reach 25 percent of the population by 2050 (U.S. Census 2004), and increasing numbers of Latinos/as will attend two- or four-year colleges and universities in the future. Numbers show that in the fall of 2002, 1.7 million Latino/a students enrolled in degree-granting college programs. Furthermore, the Hispanic high school dropout rate in the period 1973–2003 declined from 34.3 percent to 23.5 percent among young Hispanic adults ages sixteen to twenty-four (National Center for Education Statistics 2006). Although this figure is still the highest among minorities, this decline points to the possibility of increased college enrollment of Latinos/as.

In the twelve years since President Clinton signed the order designating HSIs, social and political movements involving issues of immigration and a national language have resurfaced in the national consciousness and federal government policies. Educators at HSIs must address these issues that are inextricably linked to identity, access, opportunity, and social equity. According to Diana Natalicio, president of the University of Texas at El Paso, "To be an HSI is to be at the forefront of change in higher education because of the shift of demographics" (Brown and Santiago 2004, 21). Recently, HACU called for scholarship that will bring these institutions together to foster needed dialogues regarding these issues.

A Grassroots Movement

In her article Santiago states that the "defining characteristic of HSIs is their Hispanic enrollment, not their institutional mission" (2006, 3). Unlike historically black colleges (HBCs), which developed from the civil rights movement and whose primary mission revolved around serving African American students, HSIs are defined only through their Latino/a enrollment. In spite of this definition, however, readers will discover among our HSI composition scholars a deep commitment toward their students, evident in reflections on their philosophies and perspectives, examination of their practices, study of their engagements with students, and attention to their students' voices. This commitment helps shape HSIs to be much more than just places with 25 percent Latino/a enrollment. Instead, we can see that the personal mission of teachers at HSIs to promote meaningful learning experiences for Latino/a students constitutes what an HSI is, or ought to be. We hope that this collection can contribute to the growing conversation among compositionists and, more broadly, within institutions of higher education to achieve the dream represented by MALDEF, HACU, LULAC and others by helping to define an HSI mission—to educate all students, particularly Latino/a students.

Monolingual English Tradition

The first book to bring together HSI scholars from a particular discipline, this collection furthers the efforts to teach writing with Latino/a students. It follows in the footsteps of scholars who worked to counter the history of our discipline's role in English-only literacy instruction. Thanks to the detailed account by Bruce Horner and John Trimbur, "English Only and U.S. College Composition," we are well aware of the indictment against the English discipline as being complicit in creating "a sense of nationhood" at the exclusion of foreign languages in the quest for U.S. identity (2002, 607). We are certainly aware of the response to a monolingual pedagogy by scholars through the "Students' Right to Their Own Language" (CCCC 1974) and the National Language Policy (CCCC 1988) and decades of scholarship—by researchers and teachers such as Smitherman, Villanueva, Rose, Gilyard, Guerra, Kells, and Bizzell—devoted to the creation of a multilingual, transcultural pedagogy that addresses the needs of diverse populations.

However, we realize that much work is ahead. Smitherman and Richardson report that two thirds of the memberships of CCCC and NCTE, surveyed for their knowledge of the organizations' language policies, are not familiar with them (Smitherman 2003; Richardson 2003). Also, the renewed quest for national identity, cultural cohesion, and linguistic hegemony represents a challenge. Roseann Dueñas González notes that the official language movement and its ideologies and policies "are counterproductive to our work as educators and nation builders because [they devalue] the language and presence of minority persons in our society and in our most important societal institutions . . . [some being the schools and our classrooms]" (2003, xli). González's description mirrors what some of our authors, such as Isabel Baca and Dora Ramírez-Dhoore, personally experienced in their childhoods and adolescent years in school: The movement has reinforced a climate in which "accents and other forms of variety in linguistic expression, including syntactic, lexical, or rhetorical varieties, are discriminated against or overtly ostracized" (González 2000, xxxii).

The movement has prompted a special issue of *College English* (July 2006) designated to encourage a countermovement of teaching and research that addresses the negative effects of "English Only" efforts (Horner 2006, 569). Paul K. Matsuda states that the "myth of linguistic homogeneity—the assumption that college students are by default native speakers of a privileged variety of English—is seriously out of sync with the sociolinguistic reality of today's U.S. higher education as well as of U.S. society at large" (Matsuda 2006, 641). Bruce Horner articulates a contemporary concept of the composition classroom, promoted by Hawisher,

Selfe, Guo, and Liu: "[I]deologies, technologies, languages, and literacies form a complex, interdependent, cultural ecology of literacy both shaping and shaped by writers' literacy practices at the macro, medial, and micro levels" (Horner 2006, 570). This view of the composition classroom as a complex ecology invites those who teach growing numbers of multicultural and multilingual students to take a hard look at their work.

The Editors

As composition teachers working at Texas A&M University-Corpus Christi, we represent a diversity at various levels: geographic origins, cultural backgrounds, teaching experiences, and academic emphases. While our personal narratives represent our differences, we have found common ground in our commitment to provide opportunities for Latino/a and other underrepresented students.

Diana Cárdenas

In my seventeen years of teaching first-year writing at Del Mar College, our local community college, which enrolls a 51 percent Hispanic student population, I adopted and adapted many approaches to composition instruction to engage students—who demonstrated varying degrees of writing proficiency—in meaningful and empowering experiences. My desire to find connections to them academically and personally stems from my own background—born in northern Mexico and transplanted to Corpus Christi, Texas, as an eight-year-old girl—and the poignant middle school, high school, and college writing classroom experiences, which I record in my autobiographical essay.[2] My journey to develop English language literacies, with its insecurities and joys, influenced my search for an appropriate pedagogy; it continues to influence me today. In my upper-level composition courses at Texas A&M University-Corpus Christi, I engage students in service learning efforts that address local needs related to poverty and lack of access and opportunity in the most underserved areas of the community. These efforts help them place a human face on writing, and many of them invest personally, beyond a grade, in the effectiveness of their documents to improve the lives of others.

National figures (Canagarajah, Smitherman, Villanueva, Gilyard, Guerra) who promote a multilingual, transcultural democracy urge us to use linguistic, cultural, and pedagogical strategies to resist attitudes and practices that bind any individual or group. Like them, I am distressed about the language used to define who is, and who is not, entitled to access to education and opportunity. Reflecting on their work has helped me revision what I do in class. I am redefining learning, achievement, and citizenship by building on what students bring and engaging them in a critical examination of their individual and national identities. My aim is that they will help mold an America that allows all its people to develop their essence regardless of race, ethnicity, class, gender, and age.

Cristina Kirklighter

When I arrived at Texas A&M University-Corpus Christi, I was excited to begin working at an HSI given my interest in Latino/a issues in composition and literature. I thought that my familiarity with these issues as a result of my mother's Honduran background and my experience teaching students of Latino/a backgrounds in Florida would be enough to make for a smooth transition. I was wrong. South Texas is not Florida, and Mexican Americans are not Hondurans. Like many new faculty at HSIs, I did not know what an HSI stood for beyond the Latino/a enrollment of 25 percent definition, much less how the teaching of writing fits into this definition. I remember one day almost two years ago speaking to some of my colleagues about this issue. What prepares us in our composition area specifically to work and thrive at an HSI? Who are our HSI compositionists who work day in and day out with these populations of students, and what do they do to promote student success? In order to navigate the composition waters at an HSI, we needed answers to these pressing questions. We searched for HSI colleagues and developed this anthology project to bring their voices together. Fortunately, we found contributors dedicated to serving this diverse population of students and the innovative ways they use to promote student success.

Susan Wolff Murphy

As a white (non-Hispanic), first-generation college student, born and raised in the shadow of Stanford University in Palo Alto, California, I had little exposure to or knowledge of the issues facing Latino/a students in higher education until I became a graduate student.[3] As a master's student, I worked side by side with a young Chicana named Migdalia from California's central valley. Her family did not approve of her seeking a degree. She did not eat some days because she lived on her student worker wages and loans. At the same time she would confront her teachers in their offices when she felt she was not learning in their classes. Migdalia reminds me that I cannot patronize or stereotype students; I must respect their diversity, their challenges, and their passion for learning. When I accepted a position teaching basic writing at Texas A&M University-Corpus Christi, I encountered first-year nursing students from the Texas Rio Grande Valley and small rural towns who had not passed the standardized, high-stakes admission test (TASP). Some were in graduating classes of less than 100; some were seventeen-year-old students who were caring for dying grandparents or taking children to the emergency room in the middle of the night; many were students whose lives were filled with the demands of family, work, and school. I was unprepared in my graduate work or life history for these contexts, histories, and challenges. My coeditors and I see this volume as bringing together the voices of two-year and four-year HSI teachers who already have experience teaching this population to energize the conversation in composition about these regionally, culturally, and linguistically diverse and multifaceted students.

Our Collection

Our collection, made up of narratives, qualitative studies, and conversations that represent many years of teaching Latino/a students at HSIs, provides a variety of approaches to meet individual student needs as they connect to identity and heritage, language, and geographic region. It presents the experiences of teachers at two-year and four-year HSIs and validates their theoretical and pedagogical practices. Our eclectic voices and approaches signify the diverse complexities of our Latino/a students from many geographic areas. We are different, and we celebrate this difference out of respect for our students. We also are aware that this collection can capture only a small part of the good work being done at other HSIs and at all schools that enroll Latino/a and other non-white, nontraditional students.

Given that 53 percent of HSIs are two-year institutions (Reed 2003), a generous representation of scholars from community colleges is achieved in this collection. According to *Status and Trends in the Education of Hispanics*, "In 2000, Hispanic students accounted for 14 percent of the students enrolled in 2-year colleges and 7 percent of these in 4-year institutions" (NCES 2003, 1). These disproportionate percentages point to the strong need for collaborations between two-year and four-year HSI institutions in mentoring Latinos/as to pursue their education. Indeed, many Latino/a students who attend four-year institutions started out at community colleges. In fact, some of our most respected Latino/a scholars, such as Victor Villanueva and Cecilia Rodríguez Milanés, among others, have written about being mentored by community college teachers who encouraged them to pursue four-year degrees and beyond. According to D. G. Solorzona, "The origins of Hispanic doctoral recipients occur largely through the pipeline from two- to four-year HSIs into doctoral granting institutions" (Laden 2004). These particular students coming from the HSI pipelines and entering non-HSI doctoral institutions would benefit from our collection, finding validation and continuity to thrive in their programs.

Research regarding HSIs often presents Latino/a students as an at-risk population. Although some are indeed at risk, we also attempt to counter the stereotypes that are prevalent regarding HSIs: student underpreparedness, ESL difficulties, and resistance to education. Since experienced HSI teachers realize that they do not work with a homogenous group of students through their daily interactions, "a single teaching strategy is not appropriate for all Latino students, just as one instructional strategy cannot reach all white students" (Rolón 2003, 41). In these chapters, we do not seek consistency of one message; rather, we see the strength of this work in the diversity of approaches and theories used by our authors to address the issues central to those who teach Latino/a and other minority students. As a whole, this volume is a positive portrayal of Latino/a students and the generative teaching and learning outcomes that stem from an appreciation of difference, respect for diversity, honor for students' identities, promotion of students' right to their own language, and value for home literacies and languages.

Most HSIs are not Research I institutions; therefore, teachers at these insitutions work in colleges and universities where the scholarship of teaching is prevalent. Because we serve an underrepresented population in this country, HSI writing teachers follow an imperative to understand our students through informed research and reflection. Publishing and valuing the scholarship of teaching at and from these institutions is necessary to the creation and implementation of a critical pedagogy. We hope this collection will help inspire further HSI research in many areas of teaching and learning, even outside the discipline of English.

We would have liked submissions from Midwestern and Puerto Rican HSI teachers. Additionally, we are aware of specializations in composition studies and the broader field of the teaching of English that are not represented in this volume.

Part 1: Introductory Chapters

The chapters in Part 1 provide a complex introduction to the questions and issues within this conversation; the first examines writing pedagogy, while the second is a conversation focused on resources, politics, and cultures connected to two-year colleges. We begin the collection with these chapters so our readers will enter the conversation with a context for thinking about and discussing the teaching of writing at HSIs.

We open the collection with "Teaching Writing at Hispanic-Serving Institutions," by Beatrice Méndez Newman, a twenty-year professional of a four-year HSI in Texas. Méndez Newman claims that it is not the HSI student who needs specialized attention but the teaching practices, attitudes, and expectations that compositionists bring to the HSI classroom. Because writing reveals so much about the writer's ethnolinguistic, cultural, and academic identity, teaching writing at HSIs calls for a cultural and linguistic perceptiveness that allows the instructor to resist merging into what Michelle Hall Kells describes as "the linguistic hegemony that implicitly and explicitly shapes classroom practices" (2002, 7). Méndez Newman calls for new understandings, new pedagogies, and specialized training that can be learned from those who teach at HSIs.

Similarly, in their controversial conversation, "Teaching English in a California Two-Year Hispanic-Serving Institution: Complexities, Challenges, Programs, and Practices," Jody Millward, Sandra Starkey, and David Starkey, at two-year HSIs in California, critique the political, cultural, and budgetary issues that impact what occurs in the writing classroom and the resources committed to writing and access programs: "Two-year college students succeed *despite* the current system and not because of it." These community college teachers describe approaches that help students understand the multiple factors that affect their learning experiences and their performances. Bringing these contexts to light works against the stereotypical and preconceived notions of what faculty need to focus on at HSIs.

Part 2: We Are Not All the Same: Understanding Geographic and Cultural Differences at Hispanic-Serving Institutions

Part 2 focuses on differences of geography, culture and language. The authors here discuss the different practices of writing teachers at HSIs located in particular geographic areas who teach Latino/a populations with differing linguistic realities. By contrasting these four contributions, readers will begin to understand the linguistically, and thus educationally, diverse nature and needs of U.S. Latino/a students. Dora Ramírez-Dhoore and Rebecca Jones, in "Discovering a 'Proper Pedagogy': The Geography of Writing at the University of Texas-Pan American," and "Literate Practices/Language Practices: What Do We Really Know about Our Students?," by Isabel Araiza, Humberto Cárdenas, and Susan Loudermilk Garza, demonstrate how border universities, such as the University of Texas-Pan American, and more inland universities, such as Texas A&M University-Corpus Christi, located just a few hours from each other, are remarkably different in terms of student assimilation and matters of language diversity.

In contrast to many South Texas schools, "*Más allá del inglés*: A Bilingual Approach to College Composition," by Isis Artze-Vega, Elizabeth I. Doud, and Belkys Torres, demonstrates how faculty in Miami, with its Cuban American cultural and economic influences, are empowered to teach bilingual composition courses where Spanish can thrive alongside English. "*Un pie adentro y otro afuera*: Composition Instruction for Transnational Dominicans in Higher Education," by Sharon Utakis and Marianne Pita, teachers in the Northeast, illuminates how issues of transnationalism with the Dominican population create geographic disruptions of language, culture, and national loyalties that teachers of writing must address as they navigate these classrooms.

Part 3: Considerations for Creating Effective Writing Programs at Hispanic-Serving Institutions

Part 3 presents several contributions that describe how writing programs—featuring service learning, focused professional development activities, and bilingual, student-centered pedagogies—can work to meet the needs and missions of HSIs and their students. In "Building on the Richness of a South Texas Community: Revisioning a Technical and Professional Writing Program through Service Learning," Diana Cárdenas and Susan Loudermilk Garza examine how their technical writing program, dedicated to service learning, aligns with their university's commitment to community engagement. Technical writing students learn to invest in their predominantly Hispanic area by helping institutions fulfill their missions and making a difference.

In "It Is All in the Attitude—The Language Attitude," Isabel Baca describes how, in her ethnographic study of El Paso Community College's basic writing program, she discovers that valuing students' cultures and languages creates a safe learning environment for writing. Baca, who identifies with these students because of her similar geographic, cultural, and language background, describes the struggles she faced as a student. Her personal insights of identification add a dimension of autoethnography that enhances her study.

Barbara Jaffe's "Changing Perceptions, and Ultimately Practices, of Basic Writing Instructors through the *Familia* Approach" describes her role as an instructor in the *Puente* Project, a bridge program that has met with great success in California community colleges. Jaffe describes the training she conducts for community college teachers who want to improve composition instruction at HSIs by creating a positive environment that promotes collaborative responsibility and learning in the classroom and teacher training sessions. She depicts the impact the *familia* approach has upon community college teachers as they move through their training. She addresses what successful HSI programs can do to create a positive learning and teaching environment by valuing "*la familia.*"

Part 4: The Personal Narrative: Exploring Our Cultures as Hispanic-Serving Institution Students and Teachers

We end this collection with a more specific focus that addresses the importance of using the genre of personal narrative in classrooms.

In his chapter about using personal narratives at the University of New Mexico, "The Politics of Space and Narrative in the Multicultural Classroom," Robert J. Affeldt demonstrates that narrative can empower students to explore their cultural heritages. At HSIs, this approach is particularly important not just for students but for those who teach them as they gain insights into their diverse population of students.

Cathy Freeze, Dundee Lackey, Jennifer Anderson, Peter Cavazos, Rachel Eatmon-Hall, Misty Lynn García, Jennifer Nelson Reynolds, Sandra Valerio, Billy D. Watson, Elizabeth Worden, and Stacy Wyatt, members of a graduate Capstone course, with Cristina Kirklighter, wrote "Collaboratively Mentoring Our Identities As Readers, Writers, and Teachers: A Black Cuban, Black American's Impact on a South Texas Community." These authors demonstrate how Evelio Grillo, a black Cuban, black American memoirist, mentored South Texas graduate students to critique and reinforce their identities. They in turn mentored others within their communities. This collaboration between Grillo, a professor, high school teachers, graduate students, and high school students reveals how a well-coordinated literacy event can validate student experiences, provide real audiences for writing, generate opportunities for interinstitutional communication and partnership, and improve students' attitudes toward writing and reading.

Conclusion

We see this gathering of ideas as a celebration of the diversity of HSIs that makes us proud to serve our students. We hope that this collection will invite many other conversations, conferences, articles, and books to fulfill the promise created by the history of activism behind the label "Hispanic-Serving Institution" and thus to meet the needs of Latino/a students across the nation in all institutions of higher education. One day we hope to reflect and say, "We cannot imagine a time when this wealth of knowledge did not exist."

Notes

1. According to Santiago, the number of HSIs may fluctuate based on different criteria that serve specific purposes (2006, 8).

2. Diana Cárdenas, "Creating an Identity: Personal, Academic and Civic Literacies, " in *Latino/a Discourses: On Language, Identity, and Literacy Education*, ed. Michelle Hall Kells, Valerie Balester, and Victor Villanueva (Portsmouth, NH: Boynton/Cook, 2004), 114–25.

3. We are aware of the different capitalization patterns of the designations "Black" and "White" in style manuals. To conform to the Chicago style in our book, we used lowercase.

Works Cited

Brown, Sarita E., and Deborah Santiago. 2004. "Latino Students Gravitate toward HSIs." *Excelencia in Education, Inc. Hispanic Outlook* (December 27): www.edexcelencia.org/pdf/DECEMBER_2004.pdf.

CCCC. 1974. *Students' Right to Their Own Language.* Special issue of *CCC* 25: 1–32.

———. 1988. *The National Language Policy.* Urbana, IL: National Council of Teachers of English.

"Educational Excellence for Hispanic Americans." 1994. *Executive Order 12900. Presidential Documents. Federal Register* 59:37 (February 24). William J. Clinton.

"Facts on Hispanic Higher Education." 2004. *Hispanic Association of Colleges and Universities (HACU).* 1999–2000. (March 19). http://www.hacu.net.

González, Roseann Dueñas. 2006. *Introduction to Language Ideologies,* ed. Roseann Dueña Gonzáles and Ildikó Melis, xxvii–xlvii. Urbana, IL: National Council of Teachers of English.

Horner, Bruce. 2006. "Introduction: Cross Language Relations in Composition." Special issue of *College English* 68:6: 569–74.

Horner, Bruce, and John Trimbur. 2002. "English Only and U.S. College Composition." *College Composition and Communication* 53:4: 594–630.

Kells, Michelle Hall. 2002. "Linguistic Contact Zones in the College Writing Classroom: An Examination of Ethnolinguistic Identity and Language Attitudes." *Written Communication* 19:1: 5–42.

Laden, Berta Vigil. 2004. "Hispanic-Serving Institutions: What Are They? Where Are They?" *Community College Journal of Research and Practice* 28: 181–98.

Matsuda, Paul Kei. 2006. "The Myth of Linguistic Homogeneity in US College Composition." *College English* 68:6: 637–51.

National Center for Education Statistics. 2003. "Enrollment in Colleges & Universities." *Status and Trends in the Education of Hispanics.* NCES 2003-008. http://www.nces.ed.gv/pubs2003/hispanics/section12.asp.

———. 2006. "Dropout Rates in the United States: 2002 and 2003." NCES 2006-062. http://nces.ed.gov/pubs2006/dropout/.

Ramírez-Dhoore, Dora, and Rebecca Jones. 2007. "Discovering a 'Proper Pedagogy': The Geography of Writing at the University of Texas-Pan American." In *Teaching Writing with Latino/a Students: Lessons Learned at Hispanic-Serving Institutions.* Albany: State University of New York Press.

Reed, Shirley. 2003. Testimony. United States House of Representatives: House Committee on Education and the Workforce: Subcommittee on Select Education. Hearing on *"Expanding Opportunities in Higher Education: Honoring the Contributions of America's Hispanic-Serving Institutions."* (October 6). Edinburg, Texas.

Richardson, Elaine. 2003. "Race, Class(es), Gender, and Age: The Making of Knowledge about Language Diversity." In *Language Diversity in the Classroom: From Intention to Practice,* ed. Geneva Smitherman and Victor Villanueva, 40–66. Carbondale: Southern Illinois University Press.

Rolón, Carmen A. 2003. "Educating Latino Students." *Educational Leadership* 60:4 (January): 40–43.

Santiago, Deborah A. 2006. "Inventing Hispanic-Serving Institutions (HSIs): The Basics." *Excelencia in Education* (March). www.edexcelencia.org/pdf/Federal PolicyBrief.pdf.

Santiago, Deborah A., and Sarita Reyes. 2004. "Federal Policy and Latinos in Higher Education." *Pew Hispanic Center* (June): 1–16.

Schroeder, Christopher, Helen Fox, and Patricia Bizzell. 2002. "Preface." In *ALT DIS: Alternative Discourses and the Academy*, ed. Charles Schroeder, Helen Fox, and Patricia Bizzell, viii–x. Portsmouth, NH: Heinemann-Boynton/Cook.

Smitherman, Geneva. 2003. "The Historical Struggle for Language Rights in CCCC." In *Language Diversity in the Classroom: From Intention to Practice*, ed. Geneva Smitherman and Victor Villanueva, 7–39. Carbondale: Southern Illinois University Press.

U.S. Census Bureau. 2004. "U.S. Interim Projections by Age, Sex, Race, and Hispanic Origin." http://www.census.gov/ipc/www/usinterimproj/ (accessed March 18, 2004).

Part 1

Introductory Chapters

CHAPTER 1

TEACHING WRITING AT HISPANIC-SERVING INSTITUTIONS

Beatrice Méndez Newman

Compositionists with little or no experience at Hispanic-Serving Institutions (HSIs) quickly discover that traditional training in rhetoric and composition inadequately addresses the impact of many Hispanic students' sociocultural, socioeconomic, and ethnolinguistic makeup on performance in the writing class and on acculturation into the larger academic community. There are 242 institutions classified as HSIs—institutions at which Hispanic students constitute at least 25 percent of the student body. The most recent National Center for Education Statistics (NCES) figures show almost 600,000 students, or 42 percent, of the 1.3 million students enrolled at HSIs are Hispanic (Stearns and Watanabe 2002, 22–31). Statistics alone, however, do not even begin to prepare compositionists for an understanding of what an HSI composition classroom is like. Teaching writing at HSIs calls for cultural and linguistic perceptiveness that enables instructors to resist merging into what Michelle Hall Kells describes as "the linguistic hegemony that implicitly and explicitly shapes classroom practices" (2002, 7). New understandings, new pedagogies, and specialized training in rhetoric and composition are necessary to keep both faculty and students at HSIs from becoming casualties in the contact zone of the college composition classroom.

The Hispanic-Serving Institution Ambiance

What distinguishes the HSI composition classroom from the "typical" composition classroom? There are both obvious and unacknowledged differences. Hispanics are historically underrepresented in higher education; the graduation rate for Hispanic students is significantly lower than for white college students; many Hispanic students are first-generation college attenders and thus lack the familial support that propels the "typical" student toward college. Like many historically black colleges (HBCs), HSIs attract students whose access to higher education is limited by financial, sociological, academic, and cultural circumstances. Many of these students are underprepared for college. This reality is particularly stark at HSIs with Hispanic student enrollments over 50 percent, a total of 66 of the 242 HSIs (Stearns and Watanabe 2002, 32–36). When 25 percent to 90 percent of a composition classroom is made up of students whose backgrounds, academic preparation, and worldview are different from the hypothetical, typical college student, the classroom dynamics are significantly affected. Regardless of how student centered or apparently professionally prepared a compositionist is, teaching at an HSI requires adjustments of all sorts.

With an 87 percent Hispanic enrollment, my South Texas, "borderlands" institution, the University of Texas-Pan American, boasts one of the highest Hispanic student enrollments among four-year institutions in the country, and according to institutional data, we have the highest Hispanic enrollment among four-year institutions in Texas (UTPA Student Profile 2005).[1] The extent to which these demographics affect the composition environment can be partly understood through the reactions of instructors attempting to negotiate the HSI classroom experience. One of my colleagues, a white, thirty-something male, talks frequently about the experience of teaching in a composition classroom in which he is the only white person. Another white colleague, as he comes to the end of his first semester at this institution, laments that the students' lack of academic preparedness translates into hours of one-on-one conferencing, which cuts into his research and scholarship time, and he is beginning to feel considerable stress about meeting departmental and institutional expectations for tenure given the real-time demands of teaching. "No one told me how much time I would spend teaching here," he said. Other instructors, even those who have taught for years at this HSI, bombard their students with grammar drill sheets, hoping to get them to write "at least one correct sentence."

It is difficult not to rely on Freirean constructs in attempting to understand the HSI environment. There is, when the instructor is white, a profound *difference* between the teacher/authority figure and the learners. The impact of the white teacher on a class of mostly Hispanic students is one of the differences we do not discuss, one of the unacknowledged differences, because we have not really looked at the experience of being a Hispanic student or being a white teacher in a classroom of mostly Hispanic students. If education is viewed as a route toward empowerment and toward freedom from oppression (economic, social, political, or whatever other form in which oppression may be cast), it is difficult to ignore the anecdotal and statistical evidence that shows that at HSIs, the educator who functions in Freirean terms as "liberator" is white, while those being "liberated" from "oppression" are Hispanic. According to Stearns's and Watanabe's NCES report, of the 34,028 faculty members employed by all HSIs, 4,363 (only 12 percent) were Hispanic (2002, 66). A compositionist at an HSI does not have to be Hispanic to be effective in the writing classroom. However, awareness of Hispanic students' cultural and ethnolinguistic identities should figure prominently in the construction of the writing classroom community, regardless of the instructor's ethnicity. Freire advocates understanding the behavior, view of the world, and ethics of the "oppressed" in order for transformation of the environment/world to occur (1997, 36, 37). In the HSI composition classroom, this calls for sometimes extraordinary effort on the part of the instructor to infuse cultural understanding into pedagogy and curriculum.

It is, no doubt, somewhat extreme to view students as "the oppressed," but we are invoking Freirean terms and attitudes in our attempt to identify the difference between a "traditional" composition classroom and an HSI classroom. In her examination of the "postmodern" composition classroom, Xin Liu Gale proposes a complex paradigm for reconstructing and redefining the student-teacher relationship, interestingly relying on terminology that reflects Freirean pedagogy (edifying, emancipatory, enabling). Both Gale and Freire lead me to conclude that in effective teaching and learning pedagogical content is far less important than pedagogical attitudes. If an environment of trust and respect is not established in the classroom, little if any learning will occur. And in the HSI classroom, that trust and respect are fostered to a great extent by the instructors' understanding, exploration, and appreciation of the Hispanic culture.

Let me return to the difference between the HSI classroom and the "traditional" composition classroom. Many of the students who populate our HSI classrooms have not been raised with the expectation of attending college; in fact, in many traditional Hispanic families living in borderlands areas and urban areas with high Hispanic populations, college attendance is viewed as delaying one's entrance into the workforce. Thus when young people from such families attend college, they are, to some extent, inviting the criticism of their families because of the financial strain their college attendance causes. And there is little family "buy-in" into the students' college experience; necessarily, this creates conflict for the student: family expectations constantly conflict and compete with academic expectations, a conflict manifested as an apparent inability or unwillingness to attend class regularly, to complete assignments on time, and to participate wholeheartedly in the classroom experience. In effect, Hispanic students from strongly traditional families must negotiate two "contact zones": their own family environment and the institutional environment. The students' families interpret their attempts to acculturate into institutional success as rejection of family and culture, while instructors construe problematic composition classroom performance as an indicator of general academic inadequacy. Adapting the contact zone metaphor for this scenario (Pratt 1991), we recognize the discomfort Hispanic students must sense as they recognize that the demands of one authority (family) frequently contradict the demands of the academic authority.

Compositionists at HSIs should have some understanding of how cultural and familial expectations shape the Hispanic student's classroom experience. In traditional Hispanic families, young people are raised to unquestioningly accept authority figures, and this includes maintaining silence, refraining from questioning what the authority figure says, and accepting the "judgments" (grades) meted out by the teacher/authority figure in the classroom. In Freirean terms, this can result in "rebelliousness" manifested as students' apparent refusal to participate in class discussions, resistance to arranging office visits with an instructor to discuss a grade, failure to ask questions about assignments, and many other behaviors that easily erode student success. When I served as writing center director several years ago, I worked with Josué, a first-year student whose essays were consistently graded D and lower, by an aging white instructor, an error-hunter who graded only grammatical and mechanical aspects of his students' essays. When I urged Josué to arrange an office conference with his instructor, he refused, saying that he did not like to associate with people who "put him down." Josué may not speak for all HSI students, but his resistance to meeting with his instructor suggests that he felt "oppressed," that his instructor was "hinder[ing] his pursuit of self-affirmation" (Freire 1997, 37). At HSIs, instructors who do not aspire to understand students' worldviews, behaviors, and ethics can easily thwart students' efforts to succeed academically and might instead misinterpret certain student actions as academically self-destructive behavior.

In Their Own Voices: Hispanic-Serving Institution Students Talk about Education

Who exactly is the HSI student? Student voices are our best source for illuminating the obstacles, the circumstances, the cultural pull/drag, the fear of impending and historical educational failure that HSI students must negotiate to persist and succeed in their education (Newman

2000). I offer the comments of three students, in their own words and their own language, whose perspectives can help HSI compositionists understand how cultural conditioning impacts Hispanic students' college experiences:

> *Student 1/Voice 1*
> My father was raised in a ranch outside of Edinburg. He was raised with the view that education got you nowhere, but hard labor work is what made you succeed. Like his parents who cared nothing for school, my father dropped out of school in sixth grade and has worked all his life. Like many hardworking families, education was seen as a bother not a priority. Today it is early college preparation in junior high and high school that must be enforced to students. Who knows, maybe if my father was given the right road to education he would have been a successful business man than a 53-year-old disabled alcoholic.

> *Student 2/Voice 2*
> The majority of the population [at UTPA] are Hispanics, and most of them were brought up and taught that work is more important than education. A friend of mine works with HEB Food Stores, and his mother told him to quit school because he had a real future with HEB. I thought it was sad that a parent would tell their child to give up his education and found it even more disappointing that he actually obeyed. Students often fall into this category of wanting the money more than learning, not realizing they are only hurting themselves in the future.

> *Student 3/Voice 3*
> Being that I am Hispanic and female, the traditional values that were instilled in me as a child was finishing high school and getting married. My mother raised me with the same beliefs she was raised, which were that after you marry, you stay home and take care of your children. If your spouse wanted to reach for a higher education, it was okay because he was securing the home and hoping for a better future. Although women have come a long way in being equal in society, there are still those who think that high school education is enough and should not attend college, or drop out before they ever have a chance to experience it.

The voices of Hispanic students at HSIs point to a complexity of obstacles that I do not believe current rhetoric and composition training addresses or is even attuned to. "We know of the Latinos and Latinas in our classrooms," write Kells, Balester, and Villanueva (2004) in the introduction to *Latino/a Discourses: On Language, Identity, & Literacy Education.* "We know of their linguistic complexity, but we haven't yet found ways to translate this knowledge into classroom practices that aren't still founded on an assimilationist set of assumptions" (2). Linguistic complexity is only part of the HSI picture: teaching composition requires an almost supreme teaching effort on the part of compositionists as they superimpose awareness of the students' cultural conditioning on possibly all classroom interactions. And then there is the growing awareness that the HSI student will always simultaneously exist in two cultures: the culture of home and family and the culture of the academy, with the culture of family almost always trumping the culture of the academy. At HSIs like mine, where most students live about fifteen to thirty minutes away from the institution and commute to the university daily, it is hard not to recognize the pull of the students' family. In recent semesters, I have had a student who had to take care of his toddler siblings while his mother was in the hospital with serious gallbladder problems; a student who missed class to take her grandmother to a clinic for her flu shot; a student who had to drop the course because he had to drive his mother to work at the same time he was supposed to be in class; several students in every class whose grandparents died; one student who had helped her distraught parents make funeral arrangements when the parent's parent died; and several students with other relatives who died.

At HSIs such as UTPA, which draw their students from the surrounding area, students are going to be absent because of family "intrusions." For the most part, our students would prefer to be in class attending to their education, but when family responsibilities summon them, the pull of family cannot be outdone by the pull of educational responsibilities. This preference for family should never be construed as a lack of interest in academics. The Hispanic student at an HSI located within commuting distance of his or her home literally has no choice: family always comes first.

Teaching in the Hispanic-Serving Institution Composition Classroom

Many compositionists have pointed out the centrality of the composition classroom in the student's acculturation into the university and in the development of the student's academic voice (for example, Bartholomae 1985; Beauvais 2002; Trimbur 2000). Because of the highly interactive nature of our discipline and pedagogy, compositionists can play a key role in creating an environment that the student finds conducive to comfortable assimilation into the university culture. Writing about the longitudinal study of writing development among Harvard undergraduates of the class of 2001, Nancy Sommers and Laura Saltz use the term *threshold* to metaphorically describe the position freshmen find themselves in when they first enter the university: "The first year of college offers students the double perspective of the threshold, a liminal state from which they might leap forward—or linger at the door" (2004, 125). Those of us who work with Hispanic students at HSIs know that Sommers's and Saltz's metaphor powerfully reflects the experience of many our students who are not only underprepared when they arrive at our institutions but who then fail to find appropriate institutional support required for "reconstruction of academic self-confidence [that helps them] navigate the higher education setting" (Martinez 2003, 15). The composition classroom, potentially one of the most student-centered, social sites in the students' early academic experience, could figure prominently in the HSI student's decision to persist or drop out, to cross the "threshold" or to retreat from the institution.

Compositionists at HSIs can promote focal attitudes and strategies to create an environment that fosters personal, social, and academic success for the Hispanic student, that values the distinctiveness of the student's ethnolinguistic identity, and that does not degenerate into a contact zone with the student as a casualty.

1. Avoid the English as a second language (ESL) label.
2. Understand the writing of Hispanic-Serving Institution students.
3. Establish a community of learners.
4. Make yourself accessible.

Avoid the English as a Second Language Label

A common misconception among composition instructors, both newly arrived and long established, at HSIs is that the writing of Hispanic students is best described as the writing of ESL learners. This misconception invokes a multitude of misinformed attitudes about the writing of Hispanic students and about the place of Hispanic students in the institution. The ESL scenario implies that the students are "foreigners" linguistically and culturally in the academy.

Applying the ESL designation to students at HSIs is reductive and colonial. The ESL label implies that the student is relying predictably and consciously on competence in an established first language (L1) to achieve competence in a second language (L2). The "classic" ESL scenario involves a child born into a home where L1 is the parents' language and thereby the child's dominant language. Learning L2 optimally allows the L1 speaker to function socially and economically in L2 culture and society. Learning L2, in the ESL scenario, requires that the learner be competent in L1 so that L1 knowledge can be used as a sort of scaffolding for L2 learning (Fromkin, Rodman, and Hyams 2003, 378–79; Yule 1985, 150).

Anecdotal as well as demographic evidence shows that at HSIs, where the student body is drawn from an area in which the majority of the general population is Hispanic, most students do not fit this ESL speaker profile. While most Hispanic students at borderlands and urban HSIs possess some knowledge of Spanish, it tends to be primarily oral competence: they can converse more or less fluently in the variety of Spanish they speak, but for numerous socioethnic and demographic reasons, they are technically not literate in Spanish (Newman 2003, 45–46). Still, because of the ethnographic makeup of the region, for most Hispanics, such as myself, who have lived, gone to school, and worked in a borderlands area most of our lives, our *Latinidad*[2] is the most salient aspect of our identity. We do not think of ourselves as *ESL* speakers because we learned Spanish *informally* and *incompletely* in the environment of our homes and families while simultaneously learning formal, academic English at school. I say *informally* and *incompletely* as a means of distinguishing the language learning that occurs in classrooms: oral fluency gives the Spanish speaker of borderlands areas and urban areas with large Hispanic populations some intuitive knowledge of the language but not enough on which to base conscious learning in English. Thus many borderlands residents are *minimally* bilingual, and ironically, despite our *Latinidad,* we communicate in English—which under the classic ESL scenario would be our *second* language—far better than we do in Spanish, and this constitutes a reversal of the traditional ESL paradigm. Therefore, I believe we can safely and authoritatively assert that the pedagogical practices associated with ESL writing are inappropriate for the HSI writing classroom.

Understand the Writing of Hispanic-Serving Institution Students

Compositionists arriving at an HSI should know the range of writing competence they can expect in student writing. At one extreme, as the following first-year writing excerpt demonstrates, is the writer who needs significant guidance in appropriating the conventions of academic discourse but whose writing is *basic* (Shaughnessy 1977, 5–7) rather than ESL in designation:

> A Goal
>
> I have been over weight all my life. Sometimes I see my baby pictures and even than I was over weight.
>
> For many years I did not do anything about it. Until my senior year, by this point I weighted 180 pounds. I hated seeing that I was over weight by 40 pounds. I also realized that I needed to loss weight if I did not want to have problems in the future with my health.

> I started by eating less food. I used to eat up to five tortillas and serve myself twise; now I am eating less than three tortillas and serving myself only once. Sometimes I stoped eating breads. I also had my body used to eating more than three times a day. I new I had to cut that off but it was very hard. I have heard some doctors that came out in television said that breakfast was the most important meal of the day. Breakfast will help me digest the food I eated faster throughout the day; so I started eating breakfast and eat two more times afterwards, Lunch and dinner. I would eat dinner befor six o'clock so that my body would have time to digest the food I eat.

Because this essay is written by a Hispanic student at an HSI, some compositionists would automatically label it an ESL essay. There is, however, very little to mark this as an ESL essay; most of the errors are orthographic rather than phonological, and the simplistic syntactic style is typical of the insecure, basic writer.

The biggest mistake compositionists can make with a student such as this one is to mark every mistake and to overlook the important message conveyed by the essay. Ultimately, this is an essay about success: at the end, the writer says, "I still need to loss more weight but I feel lot better now that I have lost 25 pounds." Error analysis teaches us to look at the writer's achievements rather than at the shortcomings and to view "error" as evidence of the writer's growing competence (Bartholomae 1980; Shaughnessy 1977), an attitude that goes far in bolstering the student's self-confidence as a writer, promoting what Freire refers to as "pursuit of self-affirmation" (1997, 37). The assignment was to discuss a goal that had been met and to explain the strategies used to achieve the goal; the writer met the specifications of the assignment, so my comment was:

> Great essay. You've done a good job of explaining through well-chosen details how difficult it was to meet your goal. And you've done an excellent job of staying focused on your key point, that perseverance helped you meet your goal to lose weight. Before you write your next essay, please come by my office with your essay so we can talk about how to get rid of some of the language use problems in your writing.

HSI compositionists must dissociate themselves from expectations that student writing will be riddled with ESL errors, an attitude that ironically *frees* the typical composition instructor from responsibility for helping students improve their writing competence (ESL problems require expertise that the typical compositionist lacks, so this aspect of the students' writing could be perceived as being beyond the scope of the instructor's responsibilities). Above all, the compositionist at an HSI needs to learn to hear student voices and respond to the *message* rather than to what appears to be errors in the writing. When students realize that the message is as important as the form, they will work hard to eliminate the errors that interfere with the clear transmission of the message.

Those students at borderlands HSIs who have been educated in Mexican schools and have thus learned English in their Mexican classrooms *are* ESL students, but these are the exception rather than the rule in the HSI writing classroom. Their writing is true ESL writing, with syntactic, semantic, and phonological structures that show considerable reliance on L1 Spanish for construction of L2 texts (Newman 2003, 55–58). Such texts *appear* initially to be incomprehensible, as the following excerpt from an essay on the impact of tourism on the ecology of Mexican lakes, beaches, and forests demonstrates:

> The cause of not having a long-term plan of trash dumping was much pollution created a logical effect with all the trash that were placed in clandestine trash dumps that were contaminating the river and the fauna. Many animals got intoxicated by eating garbage putting in risk the preservation of the blue fish, bears, snakes, deers, and other kind of species. In consequence of that, the food chain was altered producing disequilibria reducing the humidity of the forest.

The typical HSI composition instructor is unlikely to encounter too many texts that look like this one. HSI students with language interference problems of the extent shown in this passage are keenly aware of their problems, and they rely on institutional resources, such as the writing center, to help them overcome these problems.

Having some knowledge of Spanish clearly helps in interpreting the student's message in such texts, but for instructors who are not bilingual, there are approaches that can keep such HSI students from feeling marginalized or misunderstood. I suggest not putting a grade on essays with this degree of L1 interference problems; instead, composition instructors could invite this student in for a conference. Instructors should ask students to orally convey the ideas and points they are attempting to make in their essays. With appropriate questions, the instructor can easily determine what the student is trying to get across through the written text. But there also should be a concerted effort on the instructor's part to warn the student about the problems of directly translating Spanish words into English. "Clandestine," "intoxicated," and "disequilibria" are direct translations of Spanish words, but in English, the denotations and connotations of these words are inappropriate for the context in which the student is using them.

Giving the student an opportunity to rewrite the essay after the conference will do much to bolster the student's sense of membership in the institution. We need to remember the vulnerability of writers, the way we are connected to the words we produce, the connection between who we are and what we write. As compositionists, we need to dignify the writing of our HSI students by recognizing that they are writers just as we are.

At the other end of the HSI writing spectrum is the student who has learned how to integrate his or her *Latinidad* into writing assignments. The following excerpt is from an essay written in response to Gary Soto's "The Jacket." Felipe, clearly a more competent writer than the other two students whose writing we have just examined, incorporates humor, rhetoric, Spanish expressions, and insights about adolescence to produce an essay that engages us rhetorically, aesthetically, and personally:

Red Baron with Yellow Teeth

> One day, *Apá* tells me "I have a surprise for you. You are going to help overhaul a car for a woman who is going to give us a real nice truck as payment." "WOW, a truck!"
>
> When I went with *Apá* to deliver the repaired car, I vainly searched for my truck. Anything resembling a vehicle was a stacked heap of metal . . . the dark green truck was on the losing side of a war with metal termites; huge canon holes spotted the truck while a bomb had damaged its right wing. I was afraid to inspect on top for fear of what I might find there. Two flat tires on one side tilted the truck as if a ship had just been torpedoed and was sinking into never-never land.
>
> After a few weeks of repair, [the truck] was ready. . . . School had started and *Apá* dropped me off at school in the gray-green jalopy. To avoid being seen by friends, I asked my father to drop me off near the playground. . . . He complied for awhile until one day he looks at me and asks "*Te da verguensa?*"
>
> One Saturday, *Apá* left early in the morning to "pay bills." I knew he would be gone the whole day wetting his whiskers at his favorite watering hole. *Amá* would be busy watching her *novelas,* so I was safe from her. After *Apá* left, I, the great Rembrandt ran to the *cuartito* to gather my supplies. I had gathered two gallons of fire engine red paint and one-half gallon of yellow. *Apá* had various sizes of paint brushes, rollers, and cans of thinner in the *cuartito.* I brushed and rolled the truck from top to bottom in red. I opted to paint the grill and hub cabs in yellow paint. When *Apá* arrived, he was too drunk to notice the truck while *Amá* just grinned and made no comment. In the morning, after eating his Sunday *menudo,* he walked out to the carport to get his tools for work on the house. He returned shaking his head and said nothing.
>
> The following Monday, *Apá* drove me to school in what I now thought of as "The Baron." I noticed people looking funny in our direction. They had huge grins on their faces and the older kids were laughing. Teachers that had never noticed me before smiled at me. I heard one kid ask another, "Who the hell paints a truck with paint brushes and rollers?"

> "Yeah, you can see the brush and roller lines from here. And, check out that yellow grill; that is so stupid! It looks like it has yellow teeth."
>
> To add to the humiliation, *Apá* decided to place an ugly metal pole on each corner and add a plywood roof to provide shade for fishing at the *arroyo* and the beach.
>
> My father kept the truck until I entered my sophomore year. Dad did not have to drop me off at school after entering seventh grade; the yellow school bus took over the work of humiliation. He finally got rid of the truck by giving it to his nephews in Matamoros after he bought a new, white Ford F150.

Though not a "perfect" essay, this text does show the writer's engagement with the topic and his awareness of the reader who will read the words. He takes risks, using Spanish words and phrases that he does not translate, revealing intimate information about his family, and trusting the reader to understand his teenage angst. Felipe, clearly striving to make an impression on his reader, is a confident user of language and rhetoric, an HSI student whose ethnicity figures prominently in the production of this text and who somewhere in his college experience developed the confidence to merge his ethnicity into his writing assignments.

Establish a Community of Learners

An important aspect of creating a community of learners is to foster an environment in which students feel comfortable talking, in which they do not just recede into the background because the instructor does not know they are there. So on the first day of class I have everyone complete statements designed to share something about their goals or interests, guaranteed to engage their classmates' attention and in some way relate to the content of the class. Typical statements are:

- Five years from now, I hope to be . . .
- When I have time and money, I hope to visit . . .
- My favorite place in the world is . . .
- The best thing I've ever written was . . .

I sit with my students in a circle, into which we have arranged the desks, and I complete my own statement as we try to get to know each other.

I use this exercise to take roll on the first day and to begin to learn students' names. As they introduce themselves prior to completing their sentences, I repeat their names and make annotations on my roll sheet about the pronunciation of their names and about their interests. A note about pronouncing names: making a concerted effort to learn the pronunciation of Hispanic students' names goes a long way toward creating a classroom community of learners. Hispanic students (and adults) are used to having their Hispanic names "mangled" by non-Hispanic instructors who are unable to manage the orthography and phonetics of Spanish names. When I encounter a particularly phonetically challenging name, I actually use phonetic symbols to remind me how to pronounce the name next time. And, I believe it is damaging to students' self-concept to have their Spanish names replaced by an Americanized nickname or translation to ease the instructor's management of the name.

For the first few weeks of the semester, I try to have some sort of socializing activity to build students' confidence in themselves as members of this classroom community and to reduce the shyness many of them feel about speaking out in class. On the day that their first assignment is due, a personal essay in which they discuss their goals for the semester, I give them about five minutes to select a short passage from their essays that they are willing to share with their classmates. Then they read this short passage orally. This could be a very intimidating exercise, but I make sure that I respond warmly and attentively to their statements, and when appropriate, I provide details on how our class will help them meet their goals. Throughout the first few weeks of the semester while we are getting to know each other, I remind students of the importance of their voices, telling them that my voice should not be the primary voice in the classroom, that I will learn from them as much as they will learn from me. I also tell them that I love walking into a classroom where the students are buzzing in conversation, a situation that can occur only if a community of learners has been established. Here is what one of my students had to say about the impact of this community environment on her growth as a student:

> The fact that I managed to make friends with some of the other students helped a great deal in how I came to view the English 1302 class. No longer was there the dread of going to class like in some other subjects but a certain expectancy to meet with the other students so that we could talk about the previous assignments, or to just pass ideas around about what we were going to write about on our next assignments. The fact that we talked about our essay grades and noticed one another's improvements is another reason I enjoyed this class so much.

Beyond the initial "getting to know each other" activities, instructors should welcome the expression of responses to texts, to topics of discussion, and to other students' comments. If students have a pet peeve about the way instructors conduct discussions in classrooms, then it is probably the mixed messages sent when an instructor asks for students' opinions about a text or topic and then proceeds to tell the students that their opinions are wrong. My students tell me that when they are told that their *opinions* are wrong, they almost never speak up in class again.

knowledge (Clark 2001, 33; Gale 1996, 2). In extreme applications, however, a writing conference that follows a nondirective format can be frustrating for students, particularly those whose competence in written English is limited. I have pointed out elsewhere that Hispanic students who are brought up to respect the authority and knowledge of the teacher or professor or tutor have difficulty engaging in nondirective tutoring, and they end up feeling that the professor, whom they have approached for answers, is instead *withholding* knowledge and information from them (Newman 2003, 58).

I use an aggressively *directive* approach in my conferencing. My student and I sit in front of my computer screen looking at the text he or she has brought in. I am very careful to treat each student as a dignified writer. First I read the whole text without doing anything other than making phatic comments to make sure my student knows I am engaged in the text ("Hmmm. . . . Wow. . . . This is a great example of a compound/complex structure. . . . Did you mean this in an ironic sense, because if you did, it's rhetorically powerful"). Then I paraphrase major sections of the text to show my student that I am paying attention and understand what he or she is saying. When there are obvious problems likely to interfere with understanding, I *explain* the error, ask the writer if she or he understands the cause of the error, and then show the writer how to correct it. Since I am sitting at the keyboard, I move over and have the student make whatever changes he or she wants to record. As I see areas that need specific attention, I ask the writer if it is okay if I embed in the text suggestions for improvements. I highlight these comments to distinguish them from the student's own writing. At the end of the conference, I save the conference text as a different file on the student's disk to preserve the integrity of the original text.

I suspect that most instructors would find this approach to conferencing too intrusive. It is far more time consuming than the nondirective conference that usually begins with "Do you have any questions?" or that has the instructor focusing on errors and ultimately making the writer feel incompetent and reluctant to come back for more conferencing. I want my students to think of themselves as writers, but if I do not treat them as writers, they will always see themselves in the position of supplicants, of students who want to do only what the professor wants so that they can pass. To encourage them to see themselves as writers, I identify the rhetorical strategies I see in their writing; I point out particularly effective syntactic structures; I praise them for integrating sophisticated vocabulary into their texts; I ask questions about the ideas they are posing, not to point to weaknesses but to show that I am engaged as a reader. Only after I have responded as a *reader* do I respond as a teacher and editor. And, probably because of my writing center director background, I never mark on a student's papers during our conferences; instead, when we need to deal with a problematic structure, I hand the student a highlighter and a pen to annotate the target structure for later correction.

Although I use a directive approach in my conferencing, the outcome seems to be development of independence and confidence in the writer, as Olivia's comment shows:

> "No more writing assignments!" That is what I used to say to myself in the past, because I really hated writing. I dreaded having to sit and think, and think, and think of what to write. To me, it was the hardest thing ever, but not anymore. This semester I have learned the skills I need to be a better writer; I have gotten better grades than ever; I have accomplished all the goals I set for myself, and because of it I know that I will continue to improve as a writer for the rest of my academic career.

For Olivia, the first-year writing class is a stepping-stone to success in the rest of her academic life. This realization came about, in part, I believe, because of the effort I exerted in guiding my students to learn their strengths in writing, to see their weaknesses as surmountable problems, and to help them find their voices as writers.

Conclusion

Compositionists arriving at one of the 242 HSIs in the United States should not have to spend the first few years of their teaching experience figuring out how to teach Hispanic students and how to adapt their pedagogies to the cultural, socioeconomic, and ethnolinguistic features that so richly color the experiences and writing of Hispanic college students. Compositionists at HSIs must look to their students and must truly listen to their voices to understand who their students are and how to respond to their needs. Furthermore, those of us who have taught long and successfully at HSIs can offer explicit and implicit direction in creating approaches to teaching composition that will enable Hispanic students to find their voices as writers, as members of the academic culture, and, eventually, as productive, significant participants in society at large. Composition scholars researching issues of diversity and postprocess theories know the value of critical reflection in fostering professional and pedagogical growth in the context of cultural awareness. Compositionists, especially those at HSIs, should juxtapose traditional understandings about teaching, learning, and writing with new understandings about access, agency, and academic success for Hispanic students. Such reflection can serve as scaffolding for transforming our HSI classrooms into sites of learning where teacher and student collaborate to reach new understandings about writing, self, culture, and identity.

Notes

1. The University of Texas-Pan American in Edinburg, Texas, is located approximately ten miles from the Texas-Mexico border. In 1999, the latest year for which U.S. Department of Education statistics are complete, UTPA had an 87.1 percent Hispanic enrollment, with 10,950 Hispanic students. Only two other public four-year institutions compare in percentage and numbers to UTPA: the University of Texas at El Paso, with 10,005 Hispanic students for a 68.1 percent Hispanic enrollment, and Florida International University, with 16,495 Hispanic students for a 52.7 percent Hispanic enrollment (Stearns and Watanabe 2002, 32–35).

2. I first encountered this term in Michelle Hall Kells's (2002) "Linguistic Contact Zones in the College Writing Classroom." It also is used in the introduction to Kells, Balester, and Villanueva's (2004) *Latino/a Discourses: On Language, Identity, & Literacy Education.* The term is not defined in either of these contexts, but it is clear that it refers to the *consciousness* and *profound awareness* of being "Latino/a," an identity-shaping awareness that pervades all aspects of the Hispanic individual's life. Because of the historical and political associations that the term conjures (Kells, Balester, and Villanueva 2004, 2–3), it is a far richer, more appropriate term to describe our roots than any other neologism, say, for example, "Hispanicity" or *Chicanismo.* "*Latinidad*" is a Spanish word, and it allows us to label our cultural awareness and identity with a term that must be uttered with the cadences and fluidity of Spanish pronunciation and the remembrances of all that our culture means to us.

Works Cited

Bartholomae, David. 1980. "The Study of Error." *College Composition and Communication* 31:3: 253–69.

———. 1985. "Inventing the University." In *When a Student Can't Write: Studies in Writer's Block and Other Composing-Process Problems*, ed. Mike Rose, 134–65. New York: Guilford. Rpt. in *Cross-talk in Composition Theory: Reader*, ed. Victor Villanueva, 589–619. Urbana, IL: National Council of Teachers of English.

Beauvais, Paul Jude. 2002. "First Contact: Composition Students' Close Encounters with College Culture." In *Professing in the Contact Zone: Bringing Theory and Practice Together*, ed. Janice M. Wolff, 21–37. Urbana, IL: National Council of Teachers of English.

Clark, Irene. 2001. "Perspectives on Directive/Non-Directive Continuum in the Writing Center." *The Writing Center Journal* 22:1: 33–58.

Freire, Paolo. 1997. *Pedagogy of the Oppressed.* Revised 20th anniversary edition. Translated by Myra Bergman Ramos. New York: Continuum.

Fromkin, Victoria, Robert Rodman, and Nina Hyams. 2003. *An Introduction to Language.* 7th ed. Boston: Wadsworth.

Gale, Xin Liu. 1996. *Teachers, Discourses, and Authority in the Postmodern Composition Classroom.* Albany: State University of New York Press.

Kells, Michelle Hall. 2002. "Linguistic Contact Zones in the College Writing Classroom: An Examination of Ethnolinguistic Identity and Language Attitudes." *Written Communication* 19:1: 5–42.

Kells, Michelle Hall, Valerie M. Balester, and Victor Villanueva. 2004. "Introduction: Discourse and 'Culture Bumping'." In *Latino/a Discourses: On Language, Identity, & Literacy Education*, ed. Michelle Hall Kells, Valerie Balester, and Victor Villanueva, 1–6. Portsmouth, NH: Boynton/Cook.

Martinez, Maria D. 2003. "Missing in Action: Reconstructing Hope and Possibility among Latino Students Placed at Risk." *Journal of Latinos and Education* 2:1: 13–21.

Newman, Beatrice Méndez. 2000. "In Their Own Voices: Student Stories of Attrition." Paper delivered at the 2000 conference of the National Association of Developmental Educators. Biloxi, Mississippi.

———. 2003. "Centering in the Borderlands: The Writing Center at Hispanic-Serving Institutions." *The Writing Center Journal* 23:2: 45–62.

Pratt, Mary Louise. 1991. "Arts of the Contact Zone." *Profession* 91: 33–40.

Shaughnessy, Mina. 1977. *Errors and Expectations: A Guide for the Teacher of Basic Writing.* New York: Oxford University Press.

Sommers, Nancy, and Laura Saltz. 2004. "The Novice as Expert: Writing the Freshman Year." *College Composition and Communication* 56:1: 124–49.

Stearns, Christina, and Satoshi Watanabe. 2002. *Hispanic-Serving Institutions: Statistical Trends, 1990–1999.* Washington, DC: National Center for Education Statistics. NCES 2002-051. U.S. Department of Education. http://www.nces.ed.gov/pubs2002/2002051.pdf (accessed December 21, 2005).

Trimbur, John. 2000. "Composition and the Circulation of Writing." *College Composition and Communication* 52:2: 188–219.

UTPA Student Profile—Fall 2005. 2006. Who Goes to UTPA? The University of Texas-Pan American Office of Institutional Research and Effectiveness. http://www.oire.utpa.edu/studentprofile.htm (accessed January 9, 2006).

Yule, George. 1985. *The Study of Language.* New York: Cambridge University Press.

CHAPTER 2

TEACHING ENGLISH IN A CALIFORNIA TWO-YEAR HISPANIC-SERVING INSTITUTION

COMPLEXITIES, CHALLENGES, PROGRAMS, AND PRACTICES

Jody Millward, Sandra Starkey, and David Starkey

David Starkey: Jody and Sandy, you have dedicated your careers to the working poor. Given the racialization of poverty in California (and Santa Barbara), that means primarily Latinos/as. You have directed programs, collaborated in state and national conference presentations, and promoted teacher training on local, state, and national levels with a comprehensive booklet that includes theories and principles of multicultural pedagogy and an anthology of assignments. I would like to draw on your experience to frame the issues that two-year college teachers address at Hispanic-Serving Institutions (HSIs) such as Santa Barbara City College (SBCC).

Your key commitment has been to SBCC's Multicultural English Transfer (MET) program, which offers a designated strand of reading-writing courses from two levels below transfer through transfer composition. Our faculty sequences classroom and writing assignments within each course and across course levels based on principles we have identified that help underrepresented students succeed. Briefly, these include building a classroom community, linking students to campus resources, promoting student participation within the academic community, and encouraging students to build bridges between the academy and their familial, cultural, and linguistic communities. We meet monthly to discuss pedagogies that encourage individualized instruction and student success. With a 27.8 percent Latino/a enrollment, SBCC is designated an HSI. How would you describe our students?

Jody Millward: When I think of our students, I picture a concentric circle with the student in the middle. Then I picture the family and local community in the next circle, the academic community in the next, and the political and economic context in the outer circle. I realize that at times our students feel those circles collapsing in on them. I often do this as an exercise in my classes, having students write their individual characteristics of each circle, and then we do a joint diagram. Patterns emerge, and we begin to realize the many challenges each student faces and, thus, our pedagogical challenges. Our students do not operate in a vacuum, and while the complexity of their lives can (and does) enrich their classroom contributions and writing, those very complexities can derail them.

David: And these challenges may be invisible to instructors who have never faced them in their own academic careers.

Jody: Right. Let us adapt the diagram and put the two-year college instructor in the center. She or he would define the self in terms of age, gender, ethnicity, family structure; the next circle would be the classroom—number of classes, total number of students, student characteristics. Many teachers view each student as an individual and believe each class has its own personality. Of course this is true. Still, we can identify patterns and develop strategies that will allow us to provide individualized instruction. I have just finished the "2005 TYCA Two-Year College Facts and Data Report" as part of a CCCC's Research Initiative grant.[1] The demographic information warns that we cannot afford to hang on to notions of the traditional college student. Nearly 90 percent of the two-year population has a nontraditional marker.[2] In 2003, community colleges enrolled nearly 60 percent of all Hispanics and Native Americans and nearly half of all blacks and Pacific Islanders nationwide.

Given California's location (bordering Mexico and on the Pacific Rim), we can predict that our classes will not be "traditional." A 2005 study shows that nearly half of all California ninth graders are low income and will not complete four-year university entrance requirements. As an additional risk factor, Latinos/as comprise nearly half of the English Language Learners in the K–12 population (Beachler et al. 2005, 3). As Beatrice Méndez Newman notes in her chapter, 42 percent of all HSI Latino/a enrollment is in California. Peter Schrag reports that "80 percent of all California Latino[as]" enroll in a community college, "four times as many [as in] UC, CSU, and all California private colleges combined" (2004, 2). Sandy's research indicates that we will have ESL, bilingual, and Generation 1.5 Latinos (students whose native language is not English, but who have been educated in the American K–12 system) in our classrooms, and the linguistic challenges differ drastically. That may be why Hispanics are "over-represented in basic skills courses" (Beachler et al. 2005, 6).

Sandra Starkey: The major challenge for two-year college teachers is the diversity of students in foundational (i.e., developmental) composition classrooms. We have students with vastly different needs and expectations: reentry students, international students, immigrant English Language Learners, Generation 1.5, special needs students, local students with family responsibilities, parents, the "traditional" 18-year-old high school graduate financially dependent on his or her parents and, yes, the "unmotivated" community college student—with a variety of goals (certificates, AAs, transfer). Teachers wonder: What is the best text and curriculum? How strict should my attendance policy be? How much group work or conferencing should we do? How much should I focus on grammar? What benefits one group may disadvantage another. While we may know that every community college student needs a great deal of individualized attention, our SBCC full-time course load for at least one semester a year is minimum 100 students (all foundational courses), maximum 144 students (all transfer level). I have become an informal counselor, advising students on required classes and what majors they may pursue and informing them of financial aid opportunities. Nothing in graduate school prepares us for these multiple roles, and not all teachers are willing to take them on. For example, we all feel more comfortable advising the English major. Now consider the realities for most Latinos: many feel they must pursue careers that will support their families (both immediate and extended), and many Latinos/as have underestimated their ability to transfer. We cannot ignore the fact that a certificate or an AA could provide them with emotionally and financially fulfilling careers. But as teachers of students we fear we underserve; we all want to increase the transfer rate of Hispanics.

A handout about Latino/a students, brought back from the 2004 conference sponsored by UCLA's Student Transfer Outreach and Mentor Program and circulated by our president to faculty, students, and community members, rightfully caused quite a stir. According to this report, in California, of 100 Chicano/Latino students enrolled in elementary school, 46 graduate from high school. Of those 46, 26 pursue higher education; 17 will attend community college; 9 a four-year school. Of the 9 at the four-year university, 9 stay. Of the 17 who choose a community college, only one will transfer. The fact that the UC schools are better at retention is, I think, in part because they have more material resources (mentors, peer tutors, etc.), researchers who dedicate time to the subject, and admissions criteria that tend to eliminate students with multiple risk factors (linguistic, class, and family responsibilities). But these data show that Hispanic students need to be made aware that transfer is, indeed, an option.

Jody: And now we are addressing the outer circle of my original diagram—the political, cultural, and economic. National media now celebrate two-year colleges as the locus for retraining displaced workers and as an economically sound way to prepare students to transfer to a four-year university. But nationally, and in our own state—despite the fact that the California Community College system enrolls more students than any institution of higher learning—2004 budget cuts meant that we could not offer classes critical to job enhancement (in ESL, certificate, and associate programs), and so California community colleges turned away an estimated 175,000 students (Hayward et al. 2004). And this is a national trend. In "The Silent Killer of Minority Enrollments," Jamilah Evelyn warned that the "threat" to diversity is state budget cuts, which "fall disproportionately on minority students." In 2003, Mark Drummond, chancellor of Los Angeles CC District, a district that enrolls more than three times the number of Latinos/as than all UCs combined, estimated that his district would turn away "some 6,000 Hispanic students—more than five times the number of [UCLA] Hispanic freshmen" (quoted in Evelyn 2003, 2). This community college district enrolls more than three times the number of Latinos than all UCs combined.

Our students succeed despite the current political, economic, and cultural climate—not because of it. They understand the politics behind citizenship laws, immigration laws, profiling, the cuts to financial aid and scholarships, English only in K–12, the revised transfer requirements of UC and CSU, and the funding discrepancies between four-year schools and two-year colleges. Students of color—especially Latinos/as, given the legislation adopted in the last decade—are sent a message that education is not meant for all. If students stumble or fail, it is not because of lack of money or resources for them or their teachers, but because they—as individuals—cannot cut it, while others obviously can. Clearly, we have a lot of data. What we do not have is a clear analysis of what happens as these forces intersect and how to change our pedagogy in ways that will enable students to realize their academic promise.

David: As a university hire and a scholar in comp theory, I wanted the information you talk about here. At the universities where I taught, I was used to low drop rates and high retention. At SBCC, I saw immediately that what I had been told about CC students' low "skills level" was not true. So I knew I had to pay attention to the affective factors. I also discovered that incorporating these issues of dropout rates and retention as topics for class analysis allowed students to situate themselves. Defining shared personal and political challenges allows them to address those challenges. I am thinking, Jody, of your brainstorming assignment, "What can't be changed or chosen after birth?" Students respond with time and place of birth, family structure, class, gender, ethnicity, and genetic makeup. They fill in specifics for a cluster of these items and predict something about that "person"; then they change at least three of those elements for a second cluster and predict something. This exercise generates discussion about the intersections of class, ethnicity, gender, status, and so on. Students also agree that not everyone born in a similar time with similar circumstances will have the same "fate" and talk about choices, challenges, and the interplay between the self and "outside forces."

Yet if we are going to talk about students in communities, we need to identify the differences between the four-year and two-year academic cultures. The University of California, Santa Barbara (UCSB), like many four-year institutions, provides first-year students with the multiple benefits of dorm life. Resident assistants serve as mentors who can provide immediate assistance, linking students to campus services when financial or academic challenges arise. In the dorms, peers share information on tests, teachers, financial aid, clubs, and on-campus jobs, and they often form informal study groups. Most importantly, they are in a culture that says academics come first. Twenty-four/seven, students are studying on campus—in the dorms, library, and computer labs. Our students come to campus, drive to a job, go and pick up a child or a sibling, and rarely have a "room of one's own" for thought and reflection. Our two-year college libraries and labs have limited hours. While it is difficult to bring these benefits to students through classroom assignments, in conjunction with teaching critical thinking, computer literacy, reading, writing, and research, students give high marks to those types of assignments in course evaluations. In a sense, we are giving them the tools they need to decode academia.

We must acknowledge that these cultural differences affect student performance. In the three years I taught at UCSB, I noticed that students in their Writing 1 (the equivalent of our Fundamentals of Composition) course had a much stronger sense of the consequences of not completing their assignments. The UCSB students had been trained in high school to get the work done, turn it in on time, show up for class, and so on. Clearly they possessed study and time-management skills that many two-year college students have never learned. Consequently, the "remediation" their writing required was much easier to accomplish, because they understood most of the codes needed to successfully negotiate the institutional requirements.

Similar to the students Méndez Newman teaches, SBCC students often use a different calculus to determine priorities as they juggle their personal and academic lives. I need to remind myself that going to work to make enough money to pay the rent or the electricity bill may, indeed, at least in the short term, appear more pressing than handing in Essay #3 on the day it is due. Although, of course, when they do have time for reflection—whether it is through class discussions or essay assignments—our students are as intellectually incisive, if not more so, than their four-year counterparts.

Jody: At UCSB, I taught full-time in a program designed to promote the success of underrepresented students (now called A.C.E.). I rarely lost a student, maybe one or two in an academic year. In my first semester at SBCC, I lost three in the Fundamentals course alone. They just stopped coming. Like you, I found their skills sets were not that different from those of students at four-year schools. As a teaching assistant at UCSB, I had two Latinas from an inner-city Los Angeles high school in my Writing 1 course. Their scores, in the language of the time, defined them as "borderline." Their high school English teacher attended a welcome function and celebrated their preparation. When I received their first essays, I was astonished by her characterization. However, within two quarters (students in this program could choose to stay with the same teacher), I used the same glowing language in their recommendation letters. They caught up. Our students do too, but it takes longer because often they interrupt their comp studies. Some "take a break from English" because they perceive comp and math as work intensive and as gatekeeper classes. Others dip in and out during the semester because they are sideswiped by life or, as the semester wears on, realize that while their outside responsibilities have not lessened, their work in classes has intensified—particularly in disciplines that rely on a few major tests or one long paper to assess student knowledge of a specific subject. Given the sequential nature of our classes, students with multiple responsibilities find meeting every deadline nearly impossible. They can "catch up" and get the work done but miss the benefits of the recursive nature of the writing process. The MET faculty have experimented with ways to build flexibility into the course structure (e.g., permitting one late paper, no questions asked, or accepting the final draft at the end of the assigned week). I accommodate those with emergencies by letting them complete portions of the course online. One woman finished the course work early and brought her newborn in on the last day for all of us to meet. But perhaps we could do more. Given the realities of students' lives, how do we incorporate prewriting, live peer response to drafts, metacognitive assessments of writing process, and so on? Is offering the course traditionally while working online with individual students doable (given our workloads) or good pedagogy, since the MET faculty view composition courses as a pathway into the campus community and craft assignments to help students integrate multiple social identities?

Sandra: If I may, that goes back to an early point I made. There is little research into this critical issue. While four-year college students often enter with a history of success and nurturing and have some knowledge of how to decode academic conventions, our students (particularly first-generation with linguistic and cultural differences and mixed experiences of success in K–12) enter with very different attitudes. Some believe knowledge is self-achieved and assume, "I must be able to do it all—work, family, and a full-time load—or I'm not college material." Others think they will test the waters and any failure confirms they are not "college material." This viewpoint is a key difference. Yet the literature does not address how these beliefs affect both individual performance and classroom dynamics. Jim Cummins's (2001) "Empowering Minority Students" shows that school failure among minority groups has much to do with the relation of that group to the "majority" group. If the minority group is viewed as a low-status one in the larger society, then failure rates, not surprisingly, are much higher. An oft-quoted study involves Finnish students, defined as "low status" in Sweden, who had high failure rates in comparison to Finnish students in Australia, where they were viewed as "high status" (53). When a person's language and culture are devalued by the culture in power, the impact is tremendous. That is why we need to pay attention to the cultural, economic, and political forces affecting our Latino/a students.

David: Having taught in Finland, I find that a particularly telling example. From the average American's perspective, both groups are "Scandinavians," basically indistinguishable from one another. And yet there is a marked tension between Swedes and Finns, particularly among the working classes. Yet I am aware of no research focusing specifically on two-year college Latinos/as in terms of who succeeds and why and what role composition courses play. Instead, we find ourselves gleaning what we can from four-year studies or localized examples of two-year college successes. Both types of research view students through the lens of a particular community—ethnicity, class, first generation. But how do we help individualize instruction for our Latino/a majority with their varied linguistic and cultural backgrounds?

Jody: What comes to my mind is Ann M. Penrose's (2002) study on first-generation students. She provides valuable information on how home and academic cultures diverge by identifying the commonalities of First Generation college-goers (FG) that differentiate them from their peers:

- discontinuity between home and school culture, between the norms of the neighborhood or family and those of the academy
- sensitivity to social and academic factors that will distinguish them from their classmates
- more likely to notice distinctive features of academic discourse
- significant differences between literacy practices at home and school
- contrast between intuitive models of literacy and formalized expectations of academia
- tension between the personal, emotional voice and the dispassionate language of academic analysis

Penrose notes, "By virtue of their decision to attend college, these students have not only entered alien territory but distanced themselves from the understanding of family and friends" (2002, 439), and she suggests that because "literacy practices enact the values and customs of a community, they represent a critical site of vulnerability for those who are uncertain of their membership." Penrose concludes that "FG students do not bring . . . insecurities with them to college," but develop them afterward (2002, 457).

Yet reports of students and faculty in the MET program challenge these assumptions. In general, first-generation two-year college students tend to be tentative upon entry; as they experience success, however, they blossom. Latino/as in particular see that they can recover and pick themselves up when they fall, an experience they often feel was denied them in high school. In the last three years, many of my Latino/a students have transferred, with mixed success, in their first semesters. Just off the top of my head: to UCSB, Juan in computer science, Eduardo and Napoleon in business; to Cal Poly in San Luis Obispo, Jose and Miguel in engineering, Leah in landscape architecture, and Denova in nutrition; to UCLA, Ernesto in premed and Margaret (whose major I do not know). And currently, Antonia, Jorge, Blanca, and Lily are in graduate schools. I knew these students well. When they graduated from SBCC, each saw bilingualism as a strength; several had drawn their families and neighborhood friends into their study time. Two women convinced their mothers, Mexican immigrants, to enroll at SBCC. When I went to their graduations, I met their extended families. Some had traveled from Mexico. These students were proud and confident. Rather than developing insecurities during their two-year college experience, they developed great confidence.

A 2002 study of "high-risk" two-year college students and recent transfer reports confirm this anecdotal information. A study of high-risk two-year college students found that while students are "more likely to find their exams challenging," they are

> much less likely to come to class unprepared, are more likely to ask questions and participate in class discussions, [and] are more likely to prepare two or more drafts of a paper or assignment before turning it in. They are more dedicated to studying despite the number of hours they work (79% . . . work more than 30 hours per week compared to 6 percent in the low-risk group [and] devote as much time to preparing for class as their lower-risk classmates do). (Penrose 2002, 9)

That is great news, important news. It suggests that many first-generation and/or reentry students do not underestimate the time and effort that success will take or undervalue the pride and confidence that such success brings.

On the other hand, four-year colleges tend to underestimate the burdens our transfer students carry. I just had lunch with one of my former students who graduated from UCLA within two years of transfer while working forty hours a week to support herself. The senior survey she received asked students to check hours a week worked—forty hours was not an option. On the upside, she was personally proud of her accomplishment and confident that because she had done what UCLA apparently believes is inconceivable, she can handle anything. On the downside, this is a clear example of how elite institutions render many students invisible. As we often ask in MET, are opportunities limited for students with several high-risk markers? This, too, is the type of research that needs to be pursued.

Sandra: I have had that experience—the experience of watching confidence, particularly for Latino/as, increase as they build bridges between their home and academic cultures. Yet I fear we are so focused on transfer, we sometimes forget to ask, "What happens to them once they get there?" I have been working with a UCSB outreach group that involves the university, the two-year college, and local high schools, and I have learned a lot about the preconceptions and biases university faculty have toward these students. The leap from the two-year college to the university is almost as traumatic as the leap from high school, yet the university is just starting to put into place the orientations and community building for transfer students that is so integral a part of the freshman experience. Starting a dialogue and maintaining connections between these three institutions is so important to our mission.

Jody: We also have some hard data: nationwide, transfer students have an 80 percent persistence rate; but we also know that while 35 percent of upper-class and 21 percent of middle-class students transfer, only 7 percent of the working poor do so (Millward 2005, 8). As you noted earlier, the racialization of poverty in states such as California makes Latino students woefully underrepresented in transfer. Crossinstitutional partnerships are key. For me, the paucity of such programs nationwide shows the conservative nature of the academy. Embedded within academia is the cultural norm of the "traditional" college student, a mere 27 percent of the national college population (Millward 2005, 5). In this model, a financially independent college student, living on campus, completes the bachelor's degree within four years and then enrolls in another institution for graduate work. This certainly does not honor the very real family and economic responsibilities of many "nontraditional" two-year students who have obligations that keep them local. A formal collaboration, programs with articulated goals, would provide two-year college students with the support and expectations they need for success within their local communities through the bachelor's degree and beyond.

Sandra: In the meantime, we need to adapt four-year research and create a pedagogy that allows students to integrate their home culture into every level of their academic experience from the moment they enroll in a two-year college. English classes are uniquely situated to help them do just that.

David: MET does just that. For example, we know retention rates go up when students feel connected to the campus community. But we do not have a multicultural center, and often students feel they do not have time to participate in tutoring much less join campus organizations and clubs. Sandy, your "treasure hunt" assignment directly addresses student awareness of campus resources. You provide hypothetical case studies of students whose challenges affect their ability to focus on school. Working in collaborative groups, they research which agency on campus would best assist that student, report back to the class, and then write a paper on a friend or peer and provide advice to that student incorporating what they have learned. For me, that stands as a model (among many) of what the MET faculty have done over the years. You get students into the offices, talking to faculty, staff, and fellow students, and then place them in a position of authority and give them a context of helping someone else. That makes the writing authentic. The end result is that students realize services and networks can save them time and money by helping them resolve issues that may cause them to underperform or drop a class.

Sandra: You are right, David. MET has made a difference. As someone who has taught in the program for over a decade, what I most value are the monthly faculty discussions. We have at least ten faculty (more in the last few years) volunteering for the program. Hearing challenges, assignments, research, and insights from part timers, new teachers, and senior faculty provides the support we need to experiment. Instructors have the right to share what did not work. We do not discuss personalities or self-defined "failed experiments" outside of our meetings. We are, I think, constantly striving to provide what Méndez Newman calls for in her chapter—adjusting our pedagogy rather than defining students by the deficit model. The cornerstone program principle, "No student comes to SBCC hoping to underperform, fail, or drop out," drives our classroom efforts. As a faculty, we practice what we preach to students: pause, assess, ask for help, and regroup. We all rely on each other.

Jody: MET's frank exchanges help mitigate the isolation that two-year college teachers often feel when facing the multiple challenges of their classrooms. As David was talking about how we as teachers adapt assignments to our population, I thought about the career assignment, something I (like many others) used over a decade ago at UCSB. Louis Attinasi's (1989) study shows that choosing a major is a key retention factor: students who discover they do not like their majors are at risk, and those who do not choose a major miss a path into the academy. Four-year students seem to have the confidence to experiment and change majors and the family support when they do so. It is not necessarily pleasant and can make them feel at sea, but their strategies for addressing this core issue are, in general, effective. But first-generation students do not have a full understanding of the range of majors available. For example, I had a Latino who designated computer science as his major because only one member of his family, a cousin, had gone to college and that is what he had done. But he hated the field, got poor grades, and was thinking about dropping out. If we had not had career assignments in our sequence, I know he would have dropped. The assignments gave him a way to analyze his choice. When I started here, only MET transfer classes donated time to the major. Now MET pretransfer reading classes have students do collages, pretransfer composition courses have them do interviews with those working in the field or career center research, and then we have the transfer-level paper that incorporates interviews and research requiring students to "translate" the bureaucratic language of the database and the informal language of the interview into an "I-search" paper. If an understanding of the college culture and confidence inspires Latinos who chose a certificate or an associate's path to set higher goals as studies suggest (Hochiander, Sikora, and Hom 2003, 13, 15–16), then it is critical to show students their options.

Sandra: Yet this assignment is particularly difficult for Latino/a students, even as we attempt to celebrate the languages, dialects, and personal heritage they bring to the classroom. For example, students with a rich language history who engage in "code switching" are performing a complex linguistic task that can enrich their writing. Many Latinos/as have a difficult time controlling the voices that emerge in the database information and the interview language of practitioners who often are Spanish speakers. We must, though, be teaching them the language of the "academy," and we will disadvantage them if we do not make this code explicit, as Lisa Delpit (1988) points out. We really cannot afford an either-or approach; we need to give students the tools they need to gain access into four-year universities, and we need to do so by building on the literacies they bring into our classrooms. Yet consider the linguistic diversity within our classrooms. We have Generation 1.5 and immigrants from different states (and thus dialects) of many different Spanish-speaking countries. In addition, we have students who are highly literate in their native language but have had only two or three years of ESL instruction; and we have students who speak both languages but have little formal instruction in either language.

Jody: Few of us have the linguistic training we need. Knowing Spanish may help, but we need more training to better identify the varied patterns students rely on when they frame an essay, choose a level of diction, construct a voice, and wrestle with sentence-level issues. Some of what I have read has helped—in particular with how students structure an essay, oral markers, conflating formal and informal diction—but I suspect that student linguistic patterns differ based on how the factors Sandy identified are combined.

Sandra: This has got to be our biggest challenge, and my sabbatical project on Generation 1.5 shows there is no magic bullet. It does confirm, however, that the diversity of the students' language experience/ background mandates that we work with each student individually.

David: You are saying that the one-to-one conference on an essay draft, which we already know to be an essential part of any basic writing course, is even more crucial in linguistically diverse classes.

Sandra: Yes. My sabbatical has shown me the value of individualized, detailed linguistic profiles. For example, many of our older, reentry, or fairly recent immigrant students have problems with verb tense, agreement, articles, and idioms. These students, whose primary language is Spanish, have problems producing the U.S. deductive "academic" essay, since Spanish has a very different discourse pattern. Yet many 1.5 students use English as their primary language. They speak Spanish only at home and in a limited fashion with their peers, and they may feel increasingly unable to communicate complex feelings in Spanish, which can be very painful. This inability can create unconscious or conscious ambivalence about gaining proficiency in academic English. The students, as we know, may use various dialects, including Spanglish, Chicano English, Chicano Spanish, and mixtures of these. But many times they are actually more proficient in English than in Spanish, although they may identify themselves as "bilingual." Often the problems will be with word choice and clarity as the students reach beyond their common oral language to an "academic register." We will also see run-ons and fragments, typical markers of the oral style. As Maria Montano-Harmon (1991) reminded us in our MET training session some years ago, code switching—going back and forth from an informal, oral style to a more academic (or an attempt at an academic) register—generates such errors. Of course, we also have Latino/a students who do not speak Spanish at all. We have to be very careful about making assumptions, as Araiza, Cardenas, and Loudermilk Garza point out in this volume. We need to know the linguistic background/profile of each student.

Pedagogy, both classroom activities and writing assignments, can make a difference. In each course of our sequence, we focus on language registers. In my pretransfer level, for example, I have students identify a conflict they are having either at work, in college, or in a group where they volunteer. They write a letter to a friend describing the challenge, write a letter to the person responsible for change in the group, and then analyze the differences between these registers. Jody and I have both used Tan's "Mother Tongue" and then had students identify the different languages they use in academic, work, family, and peer communities. And I have used Jody's assignment, where she gives students the option of translating a poem and then analyzing the choices they made in doing so and why. That way we have students themselves subvert the notion that speaking two languages is a disadvantage, and we try to have monolingual students see that they too have several codes by virtue of the registers they choose to use.

Jody: In my second-semester transfer course (lit and composition), I teach a series of poems about language learning. Students love Pat Mora's *Elena.* On the surface, it is a simple poem about a mother from Mexico who is trying to learn English. Her husband speaks only Spanish and does not want her to learn the new language. Her children speak more and more in English, and, like the neighbors and storekeepers, they laugh at her attempts to speak English. She ends up locking herself in the bathroom to study privately to avoid the tensions in the house. This literature allows us to discuss the cultural assumptions her children have absorbed—the fact that those who speak Spanish are less intelligent. We analyze her husband's view; he faces that attitude every day in the work world and so feels that English provides his family with a way to separate from (even look down upon) him. Students may interview friends or family who immigrated here about their experiences to determine which cultural assumptions remain and which have changed since the poem was written. They also can survey students who grew up in homes where English was not the first language to determine when they speak which language and why and what their attitudes are. These assignments allow them, I think, to gain a broader perspective on the issue. It is interesting how many write in their journals about their personal feelings when they see their parents dismissed in stores, doctor's offices, and so on.

Such assignments also allow us to discuss the causes and functions of student silence. The early studies about the silence of minority students in the classroom remain relevant: Students fear being misunderstood because they speak with an accent and may fear that asking a question or having their responses challenged will confirm for themselves and others that they do not belong in college (Saufley et al. 1983, 48). Culture has a marked influence too. Despite my encouragement, I had a young Latino who first spoke in the last third of our second, eighteen-week semester together. He later told me that his father had forbidden him to talk in a class, because "only God and the Norteamericanos know." Now I incorporate readings, research, and the option to write on this theme of student silence. Students can see that silence is often tied to cultural beliefs.

They see that in the United States (as the popularity of talk shows confirms) "everybody has a right to their own opinion and to express it," while other cultures may find our behavior rude or arrogant.

David: While all of us in MET require classroom participation, we have developed ways to lower the risk level for students beyond group presentations. For example, students can present each other's work, design the way the audience is seated, use technology to remove the focus from the speaker, or even sit to the side while a peer writes the main points of the presentation on the board. This flexibility allows students to assert authority while providing them with the safety they need to do so.

Sandra: We have made tremendous progress in this area, but it is an issue we need to address in every class, and it reflects the importance of building bridges between the home and the academic cultures. When we do that, students will more likely take risks in terms of the topics they choose and the depth of their analyses and will focus more on their writing (including word choice and grammar). For our Latino/a students, family is a support system that often carries multiple responsibilities. For example, the majority of four-year freshmen will not be called upon to interpret for their parents on a daily basis, to advise and take care of their younger brothers or sisters, and/or monitor their siblings' elementary and high school educations. First-generation students often serve as role models but cannot ignore the family responsibilities they had when in high school. Additionally, some Latinas/os face other cultural expectations: pressure to marry or lack of spousal support. On the one hand, some feel pressured to succeed in order to please the family; some feel pressured to place family above academics. The key is to show students how to negotiate between their different communities—their different linguistic, familial, class, and cultural identities. We use assignments that allow them to see that the skills or talents they develop in one arena can support their success in another. We also suggest ways to address what may seem to be competing or conflicting responsibilities between home and school. For example, we suggest that students recruit siblings or parents or spouses to help with their homework (memorization, flash cards, creating study aids, etc. and to serve as interview sources). This practice accomplishes several things at once: child care (of siblings or offspring) becomes shared study time; the students send the message that they value the history and intelligence of all members of their families; and students become active role models, sending a message that they expect children to follow in their footsteps.

David: So much of this depends upon building a safe classroom environment. Yet we do not teach in a vacuum, and racism inevitably emerges in our classrooms. We talk about this a lot in our faculty meetings. It is so damaging.

Sandra: When our students place into a pretransfer course, they know they are being defined by our state and our college as "remedial." Some white students enter the classroom, see students of color, and hear accents and immediately think, "I am in the wrong class. I wasn't assessed right." They adopt a resistant pose—sit in the back of the room and "eye roll." I will also hear comments during peer editing, or students will ask me directly, "Why should this person read and comment on my paper? They barely even speak English!" This is very troubling and definitely damaging. We try to elevate students who speak more than one language by talking about the advantages of being bilingual or multilingual, but some of our white students have absorbed the cultural stereotypes and fear that their placement in English affirms that they, unlike their high school friends, are not "college ready." They shut down or lash out.

Jody: I agree. It is an unresolved, almost under-the-radar issue. And it is complicated. Because we cannot support the racism reflected by their passive or overt resistance and because we find it personally offensive as well, it is difficult to keep intellectual distance and to parse what is behind such behavior. I believe Mike Rose (1989) gets to the heart of it when he warns, "The danger [is that students] might not be able to separate out their particular problems with calculus or critical writing from their own image of themselves, as thinkers, from their intellectual self-worth" (173).

Sandra: MET faculty speak individually to the student who makes a covert racist statement and discuss overt racist statements with the class as a whole. However, as Jody says, it is difficult at times to do this without humiliating or losing the student who made the comment. But the worst thing is for teachers to turn a blind eye because they fear confronting a student. We know of the powerful effect negative stereotyping has on student performance, and we need to determine how best to eradicate such stereotyping in our classrooms.

Jody: What is also troubling is that these resistant students who do not change their attitude end up underperforming or dropping the class when they realize it is not going to be an automatic easy "A," and that the reading, writing, and research requirements demand commitment to risk taking and growth. This stance is sometimes a defense for mainstream students, especially those who may have had advantages in place but did not gain university admission. It is usually a maturity issue. Given the realities of tracking, these students transition from high schools with little experience of diversity. Often they do not understand that college compositions demand revision, and so they do not revise. They do not understand the success of 1.5, immigrants, or other non-native speakers who welcome the opportunity to revise.

While we have developed many strategies for building community and address the limits and powers of stereotyping and intervene when we can define and name such bias, the systemic racism imbedded in our culture undercuts our efforts. The majority of whites do not voice or act on these biases, but the few who do affect classroom climate and hurt themselves. I would like to see more about this in the literature, but it is a touchy subject because of the complexities mentioned. How do we help students understand that their actions reflect an unconscious absorption of stereotypes that can derail them as easily as they derail students of color? They too hear the public voices claiming that high schools do not provide quality education, and that test scores suggest students are not as well prepared as past generations. In California, these debates include the suggestion that immigrants and English language learners are lowering the scores. This suggestion leads some white students to believe they should be stronger in English than their multilingual classmates, and when scores suggest they are not, they hear the message that they did not perform well enough in high school because they are not "college material." How do we shift the paradigm from community colleges enrolling second-class students to one that promotes the notion that integral to the college-going experience is mastering a set of lifelong iearning skills that are at the heart of the two-year college open-missions statement? Simply put, students must develop the ability to assess their own weaknesses, commit to improvement, and change perspective when the result will be personal growth and a more productive contribution to community.

David: Yet we must be careful not to mask a critical component of the multicultural dynamic, that is, the complexities of teacher-student race relations. We know those disaffected students often suggest that Latino/a and African American faculty have "an agenda" where topics on race are raised, while they seem to assume that white faculty must address these issues as part of the college curriculum. We may get some resistance to the topics, but it is not personalized. That has to make us wonder not if but how much our students of color censor what they say, especially in classrooms with white faculty. But the reality is, while students of color make up a large percentage of our classrooms, a small percentage of our faculty is Latino/a, African American, Pacific Islander, or Native American. It is imperative, then, for us to develop a pedagogy that serves our students well.

Sandra: The hiring of Latinos in HSIs must be the top priority. Sadly, though, in Santa Barbara, we just are not seeing those candidates. Teaching K–12 and at the two-year college offers little money and practically no prestige. Many Latinos/as planning to transfer want careers that offer more. Mentoring Latino/a students and making sure our institutions recruit candidates of color help. In the meantime, as you have said, all two-year or four-year HSI teachers (or any teacher for that matter) should be shocked and disheartened by the transfer rates for Latinos/as and should be actively searching for solutions within their own classrooms, among their peers, in their institutions, and in their fields of study. That is our responsibility as teachers.

Jody: The need for more teachers of color in composition classrooms—especially Latinos/as, given our high Latino/a population—is critical. What bell hooks (1990) identified in *Yearning: Race, Gender, and Cultural Politics* still holds true. And my experience in CAP has confirmed the difference that role models can make. For the past five years, I have cotaught a course with a Latino math faculty (first Ignacio Alarcon, now Monica Dabos). Our enrollment is over 80 percent Latino. We focus on the math and English sequences of required courses because transcripts reveal that students tend to focus on completing one sequence or the other, and this process delays degree completion and/or transfer. Two key elements of the program are student mentors (who attend the course and hold individual weekly meetings with their assigned peer groups) and faculty-student meetings to discuss goals, progress, and any need for assistance (academic or personal). We do not force students to disclose information but provide opportunities to discuss, in confidence, anything that interferes with academic progress. Our goal, like MET's, is to help students revision "conflicting demands," help them build bridges between their home and academic cultures, and help them construct an integrated sense of self.

Latino/a student mentors and faculty role models make all the difference. While my working-class background, large family, and strong family ties provide common ground with some students, my first line of information is always the mentors. When a problem arises and the student is invited to speak to a program coordinator, Latino/a students most often choose Monica. A well placed "I know you are having a difficult time right now. If there is anything I can do, just let me know"—without any judgment implied—gives them the confidence they need to come to me for assistance, and the dynamic shifts. Students choose the faculty member with whom they feel most comfortable, or the one who is available.

I think connections to faculty are vitally important. If we do not have enough Latino/a faculty members, then students must be aware that they can turn to other faculty and that they have the right to do so. Interacting with a faculty member begins dialogue. Some Latinos/as are reluctant to discuss family issues with outsiders.

David: Do you think the political debates about affirmative action contribute to this dynamic? And do you believe that this may be a dynamic that cuts both ways? That is, white students must assume a sense of superiority when they find themselves in classes where there are a significant number of students of color and Latino students may feel that programs designed with them in mind suggest they are not able to make it on their own and that knowledge or, more specifically, a college education should be an individual accomplishment.

Jody: Definitely. When I was working with the cofounders to design MET (Mark Ferrer) and the College Achievement Program (CAP) (Ignacio Alarcon), I was heavily influenced by Rachel T. Hare-Mustin's and Jeanne Marecek's (1988) analysis of the ways ignoring difference (in culture, resources, etc.) supports the status quo; denying an unequal playing field ensures those with power will keep power (1998, 456). On the other hand, emphasizing difference and creating separate but equal programs also support the status quo as these programs do not receive equal resources, recognition, or access, and lead to an "exaggeration of differences" (1988, 456–57). We had many discussions about how to avoid building either bias into the programs.

Sandra: MET is open to all students, and many sign up simply because the time is more convenient. When we are asked what is different about our classes by those students who simply "find" themselves in the program, we emphasize that MET is committed to recreating the multicultural demographics of our county in our classrooms and to preparing students for success in a multicultural environment. We stress that this includes access to and experience with technology (as our MET classes have guaranteed computer classroom time), a focus on transfer options, assignments that link students to the academic and local community, and so forth.

David: And while we have discussed those Latinos/as who are reluctant to seek help and those disaffected white students, in general, the collaborative projects and presentations work to build an effective, productive community. The classroom becomes a relatively safe place to explore and acknowledge difference and to work together on shared goals. And, in the final analysis, each student is individually responsible for his or her work in the classroom.

Jody: In CAP, we do not focus on economic need or ethnicity. We focus on what the literature defines as risk factors for student retention and success. The peer groups are often multiethnic: whites, Latino/as, Asians, blacks, and those of mixed backgrounds are all working more hours than they should while attending school; the parents' group pulls in men and women from different ethnicities; first-generation students will often include those from different cultures, as well as first-time collegegoers who live at home. The peer group structure, like the collaborative projects in MET, makes it safe to explore difference and serves as a support system for those with similar challenges. A core focus of the class is learning how to build networks. Significantly, students accept as leaders anyone who has demonstrated competency in math, English, or other academic areas where they are struggling. So this too affirms individual achievement. The collaboration of mentors and coordinators reinforces the notion that we all should seek help when we need it. I think if these programs focused solely on ethnicity, we might not achieve the success rates we do. And we have made a substantial difference: our retention rates hover around 90 percent for the class; our students' GPAs are consistently equal to, if not higher than, the general population; if a CAP student fails an English or math course, she or he is more likely to reenroll in that course the following semester than are students in the general population; and our students are more likely to move from part-time to full-time status than is the general population.

David: CAP has built-in structures and a great support network of Latino/a students to help address some of these issues. How do we work toward that ideal in our composition classrooms? Does it help, for example, if I share that I grew up in a working-class neighborhood in Sacramento, and that most of my friends chose to enter the workforce rather than to enroll in college? Am I conveying that I may have a clearer sense of my students' backgrounds than someone who grew up surrounded by privilege? Or, to cite another example, my Spanish is weak and that makes me sympathetic to second-language learners. Should I work on bringing it up to a passable level? If I were more fluent, would I use Spanish in class? In conferencing? Do Latino/a students see white teachers' attempts to use Spanish as somehow insulting—implying that the students are incapable of adequately communicating in English?

Sandra: I do tell my students that as a teenage parent, I chose to attend SBCC, yet I do not imply that I faced exactly the same challenges. I explain that I went through college with two babies while working part time, and I would be happy to share strategies that helped me succeed. I think it has really helped me reach out to young mothers (many of whom are Latinas). Maybe some students are thinking inwardly, "Oh, come on, another middle-class white woman who's trying to say she had it so tough." But I am willing to take that risk because I feel volunteering the information helps my students. Hopefully, I do not alienate too many others. No one has ever said so.

Jody: I believe it can help. Sandy has the highest enrollment and success rates of women with children (including single mothers) in MET and the composition program. This fact suggests that students have an effective underground network, as semester after semester her classes have a higher percentage of mothers, particularly Latinas. When I have these students in the next course, mothers and women who know they want both a family and career ask me if I knew Sandy was a mother when she went to school.

I too use my job and language acquisition history when appropriate. For example, I tell them—either in individual conferences or if it comes up in relation to a story—I was a maid, an all-night waitress, that I sold doughnuts, and that my father, a coal miner, never went to high school. They correct my Spanish pronunciation, and I admit that although I studied for years and can read Spanish, I gave up trying to speak because my accent is so horrible. Often, native speakers cannot understand me. I was too embarrassed to take the risk, and to voice my regret because "the mark of a true intellectual has always been the ability to speak two or more languages." But like the two of you, I never suggest that my experiences are the same or more difficult than theirs. They know, and I acknowledge, if they do not voice what they know, that I could afford not to risk speaking Spanish; they have to take risks in English.

My ideal is that all teachers would receive training in cultural, class, gender, sexual orientation, and learning styles differences. I would also like to see a pedagogy that allows all students to acknowledge how ethnicity, class, gender, sexual orientation, and/or different abilities contribute both to individual identity and to shaping a community. This, of course, could be interpreted by conservatives as a way to justify the denial of class and race, and on the left as my attempt to erase cultural identity because I am white. But the reality is, our students will not be (and have not been) exposed to a power structure that privileges any ethnicity but white. We have to keep teaching, acknowledge our privilege, and learn how to draw upon the strengths that diversity offers—for all of our students' sakes and our own. And students must feel free to call upon faculty for support. Otherwise, the power dynamic remains unchanged, and underserved students remain underserved.

David: It seems when there is sufficient funding for programs such as SBCC's Transfer Achievement Program, MET, and CAP, student success rates rise dramatically, particularly for Latinos/as in those programs. An extensive support network of counselors and tutors to step in and help when the instructor is overwhelmed gives us real reasons to be optimistic. But in bad budget times, that support network develops some big holes. Usually the first cuts are to professional development opportunities—sabbaticals, travel, research for program development, and pedagogy. It makes our challenge of trying to balance research with full teaching loads even more problematic. And our district is in relatively good financial shape. My question is, what is being lost in other districts and nationwide, and what can we do about it?

Sandra: I understand why this happens, but how can we keep moving forward if our faculty cannot do the research necessary?

Jody: The stopgap answer is that we do what we can in our own classrooms, in our own institutions, in our own states, and in our national political contexts because those are the outside forces that circumscribe what we can do in terms of practice and research. But I would also go back to Sandy's point about crossinstitutional partnerships. Our four-year colleagues in rhetoric and composition studies do not want to speak for us (I have heard that said in several conversations when I suggested that they focus research efforts on two-year colleges), and that is understandable. But it also renders us invisible, because we do not have the funding for professional development and research that our four-year colleagues do, and our promotion and tenure do not depend on research. Research happens despite the political, economic, and cultural context. Two-year faculty committed to research and program development focused on increasing the success of their nontraditional students often must do this work in addition to teaching heavy comp loads. In addition, working mothers and faculty of color are asked to represent their students on their campuses and in their local communities (and not all of these requests are scholarly). I remind myself (à la hooks) that I am white, now middle class, without children, a woman who can afford to volunteer time and energy to the national TYCA and CCCCs and to research. Two-year college faculty just are not there because they have high teaching loads, commitments to their students on campuses, and obligations to their local communities and families.

More importantly, the study of rhetoric and composition must include two-year college students. Journals in our field include articles on multicultural education, workplace writing, beginning writers, and so on. Two-year colleges teach an estimated 50 percent of all freshman and 70 percent of all "developmental composition," and our student demographics offer scholars (including graduate students) new areas and angles of research. My ideal, of course, would be that we were consulted in terms of what needs to be examined to promote student success in composition, and that four-year scholars would build into their grants, and so on, ways to include two-year college teachers (such as buying out some of their teaching time). A few have. But if we are to increase Latino/a student access and success, we need to be realistic. The majority of Latinos/as enroll in two-year colleges. The majority of two-year college faculty does not have the professional support needed to investigate challenges and share successes. And the data suggest that despite our best efforts, we continue to fail some Latino/a students.

David: So you would, in fact, permit, four-year college folks to speak for you?

Sandra: I would happily give my sabbatical research to anyone who could influence scholarship or political legislation that would help our faculty increase the success and transfer rates of the 1.5 generation of Latinos/as—of all underrepresented students.

Jody: And there we are. We do and share what we can in our classrooms, in our states, and within our professional hierarchy. We, like two-year college teachers in every state, desperately want our California students—the majority of whom are Latinos/as—to succeed. And that takes articulation, money, time, and research networks that cross institutions. It takes coalitions for pedagogical and political advocacy to reverse the trends of low funding, transfer obstacles, and lack of support for underrepresented students. We cannot afford to have successful Latino/a transfers remain the exception to the rule. We just cannot afford it.

Notes

1. "The Two-Year College English Association (TYCA) identifies and articulates the best theories and practices, and pedagogy in teaching English in the two-year college through regional and national conventions and a journal, *Teaching English in the Two-Year College* (*TETYC*)" (NCTE 2006). The TYCA is a constituent organization of the National Council of Teachers of English (NCTE).

2. Nontraditional markers include delaying enrollment into college, working over thirty-five hours a week, having dependents other than a spouse, being financially independent, being single parents, and/or not having high school diplomas; 64 percent of those with three or more of these markers attend a community college. High-risk students have one of these markers or are first-generation students or academically underprepared; community college students are three to four times more likely to fit this profile than their four-year peers. Over half of our students are first generation; 60 percent attend part time, 34 percent spend at least eleven hours a week caring for dependents (Millward 2005, 6, 5).

Works Cited

Attinasi, Louis C. 1989. "Getting In: Mexican Americans' Perceptions of University Attendance and the Implications for Freshman Year Persistence." *Journal of Higher Education* 60:3: 247–77.

Beachler, Judy, Deborah Boroch, Robert Gabriner, Craig Hayward, Edward Karpp, Kenneth Meehan, and Andrea Serban. 2005. "A Summary of Key Issues Facing California Community Colleges Pertinent to the Strategic Planning Process." *Center for Student Success, Research and Planning Group for California Community Colleges.* (June): 1–10.

Cummins, Jim. 1990. "Empowering Minority Students: A Framework for Intervention." In *Facing Racism in Education*, ed. Nitza Hidalgo, Ceasar McDowell, and Emilie Siddle, 58–60. Cambridge, MA: Harvard Educational Review.

Delpit, Lisa D. 1988. "The Silenced Dialogue: Power and Pedagogy in Educating Other People's Children." *Harvard Educational Review* 58:3: 280–98.

Evelyn, Jamilah. 2003. "The 'Silent Killer' of Minority Enrollments." *Chronicle of Higher Education* 49:41 (June 20). Rpt. *The Chronicle of Higher Education: Government and Politics*, 1–7. http://chronicle.com/weekly/v49/i41/41a01701.htm (accessed June 21, 2005).

Hare-Mustin, Rachel T., and Jeanne Marecek. 1988. "The Meaning of Difference: Gender Theory, Postmodernism, and Psychology." *American Psychologist* 43: 455–64.

Hayward, Gerald C., Denis P. Jones, Aims C. McGuinness, Jr., and Ailene Timar. 2004. "Ensuring Access with Quality to California's Community Colleges." Executive Summary. National Center for Public Policy and Higher Education. http://www.highereducation.org/reports/hewlett (accessed June 2005).

Hochiander, Gary, Anna C. Sikora, and Laura Hom. 2003. "Community College Students: Goals, Academic Preparation, and Outcomes." Postsecondary Descriptive Anaylsis Report. National Center for Education Statistics (June). http://www.nces.ed.gov/pubs2003/2003164.pdf (accessed June 17, 2005).

hooks, bell. 1990. *Yearning: Race, Gender, and Cultural Politics.* Boston: South End Press.

Millward, Jody. 2005. "2005 TYCA Two-Year College Facts and Data Report." (September). http://www.ncte.org/library/files/Related_Groups/TYCA/TYCA_DataReport.pdf (accessed December 8, 2005).

Montano-Harmon, Maria. 1991. "Contrastive Rhetoric and Dialect." Presentation, Linguistic Research Minority Project, UC Santa Barbara, July.

National Council of Teachers of English. 2006. "Mission and Goals of TYCA." http://www.ncte.org/groups/tyca/about/110654.htm (accessed July 21, 2006).

Penrose, Ann M. 2002. "Academic Literacy Perceptions and Performance: Comparing First-Generation and Continuing-Generation College Students." *Research in the Teaching of English* 36:4: 437–61.

Rose, Mike. 1989. *Lives on the Boundary: The Struggles and Achievements of America's Underprepared.* New York: Penguin.

Saufley, Ronald W., et al. 1983. "The Struggles of Minority Students at Predominately White Institutions." In *Teaching Minority Students,* ed. James H. Cones, 40–49. San Francisco: Jossey-Bass.

Schrag, Peter. 2004. "California's First-Generation Students." *San Diego Union-Tribune* (May 6). Rpt. SignOnSandiego.com. http://www.signonsandiego.com/uniontrib/20050506/news_lz1e6schrag.html (accessed June 5, 2005).

Part 2

We Are Not All the Same: Understanding Geographic and Cultural Differences at Hispanic-Serving Institutions

CHAPTER 3

DISCOVERING A "PROPER PEDAGOGY"

THE GEOGRAPHY OF WRITING AT THE UNIVERSITY OF TEXAS-PAN AMERICAN

Dora Ramírez-Dhoore and Rebecca Jones

What remains unspoken about the history of teaching composition at this university [the University of Texas-Pan American (UTPA)], however, is what happened to those students who never passed their composition classes and therefore never graduated from college. How these students were trained to write had very real consequences, but the training they most often received, in my view, seldom achieved the desired results. . . . It doesn't take a rocket scientist to know that there wasn't anything that a proper pedagogy couldn't potentially solve. Unfortunately, I knew nothing of such a pedagogy at that time. (Mejía 2004, 43–44)

"I want you to speak English. Pa' hallar buen trabajo tienes que saber hablar el inglés bien. Qué vale toda tu educación si todavía hablas inglés con un *'accent,'" my mother would say, mortified that I spoke English like a Mexican. At Pan American University, I, and all Chicano students were required to take two speech classes. Their purpose: to get rid of our accents. Attacks on one's form of expression with the intent to censor are a violation of the First Amendment.* El Anglo con cara de inocente nos arrancó la lengua. *Wild tongues can't be tamed, they can only be cut out.* (Anzaldúa 1999, 53–54)

As professors at UTPA, formerly Pan American University, we feel it is important to answer to the experiences of both Jaime Mejía and Gloria Anzaldúa. As teachers, we must take into consideration Mejía's inadequate preparation for teaching writing as well as the absence of pedagogies available for teaching this particular population of students in South Texas. We also must come to terms with Anzaldúa's most anthologized essay, "How to Tame a Wild Tongue," which reminds us of the implications of erasing a student's history and home language in a classroom. We want to think about a "proper pedagogy" for our students here in South Texas that gives them the tools to be successful at the university level while also being mindful of Anzaldúa's warning: "Wild tongues can't be tamed, they can only be cut out."

We arrived at UTPA from very different geographical and educational spaces. Dora grew up in a farm-working, poverty-level household in a rural Oregon town and is now working as an assistant professor in American literature, focusing on Latina/o studies in her research. Rebecca grew up in a white, middle-class family who owned their own business in a small town in North Carolina. She studied rhetoric and composition in her PhD program and now works as a writing program administrator. Dora has lived and worked in the Northwest and Southwest, and she has taught in a predominately white institution in the Midwest for six years, while completing her PhD. Rebecca has taught in North and South Carolina, working primarily with middle-class and working-class students both white and African American, many of whom are first-generation college students. We have come to see writing, and especially the discourse of the academy, as existing in a very different space here in South Texas. Nedra Reynolds (2004) reminds us in her book *Geographies of Writing: Inhabiting Places and Encountering Difference* that writing happens and exists in a particular material space. Though this space can be transformed, we must attend to the particular "politics" of each writing space (2004, 7). Reynolds explains that by examining the geography of writing and learning spaces, we can understand "border mentalities" that divide students and teachers through physical, racial, educational, or discursive borders (2004, 6–8).

The political material space of this South Texas university consists of a student body that is 87 percent Latino/a literally living on the border—both a national border (the U.S./Mexican border is about twenty minutes away) and an educational border. Some of the students are Mexican Nationals who drive across the border on a daily basis, while others come from overcrowded and underfunded local high schools. From our observations, our students have strong family obligations that nearly always conflict with their educational responsibilities.[1]

In many ways, one student's experiences demonstrate some of the barriers set forth by family responsibility. Lusila Cruz, from Dora's course, translated her experience of being a Chicana in a traditional home. She illustrated how education could not be a priority in the family for economic reasons and would not be a priority because of her gender. She discussed her chores, including having to prepare "dinner;

babysitting, cleaning house, and washing clothes" and how those affected her grades in high school. Yet she still desired an education:

> I am still living at home but I had to literally run away from home for a year to show my parents that my younger siblings were not my children. I found myself the year I moved away, it was difficult at first but I coped with the changes and came back home refreshed and ready to take on whatever my parents sent my way.

One of Rebecca's students recently commented during a conference that all of the students here would be brilliant and achieve "Ivy League standards" if they did not have to work so much! This comment illustrates the frustration these barriers often cause students at UTPA. The students can *see* how class, race, gender, and location affect their education.

Students ask both of us how their classmates compare to students at other universities and why the students at UTPA seem to have trouble with writing. Though we are isolated in many ways here in South Texas, the students have a sense that things are different. Along with our developmental coordinator, John Wittman, we have observed a higher number of underprepared writers. Though there are many average students that easily compare to students in other parts of the country and a few high achievers, each class cohort includes a larger discrepancy in writing abilities than we have previously experienced. This means that in each course, professors have to address the needs of students at many different levels—challenging the advanced student while finding creative ways to help the basic writer catch up.[2]

A recent Hispanic Center Pew report agrees with these comments and concerns, though for slightly different reasons. The 2004 report, compiled by Richard Fry, explains that Latino students entering colleges and universities graduate at a much lower rate than their white peers. The report finds that though this problem is compounded by many factors, the predominant reason is that "well prepared Latinos attend post secondary institutions that are less selective and have lower BA completion rates than similarly prepared Whites and that even when well-prepared Latinos go to the same kind of schools as their White peers, they have lower graduation rates" (Fry 2001, v). Our university is in the process of becoming more "selective" by changing our admissions policy.[3] The impetus behind this move is the desire to create a quality research-intensive university that serves a Latino population. However, we believe it is even more crucial to address the second part of the claim made by the Hispanic Pew Report—even when things are "equal," Latino students still do not do as well in their classes. Additionally, our retention rates are lower than national averages. According to ACT, the nationwide retention average for returning freshman in 2002 was 74 percent (ACT 2002). Here at UPTA we were at 66 percent in 2002 (OIRE 2003). Nearly all of these students take either developmental or first year writing courses. However, after a three year study beginning in 2000, we were down to a 45 percent retention rate after three years for the cohort being studied (OIRE 2003). For our 1999 cohort of students, we had a graduation rate of only 8.4 percent after four years, 21 percent after five years (OIRE 2003).

Mejía speaks directly to these reports in arguing for a "proper pedagogy" to help these students achieve higher graduation rates, which for many offer a measure of success (along with a job after graduation). Mejía specifically wants to see a pedagogy, which includes ethnic literatures, that also "focus[es] on the literacy of not just Latino/as but also of the indigenous folk in the United States" (2004, 52). He believes that this combination "could revitalize and change the colonialist nature of discourse and, more important, literacy studies in the Southwest and throughout the country" (ibid.). This kind of thinking is not about scores, remediation, or catching up. Instead, the focus shifts to speak directly to student need and interest. It pushes us to ask new questions, questions about how and what we teach as at least part of the answer to the problem.

These educational challenges became apparent at the university level for both of us as new professors at UTPA. For one, we assumed, incorrectly, who our students would be and that most of the students would speak Spanish. Many do not, and there is some "linguistic shame" in this for them, even as their language habits are affected by local variations of Spanish. Michelle Hall Kells reflects on the workings of "linguistic shame" in "Leveling the Linguistic Playing Field in First-Year Composition" in *Attending to the Margins:*

> He [Labov] notes speakers of nonstandard language varieties tend to misperceive and undervalue their own language varieties. This insecurity, or what I call "linguistic shame," among members of subordinate social groups is frequently reflected in negative self-perceptions and asymmetrical language attitudes: a high regard for the language of the elite class and a concomitant low regard for their own. (1999, 133)

Many students, however, are bilingual and go home each day to a space where Spanish is the only language spoken and then return to the university where Standard English is expected. When parents send their children to school or work in the school system, they must negotiate the treacherous waters of bilingual education and make decisions about language daily. These decisions include whether or not to put children in English-only courses or ease them into the transition from Spanish to English. Each local school has a different program and set of rules for this transition.

From talking with her upper-level students in a pedagogy course made up primarily of current and future teachers, Rebecca has learned that the options can be confusing and often lead to challenges for bilingual students throughout their elementary and secondary education. Rather than valuing both languages, some schools inadvertently ignore or punish students who speak Spanish at home. On the other hand, to ease the transition between Spanish and English, other schools confuse some students by switching back and forth between languages. As a result, some do not gain competency in either language at crucial points in language development. Our students often have heated debates about the issue of how to teach bilingual students that range from advocating sink-or-swim models to hopes for a more European approach that accepts multiple languages in schools (see Hacsi 2002). Dora's students also reflected the same attitudes about education and language in their written responses to the literature in her Mexican American literature course, often addressing the issues that arise when bilingual education abruptly ends for students in the fifth grade and/or the necessity of maintaining a strong home language at school. Though we do not often make clear theoretical connections in rhetoric and composition studies to work in secondary education, the effects of bilingual education theories and practices have a huge impact on the students at UTPA and other HSIs and need to be explored.

In an interview with Andrea Lunsford, the late Gloria Anzaldúa (one of UTPA's most recognized students) reflected on the discursive struggle her public education made her confront. She understood herself and the people of the Valley as "colonized people who were not allowed to speak our language, whose ways of life were not valued in this country . . . [as] a kind of international citizen whose life and privileges are not equal to the rights and privileges of ordinary, Anglo, White, Euro-American people" (Lunsford 1999, 48). Within this interview Anzaldúa elucidates, "Public education tried to erase all of that" (ibid.). We want to consider Anzaldúa's discursive struggle in relation to our students' struggle with learning an academic discourse as well as our own struggles, though from different spaces, with teaching them "writing." As educators who are trained in this discourse and often struggle with it ourselves, we want to think about the best practices for teaching writing to a Latina/o student population. In Anzaldúa's terms, how can we begin to take into account "other ethnicities . . . races . . . cultures . . . and histories" alongside the demands of both scholars and university students to perform particular standards that mark success? Even more importantly in this political-educational space, what are our options for best practices for teaching?

While there are similarities between the students at UTPA and the students we have worked with in the past, through this conversation we hope to draw out the differences that actually impact our practice. In arguing for a more useful way to solve problems, pragmatist William James explains, "The whole function of philosophy ought to be to find out what definite difference it will make to you and me, at definite instances in our life, if this world-formula or that world-formula be the true one" (1981, 27). James asks that in creating principles to act by (or teach by) we consider the real consequences of our beliefs based on an examination of real-life experience. In other words, here at UTPA we cannot rely on assumptions about students or a canon of "good" pedagogy to guide our teaching. Our teaching practices and our students' differences and especially our beliefs about these things matter when they affect the outcome of work in a class. Just being of a different race, gender, or culture does not necessarily make teaching or learning different. Instead, we must examine the particular things within a political and educational space that necessitate differences in practice and theory.

So we begin with practice and with our students' voices. Through these voices we begin to arrive at theories. Just as Anzaldúa and bell hooks find praxis by developing their theories out of their practice, we look for both our own agency and our students' through our dialogue with each other across our differences as educators. Through this, we can arrive at new theories (perhaps regional theories) that will "teach others to acquire voices without becoming *periquitas* (parrots) and to use theory to enable us to interpret what happens in the world" (Anzaldúa 1999, 47).

Dora: Letting Our Guards Down

I taught a 4000-level course focused on literacy, race, gender, and education. Of the thirty students in the course, 80 percent declared their ethnicity as Mexican American, and 20 percent as Mexican Nationals (mostly commuters from Reynosa, Mexico). The students, mostly first-generation college students with a working-class background, presented the all-too-common challenge of stepping out of a familiar discourse environment and into the "new" world of learning academic discourse(s). Less common than my experience in the Midwest were the students who held full-time jobs or careers, were parents, and were older than average students. Additionally, I had a mix of students who spoke Spanish (in a both fluent and bilingual capacity) and others who knew only English, having been "taught out of my language," as one student told me.

I soon grasped this situation and quickly realized that these South Valley students mirrored my own educational experiences: "We are your linguistic nightmare, your linguistic aberration, your linguistic *mestizaje*, the subject of your *burla.* Because we speak with tongues of fire we are culturally crucified. Racially, culturally, and linguistically *somos huèrfanos*—we speak an orphan tongue" (Anzaldúa 1999, 80). Anzaldúa calls this action "linguistic terrorism." This resonated with me during my first semester at UTPA as I met students who were fluently bilingual, those who were monolingual (mostly English), and those who were comfortable with code switching. The students presented their language experiences as directly related to their cultural experiences, adding to my understanding that these students' writing skills were being linguistically challenged by both internal and external dynamics. I noticed that regardless of their spoken language or writing ability, the students struggled to construct their identity in the classroom and in academia through written language. I wondered how the Spanish speakers constructed their identity in relation to writing Standard American English.

I tie this into the introduction of *Attending to the Margins,* where Kells and Valerie M. Balester examine *la frontera* as *border,* and ask how and "if our metaphors have become our myths, our disabling fictions. Has our notion of *la frontera* as border inadvertently advanced the construction and perpetuation of a host of disabling fictions?" (1999, xix). When the myth of "margin as frontier" works in conjunction with "linguistic terrorism," students are placed in a precarious place when it comes to their education. It creates disabling fictions in our students' minds. If our students who speak Spanish or any variant of this language are going to believe that they are not good writers, then this position defines how students perceive dominant society, how they perceive education and their place within it, and how they perceive success. In essence, the students' language and their comfort within or against an academic discourse force them to wear multifaceted masks.

Students come across two concepts, "linguistic terrorism" and "*la frontera* as *border,*" when I teach Kells's and Balester's and Anzaldúa's texts in my upper-division Mexican American literature course. My choice in texts speaks to Mejía's push for students in South Texas to read texts that are about them so we can work "toward composing ourselves lest we be composed by others" (Lunsford, qtd. in Mejía 2004, 53). Students often are compelled to tell me that reading these texts (primarily Kells and Balester, Anzaldúa, and fictional texts such Americo Paredes's *George Washington Gomez*) has given them the ability to forgive themselves for not speaking Spanish well. Sometimes they admit to making fun of others who speak Spanglish, pocho, or mocho, or those who have forgotten their first language, Spanish, and speak only English. For the first time, some students find their voices (or sense that they are part of the linguistic terrorism for others and for themselves) amidst the dominant language of the area—whether it is English or Spanish. It is then that students find that their experiences have been given a voice, and some feel they have the choice of whether or not to cater to the dominant language—by writing in only Spanish, Spanglish, or the language in which they are comfortable. Through our discussions, presentations, and written work, I realized that much of this work is done outside of class, in students' poetry, fiction, and music. For many, this realization comes at the 4000-level (upper-division courses) and reawakens a necessary critique of their education (both secondary and college). Unfortunately, many still do not see the essay as a format that can incorporate anything besides academic discourse written in Standard American English. Perfecting this is what they desire and expect to achieve in the traditional classroom.

Minority writers often are praised for learning to write and speak well in academic language but rarely are praised for their own language or voice (the construction of the academic mask). When I focused on the differences between the students in the Midwest and UTPA, I noticed the way academic discourse complemented the spoken language of the majority in the Midwest, whereas at UTPA, the academic language clashed with the familiar language spoken. I point to this because many students in this course commented on the fact that the school or education has everything to do with whether their language is preserved or erased. In one essay, "The Lightness of Me," Amanda Quintanilla, who was no older than twenty-five, remembered:

> When I entered school, I was no longer allowed to speak Spanish and would be told repeatedly to stop. So I am told I would go home and not speak any Spanish to my mom and dad. They of course at the time only spoke to me in English and that is how I lost my fluency in Spanish. Every conversation with family would now be in English.

As the essay continued, she shares how she is able to subvert the miseducation she received by practicing Spanish with her grandparents and by buying her own workbooks, videos, and audiotapes to help regain her first language.

Many of the students understood "success" as being tied to their language skills, saying that they or their parents felt that speaking English well would lead to "better things." Some students also found it difficult to balance that definition with their reality. A recurring sentiment in students' writing was how language presented a barrier to their parents' success. They wrote about working in the fields, using *estampias* (food stamps), having to stay home because their husbands or fathers would not allow them to go to school, or having to work instead of pursuing an education—which for many seemed like an unattainable dream because of their lack of financial resources. These narratives elucidate the ways students equate success with moving out of poverty, learning English well, and rising to middle-class status. I soon realized that an education at UTPA was not about "art for art's sake," but art for reality's sake. It was about upward mobility and "making something of myself" (a sentiment often repeated by students).

Another element of "success" had notions of race, racism, language, and skin color embedded in its definition, and it involved moving out of the Rio Grande Valley to northern states for a "better" education. What was apparent within these students' experiences of moving north to get an education was a subtle (or very real?) fear of another culture—a northern culture—that often was seen as a barrier to their success. One student shared, "I went away to school for a year up in Dallas where I had several friends go up with me. Well, some of them chose not to stay because they were often made fun of due to their skin color and Spanish accents." In her essay, "Me Talk Pretty One Day," another student, Edwina Garza, explained this same realization of discomfort in a predominately white university setting: "I had come to realize that I couldn't really relate to anyone. I had never felt the need to before, but I wanted nothing more than to throw out some Tex-Mex for the hell of it. My biggest insane hope was that the City of Austin could merge with the people of the Valley." She continued by relating a story of "a childhood friend [who] left to College Station and decided to come home two years later—she too had discovered something special about the Valley in her heart that she grew to miss." That "something special" was a comfort level related to language and racial appearance. The narratives prompted me to ask how these students' experiences reflected on them as writers in the classroom. How do these students negotiate language and culture in the university system—a system that reflects the "success" model as defined by a dominant culture? Their writing shows a clear understanding of the need to "fit into" academic discourse. There is a struggle here, and one that reflects a power dynamic where one dominant group regulates and thereby influences the language and linguistic identity of another group.

Students are aware of this. These students view Spanish as a language that will not help them "succeed," even while they understand that speaking multiple languages is important. They view education as a game and "recreate" the rules that regulate when they can and cannot speak their "foreign tongue." In the essay "Dual Identity and My Struggles," one student writes, "They completely overlook the fact that I am attending college (while many of them are not) and that what I have to say may actually matter. I feel that I can never speak my mind because it will either surprise or offend them." This response shows an obvious parallel between having a voice that will be listened to and having an education. Also apparent is how the student alludes to the "Anglos" as having that power to speak, even without an education. This sentiment is repeated in another student's analysis of her linguistic choices when she places English as an academic language that she chooses not to use in her home. She writes:

> I can understand the anger [Gloria Anzaldúa] has because we all feel it at times when the pressure is building up inside of us trying to be one thing and having to be another because of your family, keeping up with both roles is tiring. What I mean is when one is in school they tend to only talk English but at home we let [our] guard down and talk Spanish and mix it with a little bit of English.

Then she goes on to put in parentheses "(Mention changing when classmates call)." That last sentence, set aside in parentheses by the student, illustrates the common misconception that one must conform to linguistic and cultural roles in order to be academically successful. This is about playing a game—one that angers her. As an educator in classrooms that will always meet "at the crossroads" of language and writing, I find that I have to *let my guard down* and begin teaching how linguistic terrorism and *la frontera* as *border* work in our students' discourse to the students. This theoretical language allows students to articulate what they already know through experience.

Rebecca: Being Brave

"Linguistic terrorism" was certainly not part of my vocabulary as I stepped into the classroom at UTPA. However, I did have an understanding of the language games that can go on when negotiating home and school language, especially when playing "the game" has real consequences for students. Working with my students in the South, the differences between home and school language were more about dialects (dialects I happen to cherish and value) and the idiosyncrasies of Southern conversation. Despite this understanding, I did take Lisa Delpit's warning seriously when I first read it at the beginning of my PhD work. She admonishes white middle-class professors for not recognizing their own position of power and especially for not sharing their knowledge of the discursive strategies of this position, explicitly, with their students who are not part of the "culture of power." In one part of the argument, Delpit explains that the process approach to teaching writing ignores the fact that many African American students are more accustomed to direct discursive strategies and may view student-centered approaches as passive and confusing. Delpit's article offers two important ideas that relate to my teaching at UTPA: "[I]t is impossible to create a model for the good teacher without taking issues of culture and community context into account," and it is fine to "[t]ell [students] that their language and cultural style is unique and wonderful but that there is a political power game that is also being played, and if they want to be in on that game there are certain games that they too must play" (1997, 578–81). Through this article we both hope to work toward Delpit's first point, to take context and community into account. It is the second part that bothers me: teaching and learning as a high-stakes game. Wendy Ryden argues that Delpit's stance can be problematic

> as long as teachers merely expect and are expected to transfer the knowledge attached to their privileged position rather than to participate in dialogic writing with their classes that goes beyond politeness and tokenism to a genuine invitation to include the knowledge represented in the competing discourses of student experience. (Marshall and Ryden 2000, 242)

Taking Delpit's warning along with Ryden's critique, I knew I needed to look more closely at my students' specific needs here at UTPA. In the South, I knew many of the students' stories because they are my own or part of the culture I experienced growing up. Now that I look back, my students in the South had different ideas about home and school language than the ones beginning to emerge for me here. Though they wanted to master school language, many had an open fondness for their home dialects. Southerners especially love "y'all" and "fix'in" and other colloquialisms that mark us as different but are not acceptable in academic prose. Admittedly, some of my African American students were much more worried about "getting it right" than the white students due to years of being battered over issues of black English vernacular. Though most students seem to intrinsically understand that writing in college is different from other kinds of writing and especially from the way they speak, in the South there seems to be an edge of defiance against the demands. At UTPA, it seems more desperate somehow. Many of these students are learning more than a new "discourse community" or dialect but a different language altogether. Daniel wrote, reflecting on grade school: "I wasn't even able to go to the restroom during class because I didn't know how to ask." These kinds of situations leave scars that follow students into college, scars that affect their confidence. If confidence is an important first step to becoming a good writer, then many of these students have missed a vital first step.[4] What follows are excerpts from a few essays my students in a composition class wrote describing their own literacy practices as well as my tentative theorizing after reading them. They teach me about what it means to teach at this particular location in South Texas—the Valley.

After a few semesters of reading their words and getting to know my students, I realize that we view each other as experts and as "other." However, the starkness of the otherness (on my part) is often eclipsed by my role as "teacher." I feel comfortable with my students and usually forget where I am after the first week of class. However, there are always moments when I remember that they have a history I do not understand. They have a language I covet. They seem very surprised when I tell them how much I wish I knew Spanish and how lucky they are to be bilingual. Until I get them as juniors and seniors, many feel like being bilingual is a disadvantage—especially those who do not speak (or get to practice) English at home. Daniel remembers lamenting in grade school: "Why couldn't God just create a single universal language?" This student explains later in his essay that learning English changed everything for him: "As the years went by I started to read and speak English fluently. I could finally express my feelings to other people and express my point of view to them. It turns out that I was way smarter than I thought. The reason my grades were so low wasn't a lack of effort but the fact that I was not equipped with the right tools." Standard English is a tool they desire, and whether or not this desire is a "disabling fiction," I must find ways to integrate it into my courses. Whatever my own reservations about emphasizing academic discourse or teaching the "dominant language" (as Dora explains), I have learned that they claim to want to know.

What I also have learned here in South Texas is how to see otherness in terms of my own experience rather than as an abstract theoretical idea. Recently a colleague in linguistics wrote a recommendation letter for me. I was surprised to read the following:

> It is important to recognize that, as a *bolilla* [Dora tells me this also can be translated as "white bread"] or "Anglo-American female" who teaches English, the language associated with education and, for some students at least, oppression, to achieve these high ratings in her first year indicates an ability to create rapport and show respect.

Though I appreciated this high praise and collegial courtesy, I was struck by the language that highlighted my own otherness from my students. I realized that in order to become a more successful teacher, I would have to see myself through my *students'* perception of me and *their* expectations for the course.

I have started to listen more to my students rather than to simply rely on what theoretical ideals I want to hold onto—generic pedagogies for "good teaching" often written by and for whites. My student Blanca tells of the battles fought by her grandparents and parents as they attempted to do migrant work in the United States while struggling with English. There were no adults that could aid with schoolwork in English: "It was up to them of whether or not he or she will be successful in the future." She goes on to discuss her troubles in bilingual classes, especially as she confused Spanish and English and felt incompetent in both. Blanca experienced the "treacherous waters" personally: "I was getting the grammar, pronunciation, spelling, everything mixed up and the little bit that my family knew wasn't enough, and they were busy working while my grandmother took care of me." Blanca hopes that "[teachers] could make it simpler in the long run to learn new strategies of learning how to read and write, for example."

Omar theorizes about the situation many students face here in the Valley through his own literacy experiences. He connects the challenges of bilingual education to its economic consequences. Omar "know[s] people my age or older who can't read or write fluently in either language." Though Omar is proud of his bilingual abilities, he understands that language problems contribute to the reason that "people in this region go unnoticed and are more susceptible to poverty." In the end, Omar believes that teachers must take up the challenge:

> So these kids grow up to be illiterate adults who have illiterate children who just let the cycle continue until some brave teacher will spend her time to try to teach this generation of well-fare takers and help them get out of the hole they were born in to.

Though Omar may utter a common stereotype at the end of this passage, the key is his belief that it takes a teacher who can connect with these students, who is "brave" to make a change, just as Blanca hopes teachers will come up with "new strategies" for teaching reading and writing. I certainly do not consider myself brave when I walk into the classrooms here at UTPA. I feel I need help. The question becomes, what does it take to be "brave" here or to teach well in this context? What do the students want, and what do they need? Are these different questions? Other students, like Richie, do not feel Omar's confidence. Richie primarily remembers the embarrassment of not being able to pronounce words "correctly":

> There was this one time, where I couldn't pronounce a word, and even though the harder I seemed to try, the harder it was for me to say it. The word was "with" and I hated that word, just because I couldn't pronounce it. I remember going home and telling my mom that I hated reading, and that I didn't see a purpose to it.

This memory affects his present performance: "It made me look at reading the way I do now, which was to read only when I had to, not because I wanted to. I guess I have to grow out of this feeling, but it's kind of hard once you've had it for so long." Whether Hispanic, white, or African American, we know that children are affected by their teachers. Richie's story of humiliation is, unfortunately, not new. The story simply comes out of a new context and with different implications.

I knew I had to ask for these literacy essays both to allow the students to express their past concerns with learning and to help me understand where these students begin when they walk into my classes in South Texas. I have done this assignment many times over the years, but it has never been as useful as it is at UTPA. Primarily, these stories have profoundly affected the way I teach my pedagogy course, Composition Techniques, for teachers of writing. Though the course is directed toward students who will teach middle and high school English, I often have many elementary school hopefuls in my class as well. I now see it as part of my job to connect these literacy essays to the way I teach teachers.

In Composition Techniques, my primary job is to offer students as much as I can, in sixteen weeks, about the theories and practices of teaching writing. The first time I taught this course during my first semester in South Texas, I knew I needed to talk about bilingual education, but I had no idea what kind of fire it would start. The students really lit up for the first time and became quite passionate about the topic. I realized that this needed to be a larger component of the class in the future sections. As I continue to teach the course, I have come to understand through listening and through research the political, educational, and ethical complexities of this topic. My students want to know these complexities so that they can address them in their own classrooms, no matter what form of bilingual education their particular district has adopted. More importantly, they can begin to combat, through more respectful pedagogies, the damaging misconceptions about bilingual students (in America) as being less intelligent and less willing to learn (see Steele 1997; Hacsi 2002). I was thrilled last year to find *Latino/a Discourses: On Language, Identity, and Literacy,* edited by Michelle Hall Kells, Valerie Balester, and Victor Villanueva. We read several essays from the collection as a way to begin discussion of educating students who speak multiple languages in the United States. Mejía's article particularly spoke to the students as he critiqued their own school. I also encourage several students to do their research paper and presentation on the topic to help extend the discussion beyond personal experience. Though we often disagree about methodologies, we all agree that the issue must become an important topic of theoretical discussion that examines best practices for students. They want to avoid, for their students, the pitfalls my freshman students have written about in their literacy essays. They want to be "brave" teachers.

The Problem of Academic Discourse

"It is in the emergence of the interstices—the overlap and displacement of domains of difference—that the intersubjective and collective experiences of nationness, community interest, or cultural value are negotiated" (Bhabha 1994, 2).

After listening through our students' voices, we revisited the theories we use to support our pedagogies to see how they work in this new context. From this, we have found that talking about "academic discourse" always leads down a path filled with wrong turns, backtracking, and dead ends in connection to the students here in the Valley. We are caught firmly in between the idea that students should be allowed to express their own language and culture and the need to teach them "academic discourse" or the "dominant language"—between the CCCC's 1974 statement on "Students' Right to Their Own Language" and David Bartholomae's classic call in "Inventing the University": "The student has to learn to speak our language, to speak as we do" (1997, 589). We worry that both of these extremes may be "disabling fictions."

As Beatrice Méndez Newman advocates in chapter 1 of this book, we have to take into account our students' voices, look at theories that speak to these voices, and then combine these to come up with new practices and possibly new theories. Though we agree on this, Dora approaches this nexus through the *mestiza* consciousness and as an interstitial space, ideas that come from a position of Chicana subjectivity as well as postcolonial studies, and Rebecca through ideas about thirdness found in followers of American pragmatism. For us, these are more like ways of thinking than exact pedagogies to follow. Hephzibah Roskelly and Kate Ronald (1998) imagine a pragmatic philosophy as the following: "Pragmatic philosophy brings this triadic process—each side tested and altered by the other and by a third principle of mediation—to bear on history, experience, self, and society" (1998, 87). Rather than merely transplant theories into this space, we need to alter both our practice and theories using our students' particular cultural space as our mediator. In this new space, we can try to avoid choosing either to teach academic discourse or value individual difference. This follows what Anzaldúa calls "*amasamiento*," or "the act of kneading, of uniting and joining that not only produc[es] both a creature of darkness and a creature of light, but also a creature that questions the definitions of light and dark and gives them new meanings" (1999, 103). As part of the *mestiza* consciousness, this act creates another space where students can make sense of the theories and pedagogies that they face in the classroom in relation to their familiar space.

Dora

When I arrived at UTPA, I was told I was an "outsider." As one administrator explained, "You've been up north too long." This phrase placed me outside of my students' experiences, making me concerned about how they would view me—a young "Chicana" radical (not a term used by most residents of South Texas). But my racial uniform (Takaki 1989) gave me entrance into a classroom and allowed students to understand that we had many educational similarities. Many of us had received impromptu speech therapy sessions from teachers attempting to erase our accents (mine came with "shopping" and "chopping"; Rebecca's student struggled to say "with"), and many of us also faced racism from teachers who did not have the pedagogical skills to work with and not against difference. We had worked with and through Spanish as a first language, and some of us had navigated the assumptions that are made about Latino/a students from lower socioeconomic situations. This dynamic made the spaces that erupt in my classrooms at UTPA energetic, troublesome, insightful, and encouraging. Through our discussions about education, I came to understand the students' perception of education as a "game." The idea that education is a game points to the differences in the languages that students and educators speak. And it is the games our students play that create unsafe classrooms.

The idea of playing a role in order to succeed and survive education continually resurfaced in my students' writing, solidifying Alfred Arteaga's (1994) point in *An Other Tongue*, that the "marginal Other autocolonizes himself or herself each time the hegemonic discourse is articulated" (1994, 16). This autocolonization influences the way students think about themselves in the academic environment and how educators perceive some students in the classroom. As Malea Powell (2004) elucidates, a dichotomous mind-set is difficult to break out of, and when course readings are based on this binary viewpoint, students are asked to find their place within very defined cultural and linguistic roles, thus making it difficult to move away from without a conscious reworking of the way we "see" and construct race, language attitudes, and definitions of "success." Thus when I examined the students' written narrative histories, I returned to Emma Pérez's (1998) use of the concept "strategic essentialism," which she describes as "practiced resistance against dominant ideologies that silence and/or model marginalized groups" (Pérez 1998, 88). The students' narratives described their experiences with language in the educational system and gave insight into the choices they have (sub)consciously made to temporarily work through an essentialized identity in an attempt to negotiate a privileged rhetoric and work within a European historical and linguistic model, thus illustrating how a language based on dichotomous thinking works in practice.

As my pedagogy developed and the semester progressed, oftentimes the students' words would echo Bhabha's (1994) words: "Colonialism often speaks in a tongue that is forked, not false. If colonialism takes power in the name of history, it repeatedly exercises its authority through the figures of farce" (1994, 85). This forked tongue is often heard in the classroom, and many non-native speakers of English and native speakers of Spanglish have learned to interpret or translate what this tongue is telling them. I argue that we must continue to reevaluate how linguistic attitudes affect students' choices, successes, and failures in the classroom because Latina/o students are often asked to mask their cultural, linguistic, and/or ethnic voices and learn to adorn a Standard American English *mask:* a game that is quickly becoming tiring. Perhaps this is the place where Anzaldúa asks that a *mestiza* develop a tolerance for ambiguity. I posit that we take her idea and take the next step forward to critically analyze how this ambiguity can move educators and students forward into that third space, the liminal space of possibility.

Rebecca

While Dora was already in tune with the possibilities of the language differences and problems these students might face, in some ways through her own experiences and primarily through her scholarship, I came to UTPA both misunderstanding my own position of power and worrying about it. Through this experience, I have been forced to "interrogate . . . the silence of whiteness in composition pedagogy" and ask myself how much of what I teach perpetuates white middle-class values and beliefs (Marshall and Ryden 2000, 240). Though I have not been oblivious to this issue in the past, I sense it physically here at UTPA, which has demanded rather than requested a confrontation with the issue. I also have realized through reading Dora's work that I have fallen into the trap of having a "dichotomous mind-set" in the classroom. My continuous references to "home" and "school" language here as being different (often implying essential differences) perpetuate the problem we are discussing. Though I understand ideas such as thinking through third spaces, resisting dichotomies, and avoiding "linguistic terrorism," these things are still difficult in practice, especially in my work as administrator, where my job is to *regulate* courses and pedagogies. I realize the irony of my wanting to help my students "find their voice" through their local culture when I have only lived here for a year and often feel as if I am in a foreign country. I also am beginning to understand my own issues with teaching straight "academic discourse." In my teaching, at times, I incorrectly conceive of "academic discourse" as only serving "hierarchical leadership, competition, stoicism, and the concealment of vulnerability," especially on those days when I attempt to teach students "the basics" of a research paper (Bleich 2001, 89). Instead, I need to remember, as Jacqueline Jones Royster (2002) explains, that academic discourse is not and never has been one master discourse but is always multiple and changing (2002, 25).[5] As Royster demonstrates, part of the problem is that both students and professors view and teach "academic discourse" as if it exists in a separate privileged space. Though reading a few different academic journals or examining new online academic discourses can quickly prove the singular discourse theory false, belief in it still exists.

Fortunately, I have realized that my actual practice has not been as dichotomous as my rhetoric here. In the class I excerpted from earlier, I chose literacy as the theme, and we juxtaposed different visions of literacy with their own narratives. We read Anna Quindlen alongside Judith Ortiz Cofer. Additionally, we read, discussed, and wrote about academic discourse. We discussed Quindlen's privileged childhood on the same day we worried about children with similar experiences as Cofer's depicted in her literacy narrative of violence and determination surrounding the educational desires of a young Latina. We read "Inventing the University" together with Brandt's "Sponsors of Literacy." I talk to students openly about "what other professors expect" and at the same time how these expectations can be arbitrary and why. I also let students experiment with language, and along with them I am learning what that means here in the Valley. I have begun to appreciate the intricacies and intimacies of Spanglish. I have realized that ethnography assignments, where voice and cultural observation are explored, offer clearer ways to navigate the space between "getting it right" and creatively exploring personal voice.

Discursive Games

When we seek discursive silence through the silencing of others, we come to regard discourse as naturally an agonistic, strategic battle of verbal wit, and we come to regard truth as but one more weapon in the arsenal of rhetorical persuasion. In such a situation discourse, indeed, life itself, can become nothing but a game, even if played for keeps (Yarbrough 1999, 211).

Through this research and exploration, we have both, unfortunately, stumbled upon the gaming metaphor as a description of the problem that connects our students' language and academic discourse. Though academic discourse does not inherently silence students, as it represents dominant discourses, we know that many students at UTPA perceive it as doing just that. In "Speak For Yourself? Power and Hybridity in the Cross-Cultural Classroom," Bronwyn Williams (2003) describes the difficult position of the colonized students who must "acknowledge that they do not understand the dominant discourse, but they must subsequently accept and complete assignments" (2003, 591). However, these classroom products are never a replication of the authority that they attempt to impress upon the students: "The consequence of this in the discourse of the colonized speaking back to the colonizer is that mimicry contains within it a mockery of the colonizer's authority" (ibid.). In this postcolonial version of the gaming metaphor, we have to ask where the student is located within this game. Certainly, silencing and mockery are not the goals of the writing classroom.

As one solution, we both talk openly about academic discourse in our classrooms as we try to admit we sometimes copy the discourse of our own miseducation—Rebecca from a discourse born out of white privilege, even though she is aware of its elasticity, and Dora from mimicking (while learning to subvert) the discourse taught to her in the academic space. Though we know, theoretically, that this can be a both/and rather than either/or situation, in practice it is much more difficult. We can feel with each paper the pendulum swing one way or the other. Is it good enough that we talk openly to our students about different kinds of writing and ask them to learn multiple discourses? Can they seriously turn in a paper with content, style, or language not considered "academic discourse" to that particular professor to another class? Another layer to this problem is that many of these students are smart but underprepared, which means it will take more time to acquire academic discourses, leaving little time for experimentation of other sorts. It becomes a question of service and disservice to the student. However, we, in the least, understand that when our students are worried about "getting it right," they are referring to Delpit's (1997) ideas. They want to be in on the game.

We are all sure we know what the game is, yet in practice it is multiple and varied, and it depends on one's position within academia. The students, especially first-year students and sophomores, do not know the game rules. If we are going to continue to use the "game" metaphor to describe the way academic discourse is taught, then we should take a look at the rules and begin to include those voices that often are excluded from the winner's circle. This is no longer about letting some students start with a handicap but about leveling that playing field and making the rules known to each of our students. As Williams (2003) writes, "If we truly want to help students grasp any kind of power, we can model for them in our own critique of our position and privilege in the dominant culture a way to consider how the culture and ideology creates and often silences them as postcolonial subjects" (2003, 607). If we continue with this line of thought, then we will be in a position of constantly renegotiating rules, an endless game of creating, observing, and breaking rules.

What if we stop thinking of gaining literacy as a game? What is in between one's own language and the most rigid academic discourses? Pérez (1999) offers the idea of the decolonial imaginary: a third space where writing can move the colonized into another space or the "interstitial space where differential politics and social dilemmas are negotiated." Pérez, echoing Anzaldúa's idea of the shadow, understands it as "intangible to many because it acts like a shadow in the dark" (1999, 6). In this shadowy realm, how do we find practical teaching strategies to get us through the day?

As Friere (1998) argues, we need to make classrooms dialogic spaces where discourses are shared and thus constantly in flux. Instead of gaming, which is linked to other war metaphors and clearly connected to ideas such as "linguistic terrorism," we should be teaching our students "discursive confidence":

> By "discursive confidence" here I do not mean the ability to persuade others to do or believe what you (already) want them to, nor the ability to "construct sentences and paragraphs" in keeping with the conventional expectations of grammar and syntax, but the ability to help others to understand the objects of your own concerns, and to seek together the common causes of your questions and problems. (Yarbrough 1999, 210)

What we have to work on is what "discursive confidence" means in each educational space. Here at UTPA, it means being able to talk about past literacy practices and to reconcile them with current expectations and to change those expectations through this interrogation.

Through this work, we have begun to realize that there is so much more to this situation that needs to be explored theoretically. For example, what do linguists or teachers of ESL have to tell us about writing and speaking practices that affect the writing practices of our students? American rhetoric and composition scholars, though usually interested in interdisciplinary work, have not thoroughly examined what these experts have to offer in theoretical terms and practices that could aid the students in South Texas. This is the next step in the process. For example, Beatriz Gutierrez, a former graduate student in linguistics at UTPA, explained in an e-mail that Spanish and American English discourses have very different conceptions of what makes a good sentence:

> For Mexicans, if a person does not know how to write long sentences, that person is showing a lack of formal schooling. Thoughts in sentences have to be explained all the way. . . . You do not have to split a long sentence, several lines long, just because of length. . . . Students do not restrict their sentences to the four types of sentences their American counterparts do.

Gutierrez adds that a bilingual education teacher noted "Spanish could not be written in short and highly structured sentences, since that is not our culture." Yet these types of sentences are precisely the kind we often demand of our students. Additionally, Dora remembers having trouble learning the concept of argument when asked to write an argumentative essay. For her, argument meant not agreeing with someone—not a kind of scholarly prose. The conventions of this prose style seemed foreign to her sensibilities both in writing and in class discussion. In this chapter, we have started the process. We have looked at ourselves and our students. We have started to listen. Now we need to reach out beyond what we already know to others who have different pieces of the puzzle.

During their educational careers, we want our students to find their place within an academic space and hope that, in turn, the space becomes more flexible. It is not an easy concept to grasp for many students and usually arrives late in their careers—that writing in the academy is not simply about filling a preordained space. We understand that academic borders often are arbitrary and inculcated with white, middle-class values. We also know it is problematic to continue to think in terms of borders at all. However, we live in a geographic space where the borders feel real, where difference is marked physically, verbally, and through the written word. Though we know our students are asking us to be brave teachers, we also know we are asking a great deal of them too.

Notes

1. According to the Office of Institutional Research and Effectiveness (OIRE) at UTPA, "Nine percent of students are employed full time and 57 percent are employed part time" (OIRE 2005). Additionally, "Forty percent of the students will be caring for a home and family while attending UTPA" (ibid.). Some are older than the typical eighteen-to-twenty-year-old college student and have decided to return to college after raising families and beginning various career paths. Nearly all of the students are first-generation college students: "Parents of 72 percent of the students do not have a bachelor's degree or higher" (OIRE 2005).

2. Two examples of this include the Nelson Denny scores generated by the reading lab for our English 1310 Developmental Reading Course and ACT scores listed on our course inventories each semester. Of the 193 students tested at the reading lab for spring 2005, 122 tested below a tenth-grade reading level, with 9 at a fourth-grade reading level. In one of Rebecca's English 1302 rhetoric courses, students' ACT scores in English range from a 9 to a 27. ACT reports that students who score below a 16 in individual areas usually are not prepared for college-level work in that area (1999). In two of Rebecca's spring 2005 rhetoric courses, sixteen students scored at or below 16. Though we realize that there are vigorous debates about the validity of these tests, especially for minority students, the numbers are

still a concern. For information about these debates, including discussions about the relationship between standardized testing and low scores for minority students, see the PBS *Frontline* special "Secrets of the SAT," http://www.pbs.org/wgbh/pages/frontline/shows/sats/, which outlines the current debate.

3. We have mixed feelings about this new selectivity. Instead of an "open admissions" policy we are moving to a "restricted admissions" policy according to the University of Texas-Pan American's David Zuniga, director of Admissions and Records. Since UTPA is the only place that many of our students will have the opportunity to go to college, we hate to see the university turn anyone away. On the other hand, we face the ethical dilemma of taking students' money to participate in courses for which we do not have the resources to help them succeed. This new selectivity is being driven by a desire to become a more research-focused institution and to raise our standards to meet those of other UT system schools. The rhetoric of this kind of move does not usually include discourse on developmental or remedial writing because the hope is that selectivity will result in students who are better prepared to succeed in college.

4. Social psychologist Claude Steele (1997) describes a phenomenon he calls the "stereotype threat." When one is part of a cultural minority that has been negatively stereotyped, especially in terms of intelligence or academic ability, Steele believes those stereotypes can affect one's performance on standardized tests and in the classroom. Taken into account when creating classroom practice, this concept offers an interesting possibility for transformative pedagogies for Latina/o students.

5. Rhetorician Malea Powell (2004) calls attention to the language of the discipline and the need for a new discourse:

> To their [Jacqueline Jones Royster and Jean C. Williams] analysis I would add that the language in which this struggle is named—dominant/oppressed, center/margins, colonizer/colonized—is itself a trap, an integral part of the rhetoric of empire. We need a new language, one that doesn't convince us of our unutterable and ongoing differences, one that doesn't force us to see one another as competitors. We need a language that allows us to imagine respectful and reciprocal relationships that acknowledge the degree to which we need one another (have needed one another) in order to survive and flourish. (2004, 41)

I advocate her idea (along with Craig Womack, Scott Lyons, and others) of pushing for linguistic sovereignty for students who are being linguistically and culturally governed.

Works Cited

ACT. 1999. "ACT Scores Show Significant Gains in 90's". *ACT Newsroom.* (August 17). http://www.act.org/news/releases/1999/08-17-99.html (accessed June 5, 2006).

———. 2002. "College Graduation Rates Steady Despite Increase in Enrollment." *ACT Newsroom.* (November 15). http://www.act.org/news/releases/2002/11-15-02.html (accessed June 5, 2006).

Anzaldúa, Gloria. 1999. *Borderlands/La Frontera: The New Mestiza.* 2nd ed. San Francisco: Aunt Lute Books.

Arteaga, Alfred. 1994. *An Other Tongue: Nation and Ethnicity in the Linguistic Borderlands.* Durham, NC: Duke University Press.

Bartholomae, David. 1997. "Inventing the University." In *Cross-Talk in Comp Theory: A Reader,* ed. Victor Villanueva, 589–619. Urbana, IL: National Council of Teachers of English.

Bhabha, Homi. 1994. *The Location of Culture.* New York: Routledge.

Bleich, David. 2001. "The Collective Privacy of Academic Language." In *Personal Effects: The Social Character of Scholarly Writing,* ed. Deborah H. Holdstein and David Bleich, 79–93. Logan: Utah State University Press.

Conference on College Composition and Communication. 1974. "Students' Right to Their Own Language." Special issue of *College Composition and Communication* 25: 1–32.

Delpit, Lisa D. 1997. "The Silenced Dialogue: Power and Pedagogy in Educating Other People's Children." In *Cross-Talk in Comp Theory: A Reader,* ed. Victor Villanueva, 565–88. Urbana, IL: National Council of Teachers of English.

Freire, Paulo. 1998. *Pedagogy of the Oppressed.* Translated by Myra Bergman Ramos. New York: Continuum.

Fry, Richard. 2001. "Latino Youth Finishing College: The Role of Selective Pathways." *Hispanic Center Pew Report.* Washington, DC: Pew Hispanic Center.

Gutierrez, Beatriz. 2005. "RE: Fwd: Mexican Academic Discourse." E-mail to Rebecca Jones. (February 27).

Hacsi, Timothy. 2002. "Is Bilingual Education a Good Idea?" In *Children as Pawns: The Politics of Educational Reform.* Cambridge, MA: Harvard University Press.

hooks, bell. 1994. *Teaching to Transgress: Education as the Practice of Freedom.* New York: Routledge.

James, Williams. 1981. *Pragmatism.* Edited by Bruce Kuklick. Indianapolis, IN: Hackett.

Kells, Michelle Hall. 1999. "Leveling the Linguistic Playing Field in First-Year Composition." In *Attending to the Margins: Writing, Researching, and Teaching on the Front Lines,* ed. Michelle Hall Kells and Valerie Balester. Portsmouth, NH: Boynton/Cook.

Kells, Michelle Hall, and Valerie Balester, eds. 1999. *Attending to the Margins: Writing, Researching, and Teaching on the Front Lines.* Portsmouth, NH: Boynton/Cook.

Kells, Michelle Hall, Valerie Balester, and Victor Villanueva, eds. 2004. *Latino/a Discourses: On Language, Identity, & Literacy Education.* Portsmouth, NH: Heinemann.

Lunsford, Andrea. 1999. "Toward a New *Mestiza* Rhetoric: Gloria Anzaldúa on Composition and Postcoloniality." In *Race, Rhetoric, and the Postcolonial,* ed. Gary A. Olson and Lynn Worsham, 43–78. Albany: State University of New York Press.

Marshall, Ian, and Wendy Ryden. 2000. "Interrogating the Monologue: Making Whiteness Visible." *College Composition and Communication* 52:2: 240–59.

Mejía, Jaime. 2004. "Bridging Rhetoric and Composition Studies with Chicano and Chicana Studies: A Turn to Critical Pedagogy." In *Latino/a Discourses: On Language, Identity, & Literacy Education,* ed. Michelle Hall Kells, Valerie Balester, and Victor Villanueva, 40–56. Portsmouth, NH: Heinemann.

Office of Institutional Research and Effectiveness (OIRE). 2003. "Stats at a Glance: Fall 2003." University of Texas Pan American. http://www.oire.panam.edu/publications/minifactbook2003.pdf (accessed October 13, 2004).

———. 2005. "Just the Facts." *UTPA Campus Report* 23:5: 4.

Pérez, Emma. 1998. "Irigaray's Female Symbolic in the Making of Chicana Lesbian *Sitios y Lenguas* (Sites and Discourses)." In *Living Chicana Theory*, ed. Carla Trujillo, 87–101. Berkeley, CA: Third Woman Press.

———. 1999. *The Decolonial Imaginary: Writing Chicanas into History*. Bloomington: Indiana University Press.

Powell, Malea. 2004. "Down by the River, or How Susan La Flesche Picotte Can Teach Us about Alliance as a Practice of Survivance." *College Composition and Communication* 67:1 (September): 38–60.

Reynolds, Nedra. 2004. *Geographies of Writing: Inhabiting Places and Encountering Difference*. Carbondale: Southern Illinois University Press.

Roskelly, Hephzibah, and Kate Ronald. 1998. *Reason to Believe: Romanticism, Pragmatism, and the Teaching of Writing*. Albany: State University of New York Press.

Royster, Jacqueline Jones. 2002. "Academic Discourses or Small Boats on a Big Sea." *ALT DIS: Alternative Discourses and the Academy*, ed. Christopher Schroeder, Helen Fox, and Patricia Bizzell, 23–30. Portsmouth, NH: Boynton/Cook.

Steele, Claude M. 1997. "A Threat in the Air: How Stereotypes Shape Intellectual Identity and Performance." *American Psychologist* 52: 613–29.

Takaki, Ronald. 1989. *Strangers From a Different Shore: A History of Asian Americans*. New York: Penguin Books.

Williams, Bronwyn T. 2003. "Speak for Yourself? Power and Hybridity in the Cross-Cultural Classroom." *College Composition and Communication* 54:4 (June): 586–609.

Yarbrough, Stephen. 1999. *After Rhetoric: The Study of Discourse beyond Language and Culture*. Carbondale: Southern Illinois University Press.

CHAPTER 4

LITERATE PRACTICES/LANGUAGE PRACTICES

WHAT DO WE REALLY KNOW ABOUT OUR STUDENTS?

Isabel Araiza, Humberto Cárdenas Jr.,
and Susan Loudermilk Garza

In order to value and build on the literate practices of the Latino students at Texas A&M University-Corpus Christi (TAMU-CC), three faculty members developed a survey that was administered to first-year students attending the university.[1] TAMU-CC is a Hispanic-Serving Institution (HSI) located in South Texas with a large percentage of Latino, primarily Mexican American, students, including many who are first generation and receive need-based financial assistance. The survey was developed to identify literate practices (visual, written, oral) in which the students participate, both inside and outside of school. The survey also asked students what languages they use to engage in these literate practices—English, Spanish, a combination of the two (code switching), and other languages. We sought to identify these practices so that in future scholarship we could develop informed instructional strategies that incorporate and value both academic and nonacademic discourses and bring them into the classroom in ways that are not alienating and not based on incorrect assumptions. We also examined the social and economic characteristics of our students to better understand their experiences. The results of the survey revealed that (1) most of our first-year Latino/a students speak only English, (2) those who do speak Spanish use Spanish less than 10 percent of the time when engaging in the literate practices identified in this study, and (3) both our white and Latino/a students have similar levels of cultural capital. Further, we held focus groups with faculty of first-year English classes to discover their knowledge of HSIs and Latino/a students. This chapter addresses widely held perceptions regarding Latino/a students, explores the disconnect between those perceptions and the realities of the students that we serve at our HSI, reveals the faculty perceptions we discovered, and shares some questions for further study.

Perceptions of Latino/a Students

Faculty teaching at HSIs may rely on the prominent discourse surrounding these institutions and Latino/a students for an understanding of the students with whom they work, but that discourse may not accurately represent the reality of the students who choose to enroll at the institution. Most of that discourse employs an "at-risk" tone, so faculty may have nothing to shape their perceptions but this negative discourse. An example of this type of discourse is a report released by the Pew Hispanic Center in June 2004, entitled "Federal Policy and Latinos in Higher Education" (Santiago and Reyes 2004). The report indicates that most Latinos/as are first-generation college students, are low income, and have less academic preparation than their peers. The report goes farther, indicating that Latinos/as are less likely to complete college through the traditional path[2] compared to whites and Asians.

An extensive body of literature (Stoops 2003; Kao and Thompson 2003; Vernez and Krop 2000; del Pinal, Jorge, and Singer 1997; Rong and Grant 1992) presents a picture of what is described as a chronic trend of Latinos/as (specifically Mexican Americans) lagging behind in educational attainment compared to their white counterparts. Complicating this portrait of the Latino/a student, current literature has begun to reveal the extremely diverse nature of the Latino/a population, found nationwide and in the state of Texas. In this book, Baca, Méndez Newman, and Ramirez-Dhoore and Jones reinforce this diversity. Yet we have found that this literature does not inform us about the Latino/a population in our Coastal Bend area. What has been written about postsecondary Latino/a students in Texas focuses primarily on the population at the border, in the Rio Grande Valley (see Farr 2001; Guerra 1998; Jiménez, Smith, and Martínez-León 2003; Moll and Gonzáles 2001). In addition to having limited knowledge of the population at the HSI where they teach, some faculty may have even less knowledge of the institution as a whole and how being an HSI shapes the mission of the institution.

Realities of Latino/a Students at TAMU-CC

Since the fall of 2001, close to 60 percent of our student population has come from the Corpus Christi metropolitan statistical area, and nearly 40 percent of the population has come from other Texas cities (Texas A&M University-Corpus Christi Planning and Institutional Effectiveness Archived Data 2006). Our Latino/a students attend schools in their local community, a fact that matches one aspect of the profile presented in the Pew report, but the students who participated in this survey started their education at a four-year college, which does not match the profile. Statistics such as those found in the Pew report and the information we gathered from our survey helped us realize that faculty who are hired to teach at HSIs must be informed of the realities of the Latino/a students at their institutions.

Language Use

The survey we conducted provided us with unanticipated results and led us to a better understanding of our Latino/a students.[3] The survey was administered to 470 first-year students, including 180 Latino/a students, enrolled in our First-Year Writing Program (FYWP) during the fall 2003 semester. The survey asked what language(s) or language varieties students used in a range of academic (writing a research paper and using the Internet for research in high school) and nonacademic (talking on the phone and reading stories) literate practices—literacies being defined in categories of speaking, listening, reading, and writing. The survey also asked a few questions about the social and economic backgrounds of the students. A majority (56%) of the Latino/a students was found to be monolingual English users, while an additional 27% reported using Spanish or Tex-Mex[4] less than 10% of the time.

As shown in Figure 4.1, first-year Latino/a students' language usage falls into two categories, those who are monolingual English and those who use Spanish/TexMex in addition to using Spanish.

FIGURE 4.1
Language Usage among Hispanic Students (n = 180)

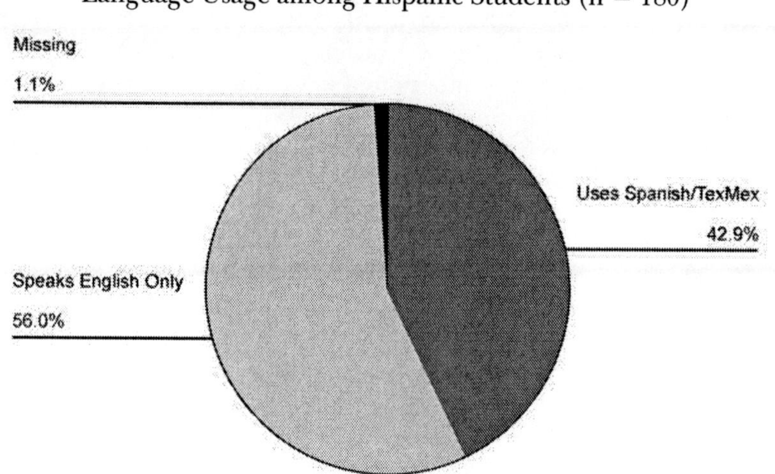

TABLE 4.1
Amount of Time Latino Students Used Spanish/TexMex during a Literate Practice (n = 178)

Column	A	B	C	D	E
Literate Practice	0.0%	0.1–25.0%	25.1–50.0%	50.1–75.0%	75.1–100%
1. Speaks on phone with relatives	116	28	18	3	13
N (%)	(65.1%)	(15.7%)	(10.1%)	(1.7%)	(7.3%)
2. Attends *quinceañera*	136	9	25	2	6
N (%)	(76.4%)	(5.1%)	(14.0%)	(1.1%)	(3.4%)
3. Gives instructions	139	23	11	1	4
N (%)	(78.1%)	(12.9%)	(6.2%)	(0.6%)	(2.2%)
4. Speaks on phone with friends	140	25	7	2	4
N (%)	(78.7%)	(14.0%)	(3.9%)	(1.1%)	(2.2%)
5. Speaks on phone with strangers	140	26	9	0	3
N (%)	(78.7%)	(14.6%)	(5.1%)	(0.0%)	(1.7%)
6. Listens to stories	141	21	13	1	2
N (%)	(79.2%)	(11.8%)	(7.3%)	(0.6%)	(1.1%)
7. Gets angry	142	22	12	1	1
N (%)	(79.8%)	(12.4%)	(6.7%)	(0.6%)	(0.6%)

Of the 180 first-year Latino/a students, 101 students (or 56.0%) reported using no Spanish when performing any of the thirty-three literate practice activities. The aforementioned figure appears to suggest that a substantial number of Latino/a students speak Spanish (42.9%). However, closer scrutiny of the data reveals that most of these students engage only marginally with Spanish. Of the remaining seventy-four students (42.9%) who do use Spanish/TexMex, none indicated Spanish language dominance. Within this 42.9%, twenty-three students indicated using Spanish/TexMex between 10–50% of the time. Fifty students (27%) reported using Spanish less than 10% of the time; only one student reported employing Spanish/TexMex 50% of the time; and no students reported employing Spanish/TexMex more than 50% of the time. Thus for most of our Latino/a students, English is the dominant language, the language within which they conduct most of their activities. Further investigation might show whether this pattern is due to assimilation, generational factors, or other issues.

The activities within which Spanish or TexMex plays a more integral, though often not dominant, role are those that do not require reading or writing in Spanish or TexMex. As Table 4.1 shows, of the thirty-three literate practices, in only seven practices was Spanish/TexMex employed by at least 20% of the Latino/a students who indicated they used Spanish/TexMex. The table shows how often Spanish/TexMex is employed in these seven practices.

In examining the frequency of Spanish/TexMex use, Table 4.1 illustrates how seldom our Latino/a students employ Spanish/TexMex: Between 65.1% and 79.8% of the Latino/a students never used Spanish/TexMex during these activities (column A). Furthermore, between 19.1 percent and 25.8% of Latino/a students used Spanish/TexMex less than 50% of the time (columns B and C combined). Between 0 and 1.7% of students used Spanish/TexMex 50–75% of the time (column D). In only one practice, "Speaks on phone with relatives," did 7.3% of Latino/a students claim to use Spanish/TexMex more than 75% of the time (column E). In six out of seven literate practices, less than 5% of the Latino/a students used Spanish/TexMex the majority of the time (practices numbered 2–7).

Cultural Capital and Scholastic Activities

Students' cultural capital[5] and high school scholastic activities also were examined in the survey. We looked at these areas based on the research in literacy studies that links the level of cultural capital and the richness of the school environment to school success (Au 1993; Jiménez 2002; Kamhi-Stein 2003; Ladson-Billings 1994; Moll 1990; Rogers, Tyson, and Marshall 2000). We asked students about the number of books in the homes where they grew up, the number of newspaper and magazine subscriptions, and the number of years of formal schooling their parents completed. We inquired about the frequency of their attendance at museums, concerts, and theater performances with their families and at school-sponsored activities, as well as their academic activities within the school setting.

First we compared the findings for Latino/a English speakers and Latino/a Spanish/Tex-Mex speakers. Here we found no statistically significant differences between the two groups. In other words, the differences that were found could not be attributable to real differences between the two groups.

Next we compared Latino/a and white students' cultural capital as reflected in their home environments. Here some statistically significant differences were observed; however, these do not necessarily reflect substantive differences. For example, the average number of years of schooling for the parents of white students and the parents of Latino/a students was significantly different. The average number of years of formal schooling completed by a white student's mother was less than fourteen while the average number of years of schooling completed by a Latino/a student's mother was less than thirteen. So in both instances, the mothers of both white and Latino/a students had only some college experience. Similarly, when examining the cultural experience of white and Latino/a students, some statistically significant differences were observed. One such difference manifested itself in the frequency that families attended concerts. Students estimated the number of times they attended musical concerts with their families when the students were between ages five and eighteen. On average, whites attended more concerts than Latinos/as, but during their childhood years the average number of concerts attended for both Latinos/as and whites did not exceed three. In other words, neither whites nor Latinos/as had extensive experiences with concerts attending their family members.

No statistically significant differences were observed in the scholastic activities listed on the survey. Overall, these results show that our Latino/a and white students are more similar than they are different in terms of cultural capital and academic experiences,[6] and both groups seem to be similarly at risk. The average Latino and white student does not have a parent who completed a four-year undergraduate program, does not have extensive cultural capital, and does not have extensive academic experiences.

Discussion of Survey Findings

We mistakenly believed that language differences factored into the success of our Latino/a students and other faculty also may be operating under similar notions. While we seek to build on language differences in a positive manner, some faculty may view these assumed differences as validation for why students do not succeed in their classes. At-risk literature supports these stereotypes. The survey results have led us to the following conclusions:

- Assumptions we made about first-year Latino/a students at TAMU-CC were faulty.
- Pedagogical strategies may be ineffective if they begin with faulty assumptions.
- Effective pedagogical strategies must be built on an accurate understanding of the student population.
- Efforts should be undertaken to educate faculty regarding their students' languages and educational experiences.

Faculty at HSIs, as well as faculty at any university serving a large percentage of minority students, need to develop a "culturally responsive pedagogy" that is "structured to connect what is being learned with students' funds of knowledge and cultural backgrounds" (Scribner and Reyes 1999, 203), but these pedagogical decisions must be based on the reality of students' lived experiences.

Faculty Perceptions

If faculty coming to an HSI assume that they need to interact with Latino/a students based on the at-risk literature, but the students do not fit those profiles, then what are the ramifications? Or, how many of us (and we include ourselves in this group) pride ourselves in acknowledging social factors such as gender and race but still have a limited understanding of what Robert P. Yagelski (2000) calls the "local" situations of our students?

Yagelski, in *Literacy Matters: Writing and Reading the Social Self,* challenges us to examine our beliefs about literacy because those views can "limit" our understanding of literate practices, which in turn will shape our pedagogical practices and also limit opportunities for student learning. Yagelski (2000) views literacy as a "local" act that students engage in to "claim agency" for themselves. He argues that our students bring unique experiences when they come into our classrooms. Therefore, we must think of them not as objects of instruction but as subjects of their own local situations, and we must construct classroom environments where they can create agency for their own purposes. Without an awareness of who they are serving, and even while attempting to be sensitive to students' needs, some faculty at HSIs may be setting up alienating and oppressive conditions if they assume differences of language and cultural capital between Latino and white students.

In order to better understand these students, some important questions need to be answered:

1. What do faculty know about HSIs?
2. Do the perceptions and beliefs that faculty have about HSIs and Latino/a students match the reality of the university and the student populations where they teach?
3. How do these perceptions and beliefs shape the teaching that occurs?

To begin answering these questions, during the spring of 2005 we conducted a series of focus groups with faculty and teaching assistants in our FYWP. Three focus group meetings, each lasting approximately ninety minutes, were tape-recorded, with the discussions transcribed the following summer. The number of individuals participating in the focus groups ranged from four to six participants. Respondents were informed that though the discussion would be recorded and referenced in future research, their identities would remain confidential.

1. *What do faculty know about HSIs?* Focus group participants' knowledge about HSIs was wide ranging. There was no consistent understanding of what it means to be designated as an HSI. Only one participant in the focus groups had any clear definition of what an HSI is. She looked it up on the Internet before she came to this university.
2. *Do the perceptions and beliefs that faculty have about HSIs and Latino/a students match the reality of the university and the student populations where they teach?* We found that some faculty did think the Latino/a students at our university would speak Spanish. One faculty member who came from a border HSI in Texas, where the Latino/a students are predominately bilingual, was surprised to find that most of our Latino/a students do not speak Spanish. Another faculty member who came from Miami, where the students switched back and forth using Spanish and English even during class, also was surprised to find that this bilingualism did not occur at our institution. The assumptions of both of these faculty members did not fit the reality of our student population.
3. *How do these perceptions and beliefs shape the teaching that occurs?* Focus group discussion of pedagogical strategies used by faculty and TAs suggests that these initial misconceptions do not carry over into the classroom. The adjustment may be attributable to the fact that faculty and TAs who teach in our FYWP become part of learning communities, so they collaborate with faculty who have prior knowledge of our students. Additionally, TAs who teach in the FYWP are required to take a practicum course, which emphasizes sociocultural literacies. The course presents readings and highlights the following concepts:

   - Respect for learning, for students, and for one another
   - Situated literacies and learning: socially, historically, culturally, politically, and ideologically
   - Writing as social action, as social practice, and as sociocognitive process[7]

   These topics offer opportunities for specific discussions about respect for home languages and literacies and help students add academic forms of literacy to their repertoires without degrading their existing literacies. Many of the TAs in the program are from the local area, so they have a lived understanding of the students at our university.

Future Research

We plan to extend this study to other HSIs in Texas, including two- and four-year schools, to see whether different institutions serve very different populations. Because one of the authors now teaches at Laredo Community College, we plan to conduct this study there. We need to know, understand, and value the cultural experiences of our students and how their experiences shape their literate practices.

While the focus groups reveal that there is an understanding of sociocultural literacies within the FYWP, we will conduct focus groups with other departments and/or colleges to determine whether what we learned is evident in other programs as well. In other words, are teachers in other programs operating under false assumptions about students' literate and language practices? We want to examine the following questions:

- What do we do in the classroom that reflects students' literate practices?
- What do we believe about student writing that is based on incorrect assumptions of language practices?
- How can we increase our understanding of our students' literate and language practices?

Conclusion

As a result of this study, we learned that we cannot make assumptions about our students' dominant languages and literate practices; rather, we have to discover their lived literacies and language use. Our goal is to ensure that faculty at HSIs will no longer be led by stereotypes of their students that are based on limited or inaccurate perceptions, but instead they will know and understand the diverse nature of the literate practices of their students and their communities. We hope to develop pedagogical practices based on that knowledge to help students succeed. These practices should allow students opportunities to build on, strengthen, and perhaps most importantly value their literacies.

Notes

1. The survey was developed and administered by Isabel Araiza, Susan Loudermilk Garza, and Susan Wolff Murphy in the fall of 2003.

2. Defined as coming straight from high school, attending school full time, and not working full time.

3. For a copy of the survey and complete findings, contact Dr. Isabel Araiza at Isabel.Araiza@tamucc.edu.

4. While we acknowledge that Tex-Mex is seen as a derogatory term by many, we chose to use the term because it would be familiar to this population, and within our region it does not carry the negative connotations.

5. The concept of cultural capital is derived from Pierre Bourdieu's (1973) work, where he examines various forms of cultural capital, such as the number of books purchased and museum, theatre, concert, and cinema attendance. In his

observations he notes that experiences such as museum, theatre, and concert attendance are closely linked to social class. The higher the social class of the family, the more experiences of "high" culture one has. This leads one to develop cultural capital—a possession of "high culture"—that is similar to the culture transmitted by colleges and universities. Thus those who possess cultural capital as a result of family upbringing are more likely to be successful in the educational system than those whose families do not offer similar forms of cultural capital.

6. Academic experiences included field trips, use of the Internet for research, writing assignments, and use of multimedia technologies.

7. Based on information from the course taught by Dr. Glenn Blalock during the summer of 2004, http://www.firstyear.tamucc.edu/wiki/Practicum04/Home.

Works Cited

Au, Kathryn. 1993. *Literacy Instruction in Multicultural Settings.* Fort Worth, TX: Harcourt Brace Janovich.

Bourdieu, Pierre. 1973. "Cultural Reproduction and Social Reproduction." In *Knowledge, Education, and Cultural Change,* ed. Richard Brown, 71–112. London: Tavistok.

del Pinal, Jorge, and Audrey Singer. 1997. "Generations of Diversity: Latinos in the United States." *Population Bulletin* 52:3 (October): 1–48.

Farr, Marcia. 2001. "En los dos idiomas: Literacy Practices among Chicago Mexicanos." In *Literacy: A Critical Sourcebook,* ed. Ellen Cushman, Eugene R. Kintgen, Barry M. Kroll, and Mike Rose, 467–87. New York: Bedford/St. Martin's.

Guerra, Juan C. 1998. *Close to Home: Oral and Literate Practices in a Transnational Mexicano Community.* New York: Teachers College Press.

Jiménez, Robert T. 2002. "Fostering the Literacy Development of Latino Students." *Focus on Exceptional Children* 34:6: 1–10.

Jiménez, Robert T., Patrick H. Smith, and Natalia Martínez-León. 2003. "Freedom and Form: The Language and Literacy Practices of Two Mexican Schools." *Reading Research Quarterly* 38:4 (October–November–December): 488–508.

Kamhi-Stein, Lia D. 2003. "Reading in Two Languages: How Attitudes toward Home Language and Beliefs about Reading Affect the Behaviors of 'Underprepared' L2 College Readers." *TESOL Quarterly* 37:1: 35–71.

Kao, Grace, and Jennifer S. Thompson. 2003. "Racial and Ethnic Stratification in Educational Achievement and Attainment." *Annual Review of Sociology* 29:1: 417–42.

Kells, Michelle Hall. 2004. "Understanding the Rhetorical Value of Tejano Codeswitching." In *On Language, Identity, and Literacy Education,* ed. Michelle Hall Kells, Valerie Balester, and Victor Villanueva, 24–39. Portsmouth, NH: Heinemann-Boynton Cook.

Ladson-Billings, Gloria. 1994. *The Dreamkeepers: Successful Teachers of African American Children.* San Francisco: Jossey Bass.

Moll, Luis C. 1990. "Social and Instructional Issues in Literacy Instruction for 'Disadvantaged' Students." In *Better Schooling for the Children of Poverty: Alter-*

natives to Conventional Wisdom, ed. M. S. Knapp and P. M. Shields, 61–84. Berkeley, CA: McCutchan.

Moll, Luis C., and Norma González. 2001. "Lessons from Research with Language-Minority Children." In *Literacy: A Critical Sourcebook,* ed. Ellen Cushman, Eugene R. Kintgen, Barry M. Kroll, and Mike Rose, 156–71. New York: Bedford/St. Martin's.

Rogers, Theresa, Cynthia Tyson, and Elizabeth Marshall. 2000. "Living Dialogues in One Neighborhood: Moving toward Understanding across Discourses and Practices of Literacy and Schooling." *Journal of Literacy Research* 32:1: 1–24.

Rong, Xue Lan, and Linda Grant. 1992. "Ethnicity, Generation, and School Attainment of Asians, Hispanics, and Non-Hispanic Whites." *The Sociological Quarterly* 33:4 (Winter): 625–36.

Santiago, Deborah A., and Sarita Reyes. 2004. "Federal Policy and Latinos in Higher Education." Pew Hispanic Center (June).

Scribner, Jay D., and Pedro Reyes. 1999. "Creating Learning Communities for High-Performing Hispanic Students: A Conceptual Framework." In *Lessons from High-Performing Hispanic Schools: Creating Learning Communities,* ed. Pedro Reyes, Jay D. Scribner, and Alicia Paredes Scribner, 188–210. New York: Teachers College Press.

Stoops, Nicole. 2004. "Educational Attainment in the United States: 2003." Washington, DC: U.S. Census Bureau, June.

Texas A&M University-Corpus Christi Planning and Institutional Effectiveness Archived Data. 2006. http://www.pie.tamucc.edu/.

Valdés, Guadalupe. 1996. *Con respeto: Bridging the Distances between Culturally Diverse Families and Schools: An Ethnographic Portrait.* New York: Teachers College Press.

Vernez, Jorge, and Richard A. Krop. 2000. "Closing the Education Gap: Benefits and Costs." *Spectrum: Journal of State Government* 73:1 (Winter): 10–12.

Yagelski, Robert P. 2000. *Literacy Matters: Writing and Reading the Social Self.* New York: Teachers College Press.

CHAPTER 5

MÁS ALLÁ DEL INGLÉS

A BILINGUAL APPROACH TO COLLEGE COMPOSITION

Isis Artze-Vega, Elizabeth I. Doud, and Belkys Torres

> *I am fifty now, maybe a third of my life left. I wonder if I'll die without ever being fluent in the language that first met my ears. English is the only language that I know, really. Yet Spanish is the language of my ear, of my soul. . . . I'm saddened by my loss. . . . [It] wasn't necessary. . . . One gives up nothing by being adept at two languages or more. One gains. So many have had to give up so much to be part of the United States.* (Villanueva 2000, 340–41)

Victor Villanueva's lament expresses the sentiments of many U.S. Latinos/as: The Spanish language is much more than a linguistic tool; it is a link to our heritage that many have felt compelled to abandon so as to succeed in this country.[1] Bruce Horner and John Trimbur (2002) chronicle this disparaging pattern of language loss in their award-winning article "English Only and U.S. College Composition."[2] After arguing that the development of composition courses in U.S. higher education was complicit in establishing our nation's unspoken policy of English monolingualism, Trimbur suggests that "where it makes sense, we should draw on students' . . . existing linguistic resources to design bilingual programs of study that seek to develop students' fluency in more than one written language and the possibilities of moving between the modern languages" (622).

With particular respect to *el español*, "the importance of developing the language resources of Latinos" has recently garnered national media coverage, working against the long-standing depictions of bilingualism as "divisive and problematic," reports Guadalupe Valdés (2003, viii).[3] In light of this increasingly receptive social climate, and in response to Trimbur's counsel and the growing number of Latino/a college students, we argue that implementing a bilingual approach to the teaching of college composition can work against our nation's legacy of monolingualism and convey respect for students' home language. Our bilingual approach can be adapted to a wide range of U.S. composition students, teachers, and writing programs—a flexibility that stems largely from the three distinct linguistic components of the composition course: the language spoken in the classroom, readings, and student writing. To reflect this structure, our chapter begins with the theoretical foundations of the bilingual composition concept and proceeds to address these three linguistic components. Isis Artze-Vega, a lecturer in the University of Miami's (UM) composition program, explains how spoken Spanish might be incorporated into the composition class. Belkys Torres then recounts her experiences teaching a literature-based writing class, also at UM, in which she used bilingual readings. Lastly, composition, creative writing, and ESL teacher Elizabeth I. Doud, who also has taught at UM, demonstrates how she promotes diglot elements in her students' writing.

Because research on the use of bilingual teaching practices at the college level is limited, we turned to the great wealth of published materials on K–12 bilingual education. And, given the considerable opposition to these K–12 programs, it seems necessary to qualify the affinities between them and our proposed course. The common antibilingual education argument that first language use in the classroom impedes students from adequately learning English is not relevant to our efforts, given that admission to U.S. colleges and universities usually requires proven competency in English, and that composition is not a *language* course per se; it is a *writing* course.[4] Indeed, a significant reason bilingual composition seems feasible is that many of the fundamental skills taught in first-year writing courses—among them critical thinking, assignment compliance, audience awareness, and providing evidence, clarity, and organization—indisputably transcend languages. In response to claims that linguistic plurality is counterassimilationist and antinationalistic, American history and statistical data prove otherwise.[5]

In the terms of the bilingual education literature, our approach would be classified in the category of "maintenance," since it presupposes that bilingualism itself is an asset, attempts to conserve both languages being used, and trusts that this approach will enhance students' academic achievement. Bilingual education author Alma Flor Ada (1995) explains that "in addition to preserving a valuable skill, encouraging the maintenance and development of the home language can foster a bilingual student's identity and self-esteem, which tend to correlate with academic success" (1995, 237). In contrast, then, to bilingual education (or ESL) courses that aim to replace the home language with English, bilingual maintenance programs such as ours emphasize the advantages of "developing the wherewithal to access not one but two social, cultural, and literate worlds as resources for . . . thinking and development" (Moll and González 2001, 157).

Our bilingual approach also presumes that Spanish is Latino/a students' native tongue, and we sustain this tenet both factually and metaphorically: census figures reveal that the number of U.S. Hispanics speaking Spanish at home rose from 10.2 million in 1980 to 24.7 million in 2000 (U.S. Census Bureau 2003). According to a 2002 national survey conducted by the Pew Hispanic Center, 46 percent of Hispanic adults speak both English and Spanish.[6] The study also found that bilingual speakers are about evenly divided between native and foreign born, so that our pedagogical model appeals to a wide range of Latinos/as. We also refer to "home language" symbolically, much like Peter Elbow (1999) employs the term *mother tongue* in his article "Inviting the Mother Tongue." He explains, "The metaphor of 'mother tongue' is no joke; . . . we experience our language or dialect not just as something we use but as a deep part of *us*" (1999, 362). Another term used for this first home language is *heritage language* (Roca and Colombi 2003).

Elbow, also in "Mother Tongue," contends that the relationship between language and self is intensified when one of the languages is "illegitimate" or discredited. He imagines what it would have been like to grow up speaking a stigmatized dialect (in our students' case, this dialect is a form of Spanish), arriving in a college writing course, and being asked to write in mainstream English. Elbow writes, "If I went along with you [the writing teacher], I would . . . have to give in to a culture that has been trying to wipe out my culture and what I experience as a part of my core self" (1999, 363). This sentiment may seem extreme with respect to a heritage language such as Spanish, but the existence and efforts of groups such as U.S. English, Inc., epitomize linguistic discrimination, and in fact contact varieties of Spanish such as those commonly used in New York and the Southwest, among them Caribbean Spanish and a variety of Mexican dialects, are often heavily stigmatized (Bean et al. 2003, 28).[7] In the academy, Latino/a students often are grouped with "basic writers" and placed in remedial courses. *The Chronicle of Higher Education* reports that more than one fourth of Latinos/as will enter college needing remedial English courses, compared to one tenth of white freshmen (Shmidt 2003). Sociolinguistics scholar Michelle Hall Kells (2002) warns that equating English skills to intellectual ability in this way can result in a "linguistic insecurity" detrimental to students' academic achievement (2002, 10).

In spite of these claims for the importance of the valuation of students' home languages, some faculty, administrators, and students might question why it is the role of the first-year writing course to provide "safety inside our classrooms for the mother tongue" (Elbow 1999, 361). Some might argue that this objective is, or should be, met by a foreign language department. We would respond that the "culture" to which Elbow refers represents not only American society but also academic culture, long disparaged for its apparent incompatibility with some students' home lives and speech. As language and writing scholar Juan Guerra (1997) recognizes, many academics expect students to relinquish their home language or dialect to adopt academic discourse. So Guerra asks, "Will we take on the role of gatekeeper, . . . or will we serve as [students'] advocates and encourage them to become agents of change willing to challenge and transform the discourse of the academy so that it more closely reflects the polyphonic discourses of their multiple and often intersecting communities?" (1997, 249). To do the latter, writing teachers must seize the opportunity presented by what is often a college-wide requirement to convince as many Latino/a students as possible that the academy views them as linguistically sophisticated and validates their skills by integrating Spanish into genuine academic activity.

Dentro del aula Bilingüe

Who might enroll in a bilingual composition class? A wide range of students: from U.S.-born-and-raised Latinos/as who are largely English dominant and newly arrived Central and South Americans or *Caribeños* who have been schooled primarily in Spanish, to perhaps even some non-Latinos/as who took Spanish classes throughout high school.[8] In institutions such as UM, a private institution, Latinos/as comprise 27 percent of undergraduates. Our bilingual approach represents one of the university's many efforts to tailor course offerings to our students' unique characteristics. Undoubtedly, developing a bilingual composition course arose out of the literacies and languages of our students and our unique local context. Miami has historically been a community in which Cuban immigrants have maintained bilingualism and political influence, and in contrast to many parts of the United States, being bilingual in Miami tends not to carry a social stigma. We recognize that this is not the case in many areas of the country where Latinos/as often are encouraged to become monolingual, yet we hope that our approach conveys an appreciation for bilingualism in the face of, and indeed to work against, societal oppression. Therefore, it is important to stress that neither the theory nor the practice of our bilingual approach limits itself to a particular geographic region or Latino subgroup.

Tailoring a class to students with varied language skills no doubt poses a challenge, but in her study of "Spanish for Native Speakers" (SNS) courses, Valdés (1995) affirms that, despite students' varying fluency levels, a single curricular sequence designed for bilingual Spanish speakers can prove effective, even within a single course (1995, 307–308).[9] Although we cannot predict college students' responses to such a course, studies have shown that high school students in bilingual programs affirm the inherent value of bilingualism and stress that both languages are important for both social *and* academic reasons. Likewise, while many non-Spanish speakers wish Latinos/as would limit their use of the Spanish language to their private lives, "Hispanics [on the whole] value bilingualism for its own sake and consider the use of both English and Spanish desirable in all domains" (Saravia-Shore and Arvizu 1992, 139).

The ideal teacher of bilingual composition will demonstrate the value of bilingualism by reading, writing, and/or speaking Spanish in order to model the value of the native language (McCarty and Watahomigie 2001, 503). We anticipate, however, that even educators who consider themselves bilingual may feel apprehensive about their qualifications. Ada (1995) acknowledges that this reaction is natural and suggests that current or aspiring bilingual teachers live, study, or teach temporarily in a country where the second language is spoken; or perhaps the more challenging (yet expeditious) alternative is to embrace this sense of inadequacy and use it to better understand students' often similar position (1995, 240). The article "Should We Invite Students to Write in Home Languages?" likewise affirms that "if a teacher doesn't know the home language or is not experienced in the home dialect, that teacher will be in the interesting and fruitful position of having less knowledge and authority about the language being used than the student has" (Bean et al. 2003, 30).[10]

After depicting a "fully" bilingual composition course in which students are invited to speak both languages in the classroom, read texts in Spanish, English, and a combination of the two, and produce written texts in both languages, we explore the "spoken language," "readings," and "student writing" factors individually.

Idiomas Coexistentes

The fully bilingual writing course would look much like an ordinary writing class since, as established earlier, many first-year writing course goals are not language specific, and because it would simply be a disservice to students to do otherwise. Developing bilingual curricula that follow the same guidelines as the nonbilingual composition courses offered at each given institution also may help prevent the bilingual approach from being classified as remedial.

Another feature that seems crucial to the success of any college-level bilingual curriculum is the element of choice—which Elbow (1999) upholds when he conjectures that students would write without resentment and more enthusiastically in a class where they could use their native voice as much or as little as they want (1999, 364). It is for this same reason that the authors of "Should We Invite" stress the word "invite" and call attention to the fact that "if choice is important, . . . in most classrooms, *students now have no choice.* That is, in most classrooms where the dominant variety of English is the norm, students feel it is wrong to write in a different dialect or language" (Bean et al. 2003, 36, emphasis in original). As such, students should make the informed decision to enroll in a bilingual composition course, *not* be placed in one simply because they are bilingual or Latino.[11]

We might also, in certain cases, encourage students to write full essays in Spanish since, as Spanish language experts M. Cecilia Colombi and Ana Roca (2003) explain, many heritage Spanish speakers struggle with formal writing, and "proficiency in academic writing is essential to gaining access to and succeeding in college and the job market" (2003, 9).[12] Later in this chapter we discuss the use of bilingual literary readings, but teachers also can ask students to read journal articles, for instance, to provide them with concrete examples of the academic register in Spanish. One common pedagogical method for overseeing the production of written Spanish used in SNS courses is to teach strategies that monitor the use of so-called "stigmatized features," much like we composition teachers advise students to avoid slang and colloquialisms (Valdés 1995, 312).[13] Elbow (1999) advocates a similar method in "Mother Tongue," arguing that instead of trying to teach students how to create works that conform at the sentence level to Standard Edited American English, we teach them "the practical ability to take whatever steps are necessary to get the desired grammar, syntax, punctuation, and spelling—*even if that means getting help*" (1999, 366, emphasis in original). In so doing, he encourages students to use their home language when writing drafts or outlines and during class discussions, and he evaluates their writing first on the intellectual level, disregarding grammar and syntax, and then assigns copyediting as a separate activity.[14] Specific pedagogical moves such as Elbow's seem fitting for our bilingual composition approach, as do two familiar composition class frameworks. The first one is the use of cultural topics, posited by Terry Dean (1989) in "Multicultural Classrooms, Monocultural Teachers," where he suggests that we "make the home language the subject of study along with the different kinds of academic discourse they will be required to learn" (1989, 28, 30–31). Along the same lines, Sandra Jamieson (1997) suggests that teachers must be self-reflexive about their choices of readings, given the danger inherent in students' "not find[ing] 'themselves'" in the readings or misrecognizing themselves "in the examples of what the text calls incorrect writing" (1997, 165).

The second framework that has proven effective in improving bilingual student literacy, proposed by Moll and González (2001), is the use of inquiry-based instruction (2001, 157).[15] This pedagogy involves showing students how individuals and communities can serve as funds of knowledge, complementing books, articles, and other traditional resource materials. Moll and González identified what is perhaps the most significant benefit of this curriculum: Since inquiry assignments emphasize the use of cultural resources, their students quickly realized that their bilingualism gained them access to two (or more) social worlds and to information monolinguals might never have discovered (2001, 157).

Teachers not ready to delve into "fully" bilingual composition, but interested in its possibilities, can nonetheless incorporate bilingual readings or exercises into their classrooms. What follows is a breakdown of the spoken, read, and written elements of the composition class, complemented by students' responses to the pedagogy, demonstrating the relative ease with which teachers can incorporate varying degrees of bilingualism into their classes.

Hablamos Español

While first researching our concept, we encountered no published accounts of anyone having taught college writing bilingually, but when discussing the matter with scholars in the field, Guerra disclosed that he and his former colleague, Elias Argott, taught a bilingual first-year writing course in 1975 at the University of Illinois at Chicago. An influx of Latino/a students and their disconcerting inability to pass a mandatory proficiency exam encouraged the two teachers to devise what became "Composition 180: The Bilingual Approach." The class included few reading materials, and students were required to write in English, but Guerra and Argott allowed them to participate in class discussion in the language with which they felt more comfortable. Despite impressive results that corroborate our current efforts—twelve out of Guerra's fourteen students passed the exam—the university refused to institutionalize the course.

Thirty years later, roughly 11 million adult English-Spanish speaking bilingual Latinos/as reside in the United States. Although our students are not enrolling in our courses in order to pass a mandatory proficiency exam, we have appropriated Guerra's efforts and modeled our bilingual composition courses after existing K–12 bilingual and dual-immersion programs that work not to transition students to English but to maintain strength in both languages (Pew Hispanic Center 2002, 2). Common techniques from K–12 programs include alternating languages by class sessions; using both languages concurrently (without translation); switching from one language to another, depending on the topic and context of the activity; and "alternat[ing] languages while working individually with specific learners to establish rapport or scaffold interaction" (Faltis and Hudelson 1998, 53, 54). Donna Christian (1996), in her study of dual-immersion education, verifies that nonverbal interaction also plays a key role in bilingual contexts. When students with varying language skills are in the same class, she explains, teachers should promote peer interaction and use "strategies that make instruction more comprehensible to non-native speakers" such as "experiential, or hands-on learning . . . [in which] students can get meaning from experience as well as from language" (1996, 71–72).

Al Utilizar Lecturas Bilingües

Alternating spoken languages in the classroom is only one way to experiment with bilingual composition. Some teachers may find it more appropriate or useful to utilize bilingual texts.[16] Although writing is the crux of any composition course, what and how students read can affect the quality of written work they produce. Additionally, as Mariolina Salvatori (2000) concludes, "Teaching reading and writing as interconnected activities . . . might be an approach appropriate to developing the critical mind—an approach that might mark the difference between students' participating in their own education and their being passively led through it" (2000, 173). Accordingly, we need to teach students how to approach written texts before asking them to conduct textual analysis. We concur with David Bartholomae's and Anthony Petrosky's (1987) assertion, that "[t]here is no better place to work on reading than in a writing course" (1987, iii). Students must be encouraged to "read as writers," to look beyond content and identify rhetorical strategies that they might apply to their own writing. In the case of bilingual texts, we encourage teachers to focus on (1) how an author manipulates and negotiates both languages to make meaning, (2) why an author chooses to work with two languages, and (3) whether or not the author limits herself or himself when choosing to write a bilingual text.

The increasing renown of Latino/a literature and criticism in the past few decades lends itself to our bilingual composition efforts, since many texts experiment with varying degrees of English/Spanish bilingualism and speak to the social, cultural, and political situations of Latinos/as in the United States. Nonetheless, one of the implicit tasks of any composition teacher who decides to use bilingual texts is to validate their linguistic distinctiveness. Although recent statistics show that "about three-quarters of Latino/a English/Spanish bilingual speakers can also read both English and Spanish," many also have been taught to esteem the dominant language over their home language (Pew Hispanic Center 2002, 2). Thus when creating a reading list, teachers should consider texts that (1) are written by distinguished authors (to establish the value of written bilingualism), (2) represent various genres (to discuss how/whether language use differs within each), (3) disclose an awareness of language, and (4) narrate a story.[17] Belkys Torres followed these guidelines when she developed a second-semester, textual analysis-based writing course at UM.[18] Given that more than one third of Miami residents are of Cuban origin, Torres decided on a Cuban American theme for the class. The following recommendations derive from her experiences in creating and teaching this course, yet they can be easily applied to other writing class topics as well.

To introduce students to bilingual reading, Pablo Medina's collection of short stories, entitled *Exiled Memories: A Cuban Childhood* (see Appendix A), is an ideal starting point because students find it accessible, regardless of their Spanish competency. While primarily written in English, Medina's work italicizes *cubanismos* and other Spanish terms and provides a glossary for easy access to cultural or linguistic explications of said terms. A work such as Medina's personal narratives also is useful for a course such as this since, as Alan Hirvela (2001) affirms, students can relate to stories because of their universal narrative form (2001, 117). Jamieson (1997) concurs, explaining that "personal narratives seem to meet the needs of a multicultural curriculum by allowing students to interact with the experiences of cultural 'others' and encouraging a student-centered pedagogy through which the students learn to value their own knowledge and feel validated by the university that has asked them to write about themselves" (1997, 155). *Exiled Memories: A Cuban Childhood* also offers a unique rhetorical tool—the glossary—with which students might experiment. Students might consider, for instance, whether or not they refer to the glossary when reading the text, whether the Spanish terms impede or enhance the meaning of the text, and whether or when it is useful to include a similar linguistic aid in their own essays.

Gustavo Pérez Firmat's book of poems, *Bilingual Blues* (see Appendix A), works well taught on the heels of Medina's text because it consciously addresses and extends the cultural, linguistic, and personal complexities that bilingual Latinos/as face in the United States. The code switching that occurs throughout Pérez Firmat's collection of poetry makes that work more challenging for the reader. It also suggests an interconnectedness and a conscious fluidity between Spanish and English. *Bilingual Blues* also voices the Cuban poet's anxieties *about* and awareness *of* his bicultural and bilingual experience in the United States, offering students an interesting forum for discussion. In Torres's experience, students are especially drawn to the poem *Nobody Knows My Name* because they relate to it on a very personal level: As they empathize with Pérez Firmat's frustration with his bicultural identity, students also begin to uncover possible reasons behind the poet's decision to write bilingually. Texts such as Achy Obejas's *We Came All the Way from Cuba So You Could Dress Like This?* or Cristina Garcia's *The Agüero Sisters* (see Appendix A) function well later in the semester when students have acclimated to the interchangeable uses of Spanish and English and can move beyond close readings to more complex textual analyses, enhanced by their increasing awareness of the rhetorical effects of bilingualism.

More importantly, the bilingualism of these recommended texts allows teachers to seamlessly incorporate discussions of critical writing with those of critical reading, since they are inextricably linked. As with many first-year students, those introduced to bilingual texts tend to examine the words on the page only peripherally at first. That is, they express their immediate reactions to the content and/or storyline—most even note the obvious use of Spanish terms—but their analysis of the reading does not generally move beyond a conversation about the characters, plot, or the "Spanish words" in the text. For example, when asked to discuss Pablo Medina's short story "Zapata," in *Exiled Memories* (see Appendix A), Torres's students noted the inclusion of Spanish words but commented that they had not really paid close attention to it, since they had understood the tale despite the terms.

One way of furthering students' awareness of an author's deliberate manipulation of language(s) while encouraging their own experimentation with language is by adapting David Rosenwasser's and Jill Stephen's (2000) "The Method," as explained in *Writing Analytically*. Torres asks students to locate the strands, repetitions, and/or binaries of the Spanish terms in one or more of Medina's short stories and to write a paragraph explaining why a particular repetition, strand, or binary seemed especially noteworthy. This adaptation of "The Method" proves effective, since as students mark the repetition of specific terms they quickly realize that the Spanish terms or idioms are not arbitrarily inserted into the story but instead strategically placed by the author at key moments in the tale to clarify meaning.[19]

Another strategy asks students to compare various writers' rhetorical moves when embedding Spanish terms in their prose or poetry. After students read works by both Medina and Pérez Firmat, for example, they form groups of three or four to compare and contrast the ways in which the writers reconcile two languages. Most groups found that both writers incorporated Spanish terms either in the absence of a viable English translation or when choosing to maintain the musicality of the Spanish term. For instance, both use Spanish terms to name typically Cuban foods—such as *ajiaco, fritas, pan con lechón*—that lack a faithful English translation and require a distinctive pronunciation. When discussing how the authors use Spanish differently, one group noted that Medina explains or defines the Spanish terms, while Pérez Firmat does not, stating that, as a result, Medina seemed more "reader friendly." Others noted that Medina only incorporated key terms in Spanish, while Pérez Firmat consciously switched between languages without warning.

In the end, the class noted that Medina's awareness of the foreignness of words such as *carbonero* and *guarapo* is implicit in his direct definition of terms within the text, and that Medina's interest in clarifying Spanish terms suggests that he writes for an English-speaking audience, or for an audience that may speak Spanish fluently, yet may not be familiar with Medina's *cubanismos.* Observing again that Pérez Firmat does not offer explanations or linguistic aids, one student astutely concluded, "He really doesn't care whether or not he is understood, because he is tired of being misunderstood and wants to write without worrying about the reader." Although the student did not find difficulty with the text—because he too is bilingual—he feared that the poet was alienating monolingual speakers of either language. Other students commented that by including Spanish and English terms that were neither explained within the text nor via a glossary (as were Medina's), Pérez Firmat manifests his own process of reconciliation of the languages.

Examining how Pérez Firmat's manipulation of language differs from Medina's and *why* this difference is noteworthy draws students' attention to the importance of audience awareness—a key objective of all writing courses. Ultimately, reading strategies such as these allow students to reflect on and experiment with the craft of embedding Spanish terms or idioms into English poetry or prose while setting the stage for students' own experimentation with bilingual writing.

Al Encarar la Palabra Escrita

In her experience, Elizabeth I. Doud has learned that perhaps the most important issue teachers should heed with respect to the use of bilingual texts is the considerable distinction between oral and written fluency.[20] Some students will be able to comprehend Spanish in readings and conversation but feel they can only write in English. In "Inviting the Mother Tongue," Elbow (1999) recognizes that "the hardest journey may be from . . . oral modes of thinking and rhetoric to written modes of thinking and rhetoric" for bilingual students who have oral fluency but limited writing skills in the home language (1999, 371). He thus corroborates the power of tapping into the "mother tongue," even for students who have limited experience writing in that language. Elbow observes that "people can't learn to write well unless they write a great deal and with some pleasure, and they can't do that unless they feel writing to be as comfortable as an old shoe—something they can slip into naturally and without pinching" (1999, 362). Bilingual writing, or diglot writing, as Doud calls it, potentially increases students' control over both English and Spanish composition because it couples their diglot writing and thinking strategies, which have previously worked separately.

Using bilingual texts in the classroom sets up models that can both demonstrate the validity of bilingual strategies in writing and introduce topics for discussion and writing projects. The authors of "Should We Invite" echo this notion, explaining that a key variable when determining whether to "invite" students to write in their home language is the language's existing usage, that is, whether it has a "settled orthography," whether reading materials are available, and whether students are comfortable reading and writing in the language (Bean et al. 2003). To increase the strength of bilingual student writing, we have used freewriting, translations, and embedding. These strategies have succeeded in ESL, composition and creative writing courses. A five-minute, nonstop freewrite, which begins with a prompt written on the board—usually an unfinished sentence, a maxim, or a question that asks students' opinion—is a good place to introduce Spanish. Because students are not required to "show" this work, anxiety about spelling is eliminated, and they can focus on writing uninhibitedly. Journaling is an extended version of the freewrite, but it more closely resembles academic writing in that it allows students to explore reasoning and ideas more thoroughly.

Another way to bring the use of Spanish into a writing course is by asking students to perform translations. Sentence-level translations can be an excellent exercise in dexterity and meaning. Some critics claim that translation is merely a rote exercise in mechanics that does not engage students with the more important rhetorical usage they need for effective writing—but studies, and our own experiences, have proven otherwise. André Lefevere affirms that "the study of translation does not compartmentalize: It unifies . . . [by forcing students] to survey, question [and] examine" linguistics, literary theory, and cultural history (quoted in Malloy 2001, 135). Elbow (1999) entertains the possibility that writing teachers use translations by citing a study of Japanese students who "developed more ideas with explanations and specifics, which captured the reader's attention, and . . . used more sophisticated vocabulary and a greater variety of form" through translation (1999, 371). Teachers can select paragraphs from class readings or give students the choice of bringing in a poem (for length's sake) of their choice, and translating engages students in dissecting both speech and meaning. While this is not an easy exercise, most students enjoy the challenge and learn a great deal about their first language use and its limitations and/or flexibility.

In addition to sentence-level translation, students can perform a global translation by preparing an outline or a draft in the home language and then translate it to English. This practice also has been found to render a more sophisticated expression of ideas. The authors of "Should We Invite," for instance, found that a Puerto Rican student who used this approach "was able to call on the richer thinking and subtler distinctions she had produced thanks to her home language" (Bean et al. 2003, 33).

The third strategy is the embedding of Spanish text and voice in student writing, which consists of placing select words or phrases in Spanish in an English-dominant text, as Gloria Anzaldúa frequently does.[21] Her borderland writings about linguistic colonialism and the power of the written word exemplify texts in which the presence of the writer's first language is essential to both the content and meaning of her argument and her authority. In the field of creative writing, embedding is taught as a method of strengthening voice, range of meaning, and rhythmic properties in nonfiction narratives and prose, as well as in free and form verse, such as in the works of Julia Alvarez or Jimmy Santiago Baca.[22] Baca, whose work is arguably defined by its bilingual-bicultural identity, admits that when he was first exercising bilingualism in his writing, he spelled many things phonetically just to get them on the page, and then he worried about the "correctness" later (quoted in Keene 1994). This writing practice is one of the most challenging parts of bilingual writing for students because it asks them to be bold with the inclusion of their first language and at the same time to monitor it for its intelligibility and appropriateness.

While there are myriad ways students can embed first language text into their work, two common approaches are to use first language words and to translate those terms into English. If students want to use a Spanish word, such as *curandera,* which might be translated into English as *healer* or *witch,* but feel that meaning will be lost by translation, then they can use the Spanish term. The obvious limitations to this translation might necessitate the use of Spanish to place the appropriate cultural significance of the word for the reader.

The use of first language in dialogue or quoted form, which allows students to represent a voice in its original state, is frequently employed when students are asked to relate personal experiences and can be effective for inquiry-based writing assignments. One of Doud's students interviewed a family member in Spanish, and she embraced the challenge by choosing to preface the relative's story in her own words in English, paraphrasing most of the responses for the reader, yet deciding to place a few of the interviewee's choice responses in Spanish. She explained that the Spanish phrasing was "too important" to exclude, and the result was a linguistically rich essay that accurately represented her relative's voice.

When using both of these embedding strategies, bilingual writers can be encouraged to contemplate the use of footnotes or a small glossary for their text to make them accessible to their peer readers (and potentially a larger English monolingual audience). And, since part of the in-class work of many composition courses includes sharing student writing with peers, revision with constructive peer critique can help students determine how a given audience responds to their bilingual usage. In sum, bilingual writing asks students and teachers to break certain "rules" they have internalized about "good writing"; it enriches the written product by expanding potential vocabulary, rhetorical strategies, and content.

En Resumidas Cuentas

Whether through writing, reading, or class discussions, we encourage all writing teachers working with Latino/a students to embrace this bilingual approach—to the extent that they are comfortable and in the way that suits their needs. A virtually effortless way to begin, applicable to all college students, is to include a statement in the course syllabus affirming students' right to their own language and encouraging them to use languages and dialects other than Standard English under certain circumstances (see Appendix B). In fact, this simple assertion alone has prompted some of our students to use their language skills in the composition class. Reading Gloria Anzaldúa's widely anthologized multivocal works and asking students to write using their own multiple voices—while making an academic argument related to this language use—functions similarly: Most students realize that they too are versed in more than one tongue, whether a language, dialect, or regionalism, and many seize the opportunity to write their own multilingual text. One of the most successful student essays resulting from such an assignment—it won our student writing contest—used English and Hebrew to argue that one can be Jewish without necessarily believing in the religion's tenets since the group has a collective history and culture that transcend faith. Although neither the instructor nor the contest judges were fluent in Hebrew, the argument was effectively supported, and all agreed that the bilingualism contributed to its unique and sophisticated style.

When embracing bilingualism in this or any other form, writing teachers also must be sure to teach the conventions of academic discourse. As Moreno (1998) reminds us, after all, "it is through this 'new language' that we give students the message that learning [it] is imperative to their success (which it is)." Nevertheless, she judiciously adds:

> We ought to also enlarge our discourse community to include their language. We don't want to render them "speechless" . . . nor do we want them to fail by hiding power relations. We instead want to make power relations more visible because then writers can learn to mix forms, co-opt style, find ways to bridge and mix the language of school and

> home. By teaching students to turn language to their own purpose, we are acknowledging and validating them, their voices, and the differences they bring to our classrooms. (1998, 50)

Integrating Spanish into college composition in Latino-populated settings moves us toward the linguistically democratic ideals that Moreno herein describes, and we hope other language groups follow our lead. Bilingual composition could then prove instrumental in student achievement, rhetorical richness, and our country's linguistic future.

Notes

Many of the concepts described in this chapter were presented (and enthusiastically received) at the 2004 Conference on College Composition and Communication in San Antonio, Texas. The three authors formed a panel, entitled "Bilingual Composition."

1. Though we are aware of the complexities of using either the term *Hispanic* or *Latino/a*, we utilize the latter in this work to include U.S.-born, immigrants, and/or international students of Latin American, Hispanophone Caribbean, and/or Spanish descent.
2. The two were awarded the 2003 Richard Braddock Award for an outstanding article on writing or the teaching of writing in the CCCC journal.
3. The NCTE also has shown increasing interest in "Students' Right to Their Own Language," recently reaffirming this 1974 resolution, and the 2004 Conference on College Composition and Communication featured the densely populated and well-received session "Cross-Language Relations in Composition."
4. As we discuss in the section *Idiomas coexistentes*, many composition scholars have considered how making Spanish a topic of the writing course might prove fruitful.
5. For instance, see Gregory Rodríguez's (1999) study for the National Immigration Forum, "From Newcomers to New Americans: The Successful Integration of Immigrants," July.
6. By "bilingual," the study means "that they report an ability to carry on a conversation in either English or Spanish at least 'pretty well'" (Pew Hispanic Center 2002, 1).
7. U.S. English, Inc., is "the nation's oldest, largest citizens' action group dedicated to preserving the unifying role of the English language in the United States." http://www.us-english.org.
8. National statistics confirm college-age students' interest in Spanish: More than 4 million high school students enrolled in Spanish courses in 2000—representing one third of students studying a foreign language and a 55 percent increase from 1990—and 7,243 Spanish BAs were earned in 2002. http://www.nces.ed.gov. And we imagine that at HSIs, non-Latino/a students might be more receptive, since many may be accustomed to Latino/a communities and bilingual environments.

9. It seems worth noting the uncanny similarities between the pedagogies of Spanish for Native Speakers (SNS) courses and those of many composition courses. According to Columbi and Roca (2003), Rebeca Acevedo reports that, "based on her experience with an advanced-level SNS class, among the strategies that can facilitate academic writing and academic language development are differentiating between oral and written registers, conceptualizing the act of writing a composition as a process, and emphasizing the importance of the reader of the text" (13).

10. This article was written by eleven scholars, including Peter Elbow and Paul Kei Matsuda, from the fields of composition, second language acquisition, sociolinguistics, and literacy studies.

11. Colleges can contact students during the summer. The University of Miami, for instance, included an invitation to enroll in the course—along with a detailed description of the class—in its summer registration packet.

12. A "heritage language" is a non-English language learned at home, and "heritage speakers" are those who speak or at least understand the language.

13. This is only one of many pedagogical elements teachers might borrow from SNS courses when teaching a bilingual writing class, so that all materials need not be created "from scratch."

14. Elbow (1999) acknowledges that his suggestions are geared to writing in dialects of English, not in a completely different language, but he also recognizes that using another language "is not such a wild idea," citing research that endorses translation exercises, which we discuss in the section *Al encarcar la palabra escrita* (1999, 371).

15. The first-semester writing course at the University of Miami, taught previously by all three authors of this chapter, is inquiry based; in fact, since the Boyer Report's promotion of an inquiry-based freshman year in research universities in 1998, this pedagogy has gained increasing support in a number of disciplines, particularly science (see the Institute for Inquiry at http://www.exploratorium.edu). The inquiry-based writing textbook, *Composing Inquiry*, is forthcoming by Pearson/Prentice Hall.

16. Bilingual texts are written primarily in English but are enhanced with Spanish terminology and/or idiomatic expressions. Another viable option is to alternate between texts written in Spanish and texts written in English.

17. All of these criteria, but the fourth in particular, are based upon Alan Hirvela's (2001) assessments in "Connecting Reading and Writing through Literature," where he makes the case for "literature-based reading and writing experiences" as crucial, since "[l]iterature is written to evoke a response on the part of the reader, and it is in the response process that the most productive and meaningful connections between reading and writing occur" (2001, 119–120).

18. Students who enrolled in the course "Writing about Literature of Exile: The Cuban-American Diaspora"—all of whom were bilingual (though not required to be)—were informed on the first day of class that reading materials were English/Spanish bilingual. (See Appendix A for the complete reading list.)

19. One student noted in his paragraph, for example, that Medina refers to the term *café con leche* whenever he is scared or nostalgic and feels the desire to go home.

20. Although this distinction is likely to be more pronounced for bilingual students, we should recall that college writing asks all students to use more formal language than what they speak.

21. We know that the embedding of foreign language text is not a novelty. The introduction of French into scholarly English language texts, for instance, has been not only a convention but a sign of erudite thinking. When running across a French expression in an academic text, we rarely squawk in protest but rather quietly seek out a dictionary and inform ourselves, as its usage is associated with the elite.

22. As in Alvarez's poem *Bilingual Sestina* or novel *Yo* and Baca's *Meditations on the South Valley.*

Works Cited

Ada, Alma Flor. 1995. "Creative Education for Bilingual Teachers." In *Policy & Practice in Bilingual Education,* ed. Ofelia García and Colin Baker, 237–244. Philadelphia, PA: Multilingual Matters.

Alvarez, Julia. 1995. "Bilingual sestina." In *The Other Side/El Otro Lado,* 3–4. New York: Plume/Penguin.

———. 1997. *!Yo!* Chapel Hill, NC: Algonquin Books of Chapel Hill.

Baca, Jimmy Santiago. 1987. *Martín & Meditations on the South Valley.* New York: New Directions.

Bartholomae, David, and Anthony Petrosky. 1987. *Ways of Reading.* New York: St. Martin's Press.

Bean, Janet, Robert Eddy, Rhonda Grego, Patricia Irvine, Ellie Kutz, Paul Kei Matsuda, Maryann Cucchiara, Peter Elbow, Rich Haswell, Eileen Kennedy, and Al Lehner. 2003. "Should We Invite Students to Write in Home Languages? Complicating the Yes/No Debate." *Composition Studies* 31:1: 25–42.

Belcher, Diane, and Alan Hirvela, eds. 2001. *Linking Literacies: Perspectives on L2 Reading-Writing Connections.* Ann Arbor: University of Michigan Press.

Christian, Donna. 1996. "Two-Way Immersion Education: Students Learning through Two Languages." *The Modern Language Journal* 80:1: 66–76.

Columbi, M. Cecilia, and Ana Roca. 2003. "Insights from Research and Practice in Spanish as a Heritage Language." In *Mi Lengua: Spanish as a Heritage Language in the United States,* ed. Ana Roca and M. Cecilia Columbi, 1–21. Washington, DC: Georgetown University Press.

Cushman, Ellen, Eugene R. Kintgen, Barry M. Kroll, and Mike Rose, eds. 2001. *Literacy: A Critical Sourcebook.* Boston: Bedford.

Dean, Terry. 1989. "Multicultural Classrooms, Monocultural Teachers." *College Composition and Communication* 40: 23–37.

Elbow, Peter. 1999. "Inviting the Mother Tongue: Beyond 'Mistakes,' 'Bad English,' and 'Wrong Language.'" *JAC: A Journal of Composition Theory* 19: 359–88.

Faltis, Christian J., and Sarah J. Hudelson. 1998. *Bilingual Education in Elementary and Secondary School Communities.* Boston: Allyn and Bacon.

Guerra, Juan. 1997. "The Place of Intercultural Literacy in the Writing Classroom." In *Writing in Multicultural Settings*, ed. Carol Severino, Juan Guerra, and Johnnella E. Butler, 248–60. New York: The Modern Language Association of America.

Hirvela, Alan. 2001. "Connecting Reading and Writing through Literature." In *Linking Literacies*, ed. Diane Belcher and Alan Hirvela, 109–34. Ann Arbor: University of Michigan Press.

Horner, Bruce, and John Trimbur. 2002. "English Only and U.S. College Composition" *College Composition and Communication* 53:4: 594–629.

Jamieson, Sandra. 1997. "Composition Readers and the Construction of Identity." In *Writing in Multicultural Settings*, 150–71.

Keene, John. 1994. "'PoetrySpeak to Each Other': An Interview With Jimmy Santiago Baca." *Native American Literatures*. Special issue of *Callaloo* 17:1: 33–51.

Kells, Michelle Hall. 2002. "Linguistic Contact Zones in the College Writing Classroom: An Examination of Ethnolinguistic Identity and Language Attitudes." *Written Communication* 19:1: 5–43.

Malloy, Mary Ellen. 2001. "The Foreign Language Literacy Classroom 'Translating Event' as Reading and Composing: Eighth Graders Read Cross-Cultural Children's Literature." In *Linking Literacies*, 109–34.

McCarty, Teresa, and Lucille J. Watahomigie. 2001. "Language and Literacy in American Indian and Alaska Native Communities." In *Literacy: A Critical Sourcebook*, ed. Ellen Cushman et al., 488–507. Boston: Bedford.

Medina, Pablo. 1990. *Exiled Memories: A Cuban Childhood*. Austin: University of Texas Press.

Moll, Luis C., and Norma González. 2001. "Lessons from Research with Language-Minority Children." In *Literacy: A Critical Sourcebook*, 156–71.

Moreno, Renee. 1998. "'Going for Broke': Valuing Differences in the Classroom." In *Situated Stories*, ed. Kathleen Geissler and Emily Decker, 44–55. Portsmouth, NH: Boynton/Cook.

Pew Hispanic Center/Kaiser Family Foundation. 2002. National Survey of Latinos. http://www.pewhispanic.org.

Roca, Ana, and M. Cecilia Colombi, eds. 2003. *Mi Lengua: Spanish as a Heritage Language in the United States*. Washington, DC: Georgetown University Press.

Rodriguez, Gregory. 1999. *From Newcomers to New Americans: The Successful Integration of Immigrants into American Society*. Washington, DC: National Immigration Forum. ERIC Documentation Reproduction Service No. ED 476 244.

Rosenwasser, David, and Jill Stephen. 2000. *Writing Analytically*. Belmont, CA: Thomson Heinle.

Salvatori, Mariolina. 2000. "Conversations with Texts: Reading in the Teaching of Composition." In *The Writing Teacher's Sourcebook*, ed. Edward P. J. Corbett, Nancy Myers, and Gary Tate, 163–174. New York: Oxford University Press.

Saravia-Shore, Marietta, and Steven F. Arvizu, eds.1992. *Cross-Cultural Literacy: Ethnographies of Communication in Multiethnic Classrooms*. New York: Garland.

Severino, Carol, Juan Guerra, and Johnnella E. Butler, eds. 1997. *Writing in Multicultural Settings*. New York: The Modern Language Association of America.

Shmidt, Peter. 2003. "Academe's Hispanic Future." *Chronicle of Higher Education* 50:14: A8.

U.S. Census Bureau. 2003. Miami-Dade County, Florida General Demographic Characteristics: 2003. "American Community Survey." http://www.fact finder.census.gov (accessed April 4, 2005).

Valdés, Guadalupe. 1995. "The Teaching of Minority Languages as Academic Subjects: Pedagogical and Theoretical Challenges." *The Modern Language Journal* 79: 299–328.

———. 2003. "Foreword." In *Mi Lengua: Spanish as a Heritage Language in the United States,* ed. Ana Roca and M. Cecilia Columbi, vii–x. Washington, DC: Georgetown University Press.

Villanueva, Victor. 2000. "On English Only." Afterword. In *Language Ideologies: Critical Perspectives on the Official English Only Movement,* ed. Roseann Dueñas González and Ildikó Melis, 333–42. Urbana, IL: National Council of Teachers of English.

APPENDIX A

Reading List: Writing about Literature of Exile: The Cuba-American Diaspora

(Readings are listed in the order they were taught in this course.)

- Arenas, Reinaldo. *Mona and Other Tales.* New York: Vintage Books, 2001.
- Medina, Pablo. *Exiled Memories: A Cuban Childhood.* New York: Persea Books, 2002.
- Pérez-Firmat, Gustavo. *Bilingual Blues.* Tempe, AZ: Bilingual Press, 1995.
- Cabrera Infante, Guillermo. *Guilty of Dancing the Chachachá.* New York: Welcome Rain, 2001.
- Obejas, Achy. *We Came All the Way from Cuba So You Could Dress Like This?* Pittsburgh, PA: Cleis Press, 1994.
- Garcia, Cristina. *The Agüero Sisters.* New York: Ballantine, 1997.

APPENDIX B

Sample "Language Rights Statement" for Syllabus

In keeping with the National Council of Teachers of English's resolution, "Students' Right to Their Own Language," students in this writing class are encouraged to make use of languages and dialects other than Standard English, albeit to a limited extent, in their essays and research. All students should, however, consult with the teacher when using a non-Standard English dialect or language to ensure that the usage is appropriate to the task at hand.

CHAPTER 6

UN PIE ADENTRO Y OTRO AFUERA

COMPOSITION INSTRUCTION FOR TRANSNATIONAL DOMINICANS IN HIGHER EDUCATION

Sharon Utakis and Marianne Pita

> *But what I needed was to put together my Dominican and American selves. . . . But the problem was that American culture, as we had experienced it until then, had left us out, and so we felt we had to give up being Dominicans to be Americans. . . . What finally bridged these two worlds for me was writing.* (Alvarez 1998, 167)

Dominican participation in higher education has increased dramatically since the 1980s. Many Dominicans come to the United States because of the higher education opportunities. But many come with the idea that their sojourn in the United States is temporary, and that as soon as they have finished their education, or as soon as they have saved enough money, they will return to the Dominican Republic. While some of these immigrants stay, others do return, and many travel back and forth from the Dominican Republic to the United States over the course of their lifetime.

Transnational migration is the term used to describe how migrants travel back and forth between the United States and their country of origin, creating communities that transcend national boundaries (Glick Schiller 1999, 19; Glick Schiller, Basch, and Blanc-Szanton 1992, 1). With more than half a million members, the Dominican[1] community in New York City is a paradigm case of this kind of transnational community, in which migrants move between the Dominican Republic and the United States, maintaining strong ties with both places. Transnational Dominicans exploit global transportation and communication networks to create a community that spans political and geographical space.

In colleges with large Dominican populations, composition teachers should take into account the special needs of Dominican transmigrants. In New York City, for example, over 11,000 Dominican students are enrolled in public colleges and universities, so writing teachers have a special responsibility to understand the Dominican experience. English instruction for immigrants has historically been designed to help students learn English, to become American, and to assimilate into the new culture. As more Dominicans enter college, composition teachers must develop critical language awareness and sensitivity to both the existing strengths and the needs of Dominican transnational students.

We teach composition to ESL students at Bronx Community College (BCC), a Hispanic-Serving Institution (HSI) whose student population is half Latino. By far the largest group of Latinos consists of Dominican students. Between the two of us, we have been teaching at BCC more than fifteen years, and during that time about three fourths of the students in our ESL classes have been Dominican.

We have developed classroom practices that build on the strengths and address the challenges faced by our transnational students, many of whom go back and forth between the Dominican Republic and New York. We argue that the increasingly transnational character of the Dominican community necessitates changes in classroom practice; composition teachers should help students negotiate the global reality of a life lived in two places.

The Transnational Nature of the Dominican Community

According to data from the 2000 census, 1,041,910 Dominicans live in the United States, making this population the fourth largest Latino group. New York City alone has 554,638 Dominicans, and other sizable Dominican communities can be found in Massachusetts, New Jersey, and Rhode Island (Hernández and Rivera-Batiz 2003).

Dominicans remain closely connected to their native country through global networks that facilitate language and cultural maintenance. In a monograph on the Dominican community in Washington Heights, Jorge Duany (1994), in *Quisqueya on the Hudson,* describes transnational communities as "characterized by a constant flow of people in both directions, a dual sense of identity, ambivalent attachment to two nations and a far-flung network of kinship and friendship ties across state frontiers" (1994, 2). Dominican transmigrants have a dual cultural, linguistic, and political life.

Dominicans place a strong value on *familismo,* commitment to extended family (Castillo 1996, 52; Pita 2000, 72). In transnational Dominican communities, many families have relatives in both countries, and strong kinship ties are maintained by regular travel. U.S. immigration policy often divides families when some members obtain visas but others do not. Even if both parents and children are in the United States, working parents often choose to send their young children back to be cared for by grandparents. With family in both countries, parents also can send teenagers to the Dominican Republic to protect them from gangs, drugs, and early sex (Georges 1990, 212). Many Dominicans save so they can buy a house and/or a business in their native country and retire there, rejoining family.

Dominican transmigrants make use of both Spanish and English in the United States. In an extensive survey of language use in the Dominican community in Washington Heights, Susan Dicker and Hafiz Mahmoud (2001) found that these migrants are moving toward acquisition of English and greater participation in the larger society while simultaneously maintaining their native language and involvement and interest in Spanish cultural activities. According to a study from the Lewis Mumford Center for Comparative Urban and Regional Research, Dominicans, in contrast to other immigrant groups, are able to maintain bilingualism even into the third generation (Alba 2004). Whether this transnational community continues to maintain its native language over the long term is a question for further research. When asked whether they planned to stay in the United States or return to the Dominican Republic, a significant number of participants in Dicker's and Mahmoud's survey made a third choice, indicating that they both planned to stay in this country and return to the Dominican Republic. Staying in this country and returning to their native country were not seen as mutually exclusive.

Transnational political ties attest to the importance of transmigrants and their remittances to the Dominican economy. The Dominican Republic changed its constitution in 1994 to allow citizens living abroad to hold dual citizenship, and in 2004, for the first time, Dominican New Yorkers voted in Dominican national elections from polling sites in New York City (Paybarah 2004). Two of the major political parties in the Dominican Republic have branches in New York, and presidential candidates conduct campaigns and raise funds in the city (Itzigsohn et al. 1999, 328–31) while New York politicians visit the Dominican Republic in order to garner support from Dominicans.

Transnational Identity

Identity is usually connected to national origin. For immigrants, a hyphenated identity is associated with a past in one country and a present and future in another. In contrast, transnational migrants are forging an identity that simultaneously spans national borders. Many Dominican migrants view their own identity positively. In a survey of Dominican high school students in New York City, Castillo (1996) found that 95 percent considered themselves "Dominicans and proud of it, regardless of where they were born" (1996, 51).

However, the process of forging a transnational identity is made more difficult by discrimination against Dominican migrants in the United States based on race and language. Racial identity is particularly problematic for these transmigrants. Most Dominicans are mulattos; in the Dominican Republic, racial categories are complex, but in the United States, dark-skinned Dominican migrants usually are categorized as black. In "Reconstructing Racial Identity," Duany (1998) attributes the segregation of Washington Heights, where Dominicans live apart from native whites, African Americans, and other Latinos, to discrimination. Segregated neighborhoods discourage assimilation and strengthen Dominican identity.

Another challenge that Dominicans face in attempting to forge a transnational identity is the difficulty of developing bilingualism, given the relatively low prestige of Dominican Spanish. In the United States, Spanish, especially the Spanish of poor and working-class immigrants, has low prestige relative to English (Dicker 2000–2001, 18). Furthermore, different varieties of Spanish have different levels of prestige within the Spanish-speaking community. Among Spanish speakers in New York, Dominican Spanish has low prestige. Zentella (1990) found that Dominicans were more insecure about their Spanish than other groups: more than three quarters of the Dominicans surveyed said that Dominican Spanish should not be taught in schools. The low prestige of Dominican Spanish makes it difficult for Dominican migrants to develop academic Spanish while learning English.

In the United States, many Dominicans feel they have to choose between Spanish and English, between being Dominican or being "American." Some Dominicans feel that in order to be accepted in this country, they need to abandon their native language and culture. The forced choice pushes others to cling tightly to their native language variety and culture, making it difficult for them to learn English. Toribio (2000) suggests that some darker-skinned Dominicans cling to Spanish because it helps distinguish them from African Americans.

Because Dominicans live in segregated neighborhoods, they have little need or opportunity to speak English. One of our students described his difficulty learning English in a Dominican neighborhood in New York:

> When I first came to this country, I was nine years old and the only thing I knew in English was how to say "I don't speak English." At that time, my father registered me for the fourth grade. I never felt frustrated about not being able to communicate with the other kids because they spoke Span-

> ish. Today I realized that was a reason why I did not learn any English in that grade. I spent six months in that school and did not learn a word of English, for the simple reason that I did not feel the need. Every time I was involved in an English conversation, the only thing I needed to say was, "I don't speak English" and someone would come out to translate. After six months, my father decided to send me back to the Dominican Republic, because I was too young and he couldn't take care of me after school. I went back with the same English I had come with.

Living and working in segregated neighborhoods, Dominicans do not have the opportunity to acquire much English, and as a result, they are disparaged for not learning English and not becoming "American" quickly or completely enough.

Dominicans in Higher Education

According to the 2000 census, Dominicans have one of the lowest rates of educational attainment of any group in the country. In 2000, only 51 percent of Dominicans in the United States over age twenty-five had completed high school, and only 10.6 percent had completed college, as compared to the overall population, with 80 percent having completed high school and 24.4 percent having completed college (Hernández and Rivera-Batiz 2003, 87). In the 1990s, George Washington High School, the secondary school in the Washington Heights section of New York City with the greatest number of Dominican students, had one of the highest dropout rates in the United States (Torres-Saillant and Hernández 1998).

One explanation for the poor academic performance of Dominicans is their resistance to integration. According to Gray (2001), "Most arrive with the belief that life in the States is temporary, that as soon as they become financially stable, and as soon as their children finish school, they will return home to the island" (2001, 182). While not all Dominican students are transnational, most new immigrants dream of returning.

However, when the educational statistics are broken down by immigrant status, in more recent years American-born children of Dominicans are attending college in much higher numbers than Dominicans as a whole. According to Hernández and Rivera-Batiz (2003):

> The Dominican second-generation in the United States has educational indicators that suggest a remarkable acquisition of human capital over the last 20 years. This differs from the overall situation of U.S.-born Hispanics/Latinos, whose educational indicators are substantially worse than those for Dominicans. (2003, 61–62).

This gain is demonstrated in New York City, where the rate at which second-generation Dominicans are attaining some college education increased dramatically between 1980 (31.7%) and 2000 (55.1%). These higher college attendance rates are linked to higher retention rates than for the overall Latino population.

Dominicans in New York City study at public institutions of higher education in large numbers: in 2000, as many as 8.5 percent of the students were Dominican, surpassing the percentage of Puerto Ricans. At City University of New York (CUNY), in fall 2001, there were 10,974 Dominican undergraduates, and a year later there were 11,214. Of those students, 67.4 percent were women (Hernández and Rivera-Batiz 2003, 57).

The high percentage of women may be accounted for by the special motivation that Dominican women have to achieve financial independence. As Dulce María Gray (2001), author of *High Literacy and Ethnic Identity: Dominican American Schooling in Transition*, and a Dominican herself, says, "Women, especially, place overwhelming emphasis on college education because they see it as the means to achieve self-sufficiency and financial independence from men and patriarchal demands" (2001, 39). For men, in contrast, pressure to work and support the family conflicts with the demands of higher education (Gray 2001; Reynoso 2004b).

At CUNY many students attempt to study and work at the same time: 57 percent of Dominican CUNY students worked in fall 2002, with 42.7 percent working at least twenty hours a week. Dominicans are poorer than other CUNY students; 63 percent of Dominicans came from households making less than $20,000 a year, compared to 39 percent of the overall undergraduate population (Hernández and Rivera-Batiz 2003, 57).

While much of the research on Latinos in higher education has focused on deficiencies, Reynoso and Gray have described Dominican academic success stories. Nelson Reynoso, director of General Counseling at Bronx Community College, and also a Dominican, interviewed Dominican English language learners and found several factors that help account for their success: supportive faculty, tutors, counselors, peers, and family. Students also reported that the college helped foster the development of a bicultural identity (Reynoso 2004a, 159–61). Gray interviewed Dominican scholars with doctorates in humanities and social sciences. She noted a scarcity of role models for Dominican students since she found only thirty Dominican academics teaching in U.S. institutions. At BCC, while there are counselors who are Dominican, there are no full-time Dominican faculty. In spite of the paucity of Dominican role models, both Reynoso and Gray found that professors, as well as parents, were critical to academic success.

Higher education opens doors for Dominican students, creating opportunities that are unavailable in the Dominican Republic. However, Dominican students give up something to succeed in higher education. They may lose their language and become alienated from their own families, yet they may never be fully accepted within academia because of their race and accent. Gray (2001) says that when Dominicans are academically successful, they "gain innumerable compensations, but . . . also pay an immense emotional price. . . . That price is the forced forging that is inherent in the process, the deracination [they] experience" (2001, 185). Education takes an emotional toll on transnational students.

The Hidden Curriculum of English as a Second Language

English language teachers have historically been responsible for teaching students to lose their foreign accents and customs and to learn to speak and act like the native born. These goals of assimilation and acculturation have, during some periods, been more overt and at other times more a part of the hidden curriculum. Whether the curriculum is hidden or overt, schools tend to reproduce the existing social structure (Giroux 1983). According to Giroux, "Instead of providing compensatory education to the students with different cultural capital, the school, while appearing neutral, asks them to think and perform in a way that is quite alien to their own background" (1983, 338). As a result, for foreign-born students, among others, this hidden curriculum casts students as deficient.

For Latinos, Americanization has required learning English and ridding themselves of their native language, an entirely subtractive approach. Critical educators argue that this approach to language education is a way of maintaining social control of subordinate groups such as Latinos, by devaluing their language, culture, and history (Darder 1995, 324; Walsh 1991, 4). Moll and Ruiz (2002) criticize the ideology that in order

> to learn English (and have academic success), it is necessary to shed Spanish and the intimate social relations created through that language. The logical extension of this ideology is the overwhelming obsession, as manifested in the schools and in the current laws in various states, with teaching the children English "as quickly as possible." (2002, 365)

Students are being asked to surrender an essential part of their identity, a demand that is particularly problematic for transnational students.

Schools also act as agents of Americanization in attempting to shape behaviors that are considered "appropriate" in the United States; in the case of adults, education is designed to prepare students for the work world. Auerbach and Burgess (1985) have critiqued the curriculum of survival ESL courses, which "prepare students for subservient social roles and reinforce hierarchical relations within the classroom" (1985, 475). While college English teachers may prepare students for better-paying jobs, they emphasize punctuality, grammatical correctness, and neat presentation of documents in order to train students to conform to the demands of corporate America.

Many well-intentioned English language teachers are unwitting collaborators in this process of Americanization of foreign-born students. Watkins-Goffman and Cummings (1997) argue that "ESL teachers should examine their teaching practice for ethnocentric approaches toward the teaching of expository writing. Epistemology is culture-driven, and we should understand that the differences in educational practices will reflect societal contexts" (1997, 11).

Based on our observations of teaching practices at CUNY, we created the following composite sketches of three imagined classroom situations to illustrate how the hidden curriculum manifests itself in the ESL classroom.

> *Professor Smith*
> Although fluent in Spanish, Professor Smith does not allow his students, three quarters whom are Dominican, to speak any language other than English in the classroom. Students are fined twenty-five cents each time they speak Spanish, even if Spanish is being used to understand the lesson, and the kitty is used to finance a party at the end of the semester.
>
> *Professor Martin*
> Professor Martin uses the theme of gender to organize the readings and essay topics in her ESL composition class. A committed feminist, she presents material that positions a liberal feminist construction of gender and family as being unquestionably superior to the *machismo* and *marianismo* considered typical of Dominican gender roles. (Pita 2000).
>
> *Professor Jones*
> At CUNY, a five-paragraph essay is the exit exam from remediation and ESL classes. Professor Jones discusses the inherent logic and clarity of this format, critiquing the digressions of Dominican students as being off the point.

Transnational students in particular need to know more than one language and culture. Each of these vignettes assumes that middle-class

American values are the norm, and that any other way of knowing is deviant. If English is the norm in the United States rather than one of the two essential languages in these students' lives, then only English is considered useful in school. If the liberal feminist construction of gender is taken as the norm, then students' own ideas about gender are inferior. If the model essay typical of undergraduate composition classes in the United States is the most logical, then students' own skills are overlooked (see Watkins-Goffman and Cummings 1997).

Pedagogy for the Transnational Community

In spite of this hidden curriculum, professors, particularly those in English departments, can mentor Dominican college students. Gray (2001) found that faculty helped Dominican students negotiate the educational system. Given how many Dominican students are the first in their family to attend college, they need the guidance of their professors to help them find available services. Dominicans who have been academically successful credit the support of faculty who took an interest in them as individuals (Gray 2001; Reynoso 2004a).

In order to be effective, professors who work with multilingual students need to problematize the teaching of English (see Canagarajah 2002; Pennycook 2001; Walsh 1991; Willinsky 1998). While learning English may help students get ahead in the United States, it may hasten the loss of their native language and strain their ties to family and community. Teaching English critically to Dominican students would mean taking into account the lived experiences of transnational students. The curriculum should integrate materials from their home country as well as the United States that are relevant to students' lives. Students in a transnational community benefit from a bicultural curriculum. Furthermore, students may be able to build on their own knowledge of Dominican history and literature (Watkins-Goffman and Cummings 1997).

A Critical Bicultural Curriculum

In our own classes at Bronx Community College, we have designed a curriculum about the Dominican Republic and the experience of Dominicans in the United States. Our intermediate-level ESL students read Fischkin's *Muddy Cup: A Dominican Family Comes of Age in a New America*, a journalistic account of a Dominican immigrant family; Danticat's *The Farming of Bones*, a novel about the massacre of Haitians in the Dominican Republic during the Trujillo era; and Diaz's *Drown*, a collection of short stories about inner-city Dominican immigrants who descend into a life of drugs and violence. Students also see *My American Girls: A Dominican Story*, a documentary about Dominican American identity. Students write essays based on the readings and video as well as on their own experiences of immigration, discrimination, and changing gender roles.

The writing and class discussion touch upon themes that are both personal and political; students are more fully engaged talking and writing about issues that they care about deeply, that touch their survival, their identity, and their anguish. In the chapter "Americanos," in *Muddy Cup*, students read about the children in the Almonte family who are struggling to learn English:

> The boy had told him how frustrated he was: that he felt his English should be better after two years in America. After school, Mauricio went home and tried to write his diary entries in English, but he didn't think they would make sense to anyone else. He watched Elizabeth, whose English compositions and speeches got better all the time, and wondered why that wasn't happening to him. (Fischkin 1997, 272)

In response to a corresponding writing assignment about the difficulties of learning English, one student wrote:

> Some times I feel frustrated and shy, in the past I used to be mad when somebody else was talking in English next to me and I could not understand what they were saying. I wanted to go back to Dominican Republic and begin a new life. . . . Some time when a couple of people were talking next to me I thought that they were talking bad about me. It made me feel upset and sad but what could I do?

This quote illustrates the traumatic experiences of students negotiating two different worlds. We have found that a critical bicultural curriculum that deals with Dominican themes and immigration helps students cope.

Emotional turmoil arises not only from the trauma of being transnational but from the racism that Dominicans face in the United States. One of Gray's informants

> disdained herself because she had absorbed "endless derogatory messages" about Hispanics. She believed herself to be substandard and unworthy. It took becoming highly literate and much introspection . . . for her to understand the power structures, the historical and psychological forces that subordinated her heritage, and which in turn shaped and determined her anguish and coming to consciousness. (Gray 2001, 214–15)

Having opportunities to reflect on the transnational experience and Dominican culture helps students make sense of their feelings of inferiority and shame and move beyond them.

Gray also found that "courses with scholarship by and about Dominicans" (2001, 110) were especially empowering for Dominican students. Professors who are able to engage their students in conversations about Dominican literature and history, especially as it relates to the history of the United States' interventions in the Dominican Republic, help students understand their "fissured identities" (Gray 2001, 76). When we focus on Dominican topics, we help students reconnect to their Dominican identity, closing the "fissure." In addition, examining this intertwined history will help students deal with the racism and anti-immigrant bias in this country.

Besides knowledge of both cultures, it is essential for transnational students to maintain and develop their native language. However, Dominican students often are discouraged from speaking Spanish. Although usually well intentioned, when teachers forbid the use of the mother tongue, students may believe their language and culture are being devalued.

English teachers also need to value the composition skills that Dominican students may bring to the classroom. In an ethnographic study of a composition class in the Dominican Republic, Watkins-Goffman and Cummings (1997) found that students learned to analyze and summarize texts. Effective teaching would identify and build on these text-related language skills.

As composition teachers, we need to respect students' right to make creative use of their native language when writing in English and resist the temptation to overcorrect. As one of Gray's informants complained, "I like to play with language and I can't do it in English. The titles of my chapters are creative and poetic. I like to use turns of phrases and themes, and I have trouble doing it in English. I also don't do it because others label my 'play' as inadequacy" (Gray 2001, 200). One way to value students' native language is to recognize when they are using a turn of phrase from Spanish that can be viewed as creative rather than awkward. For example, students in our classes have used metaphors such as "studying hard like a bull," and "My heart was beating like a horse," reflecting their rural backgrounds. Rather than helping students convert these phrases into conventional English expressions, teachers can recognize how English is enriched by students' novel word usage. Sometimes students' word choices are better than English clichés. One student wrote, "He took all the prejudice and he swallowed it," using a translation of the Spanish phrase, *Lo tragó.* Accepting the strengths that students bring from their native language can help them value it more.

English language teachers should help Dominican students in particular value their own language because Dominicans speak a low-prestige variety of a low-prestige language. Educators in the Dominican transnational community should help students become aware of the historic, social, and economic reasons for some language varieties being more valued than others. Students need to see the possibility of challenging the status quo that positions Spanish as lower than English and Dominican Spanish as lower than other varieties of Spanish.

This critical language awareness gives students the tools to understand the relationship between language and power. Teachers can promote critical language awareness by creating a space where explicitly sociopolitical and linguistic discussions can occur. For example, readings on bilingual education, the English-only movement, and assimilati on have provoked heated discussion in our classrooms. We also give students the opportunity to write about their ambivalent feelings about English and Spanish and what language(s) they hope their children will learn. Another approach to critical language awareness is described by Catherine Walsh (1991), who used sociodrama to help bilingual students "to be conscious of the sociocultural, political, and ideological context in which the languages (and therefore the speakers) are positioned" (1991, 126–27).

Dominican transmigrants are revisioning the border between the Dominican Republic and the United States. As the number of Dominicans in higher education grows, teachers at HSIs must adapt their teaching to the needs of these students. As a start, Dominican students should not be asked to leave large parts of their identity outside the classroom door, because they could be leaving outside their strengths, passions, and enthusiasm. Successful transmigrants know two cultures intimately, and so they can look at both more critically. They can cross the borders when and how they choose. Composition teachers can either reinforce the borders with red ink and restrictions or rethink their own classroom practice in order to help students make sense of their border crossings.

Note

1. We have generally used the term *Dominican* rather than *Dominican American.* Because of the transnational nature of this community, many migrants prefer the unhyphenated term.

Works Cited

Alba, Richard. 2004. "Language Assimilation Today: Bilingualism Persists More Than in the Past, but English Still Dominates" (December). *Lewis Mumford Center for Comparative Urban and Regional Research.* http://www.ecis-ucsd.org/PUBLICATIONS/wrkg111.pdf (accessed July 18, 2006).

Alvarez, Julia. 1998. *Something to Declare.* Chapel Hill, NC: Algonquin Books.

Auerbach, Elsa Roberts, and Denise Burgess. 1985. "The Hidden Curriculum of Survival ESL." *TESOL Quarterly* 19: 475–95.

Canagarajah, A. Suresh. 2002. *Critical Academic Writing and Multilingual Students.* Ann Arbor: University of Michigan Press.

Castillo, Julia. 1996. "Young Dominicans in New York City." MA thesis. Teachers College, Columbia University.

Danticat, Edwidge. 1998. *The Farming of Bones.* New York: Penguin Books.

Darder, Antonia. 1995. "Buscando America: The Contribution of Critical Latino Educators to the Academic Development and Empowerment of Latino Students in the U.S." In *Multicultural Education, Critical Pedagogy, and the Politics of Difference,* ed. Christine E. Sleeter and Peter L. McLaren, 319–47. Albany: State University of New York Press.

Díaz, Junot. 1996. *Drown.* New York: Riverhead Books.

Dicker, Susan J. 2000–2001. "Hispanics and the Spanish Language: Is Their Status Rising?" *NYS TESOL Idiom* 30:4 (Winter): 18–19.

Dicker, Susan J., and Hafiz Mahmoud. 2001. "Survey of a Bilingual Community: Dominicans in Washington Heights." NYS-TESOL Applied Linguistics Conference. CUNY Graduate Center, New York (February 3).

Duany, Jorge. 1994. *Quisqueya on the Hudson: The Transnational Identity of Dominicans in Washington Heights.* New York: The CUNY Dominican Studies Institute.

———. 1998. "Reconstructing Racial Identity: Ethnicity, Color, and Class among Dominicans in the United States and Puerto Rico. *Latin American Perspectives* 25: 147–72.

Fischkin, Barbara. 1997. *Muddy Cup: A Dominican Family Comes of Age in a New America.* New York: Scribner.

Georges, Eugenia. 1990. *The Making of a Transnational Community: Migration, Development, and Cultural Change in the Dominican Republic.* New York: Columbia University Press.

Giroux, Henry A. 1983. "Critical Theory and Rationality in Citizenship Education." In *The Hidden Curriculum and Moral Education: Deception or Discovery?,* ed. Henry A. Giroux and David E. Purpel, 321–60. Berkeley, CA: McCutchan.

Glick Schiller, Nina. 1999. "Who Are These Guys?: A Transnational Reading of the U.S. Immigrant Experience." In *Identities on the Move: Transnational Processes in North America and the Caribbean Basin,* ed. Liliana R. Goldin, 15–43. Austin: University of Texas Press.

Glick Schiller, Nina, Linda Basch, and Cristina Blanc-Szanton. 1992. "Transnationalism: A New Analytic Framework for Understanding Migration." In *Towards a Transnational Perspective on Migration: Race, Class, Ethnicity, and Nationalism Reconsidered: Vol. 645. Annals of the New York Academy of Sciences,* ed. Linda Basch, Cristina Blanc-Szanton, and Nina Glick Schiller, 1–24. New York: New York Academy of Sciences.

Gray, Dulce María. 2001. *High Literacy and Ethnic Identity: Dominican American Schooling in Transition.* New York: Rowman & Littlefield.

Hernández, Ramona, and Francisco Rivera-Batiz. 2003. *Dominicans in the United States: A Socioeconomic Profile, 2000.* New York: CUNY Dominican Studies Institute.

Itzigsohn, José, Carlos Dore Cabral, Esther Hernández Medina, and Obed Vázquez. 1999. "Mapping Dominican Transnationalism: Narrow and Broad Transnational Practices." *Ethnic & Racial Studies* 22: 316–40.

Moll, Luis C., and Richard Ruiz. 2002. "The Schooling of Latino Children." In *Latinos: Remaking America,* ed. Marcelo Suárez-Orozco and Mariela Páez, 362–74. Berkeley: University of California Press.

Paybarah, Azi. 2004. "Queens Dominicans Cast Overseas Votes." *Queens Tribune Online* (May 20). http://www.queenstribune.com/news/1095068906.html (accessed May 25, 2004).

Pennycook, Alastair. 2001. *Critical Applied Linguistics: A Critical Introduction.* Mahwah, NJ: Lawrence Erlbaum.

Pita, Marianne. 2000. "Reading Dominican Girls: The Experiences of Four Participants in Herstory, a Literature Discussion Group." Dissertation, New York University.

Reynoso, Nelson. 2004a. "Academic Achievement among Dominican English Language Learners at Bronx Community College of the City University of New York." Dissertation. New York University.

———. 2004b. Personal interview, May 26.

Toribio, Almeida Jacqueline. 2000. "Language Variation and the Linguistic Enactment of Identity among Dominicans." *Linguistics* 38: 1133–59.

Torres-Saillant, Silvio, and Ramona Hernández. 1998. *The Dominican Americans.* Westport, CT: Greenwood Press.

Walsh, Catherine E. 1991. *Pedagogy and the Struggle for Voice: Issues of Language, Power, and Schooling for Puerto Ricans.* New York: Bergin & Garvey.

Watkins-Goffman, Linda, and Victor Cummings. 1997. "Bridging the Gap between Native Language and Second Language Literacy Instruction: A Naturalistic Study." *Bilingual Research Journal* 21:4. http://www.brj.asu.edu/articles/ar3.html (accessed July 18, 2006).

Willinsky, John. 1998. *Learning to Divide the World: Education at Empire's End.* Minneapolis: University of Minnesota Press.

Zentella, Ana Celia. 1990. "Lexical Leveling in Four New York City Spanish Dialects: Linguistic and Social Factors." *Hispania* 73: 1094–1105.

Part 3

Considerations for Creating Effective Writing Programs at Hispanic-Serving Institutions

Chapter 7

Building on the Richness of a South Texas Community

Revisioning a Technical and Professional Writing Program through Service Learning

Diana Cárdenas and Susan Loudermilk Garza

Having been raised on the west side of the city, Diana remembers that not too long ago our university, located near one of the city's most expensive neighborhoods on Ocean Drive, was perceived as a "white school," an institution for the privileged. She has observed that interactions with community groups have helped begin to change the university's image. Community leaders have experienced positive results working with our students and have found that they can contribute to students' learning and civic engagement; students, who created connections or reinforced original ties to the community, learned to make a difference in the lives of others.

Texas A&M University-Corpus Christi (TAMU-CC), a Hispanic-Serving Institution (HSI) located in Corpus Christi, Texas, in what is known as the Coastal Bend area, has a "commitment to serving the intellectual, cultural, social, environmental, and economic needs of South Texas" to "invigorate and strengthen the region through its educational programs, research endeavors, and outreach efforts" (Institutional Vision and Mission 2005, 10). The university has already begun to realize its mission by becoming a positive local presence through partnerships and service learning engagements, initiated by professors, Title V coordinators, and Community Outreach directors with small and large businesses, health organizations, schools, cultural centers, not-for-profit agencies, and youth centers.

Service learning has gained momentum as a classroom and programmatic approach in the area of composition studies (Deans 2000; Adler-Kassner, Crooks, and Watters 1997), and we have found many advantages for implementing such an approach in our technical and professional writing program (TPW) at TAMU-CC. We are located in a unique geographic area: our border is the Gulf of Mexico; our port is open to international trade with Asia, South America, and Mexico; the city is located two hours from Mexico. Two military bases, refineries, health-oriented institutions, and many diverse businesses contribute to the economy. We have many needs in the community that go beyond what city, state, and county resources can cover. Thus we have a large number of not-for-profit organizations to fill the gap. The city has 280,000 residents—59.8 percent are Hispanic, 4.4 percent are African American, 34.6 percent are Anglo, and 1.2 percent are Asian (U.S. Census Bureau 2003). Hispanics[1] constitute a large professional segment, but many Hispanics also live in the poorest areas of town. The median household income is $41,000, and the per capita income is $9,000 as compared to the national figure of $14,000 (U.S. Census Bureau 2003).

When we first began teaching in the TPW program at our school, we had to address a prevailing myth among our students that no jobs exist in our area for technical writers. They believed that they would have to relocate to Houston or Dallas to secure employment. That belief was part of a broader misconception that the area lacks opportunities and resources. A survey that we sent in fall 2000 to more than 500 organizations, businesses, and agencies helped us address this misconception. More importantly, the survey began a process that led to a more positive view of our community. Rather than viewing the Coastal Bend as lacking resources with few job opportunities, as the prevalent view of areas with large Hispanic population advances, we see our area as being rich with opportunities. In the remainder of this chapter we explain how we redesigned and implemented the program to engage students in the community and promote the Coastal Bend region as a rich place at many levels.

Building a New Program

The initial step we took, sending out a survey, identified the kinds of writing done in professional work settings in the Coastal Bend area and the types of positions involving technical and professional writing. Even though small in scope (15% of 500 surveys returned), the survey revealed what we believed: many opportunities that involve writing exist in the area. More than forty different positions and corresponding writing behaviors were described by the respondents: grant writer, fraud investigator, juvenile probation officer, environmental program planner, documentation specialist, human resources personnel administrator, and child protective services caseworker. Because of the numerous opportunities in the community and the local connections and backgrounds and abilities of our students, we recreated the TPW program to focus on service learning pedagogy to take advantage of our rich teaching and learning context.

We utilize the definition of service learning advocated by Bowdon and Scott (2003): "a hands-on approach that uses community service as a vehicle for teaching specific course-based skills and strategies" (2003, 1). They note the definition, provided by Thomas Huckin, as established by the National and Community Service Trust Act of 1993, legislation that funds service learning efforts. According to Huckin:

> Service learning is a method by which students learn through active participation in thoughtfully organized service; is conducted in, and meets the needs of the community; is integrated into and enhances the academic curriculum; includes structured time for reflection, and helps foster civic responsibility. (quoted in Bowdon and Scott 2003, 1–2)

For several decades, points out Thomas Deans (2000), teachers have used three models. In model one, students write about the non-writing work they do within the community. In the second model, students study community issues, such as literacy, and do related work, for example, tutoring; in their writing they make connections between the two activities. In the third, Stanford model, students write for the community as their involvement.

Based on the third model, our approach allows students to learn and apply principles of effective written, oral, and visual communication to help local organizations achieve their missions. Writing for the community appealed to us because it engenders, as Bowdon and Scott (2003) add, a "reciprocal relationship between the university and community organizations that is ethical and beneficial to the community . . . [and] it most clearly involves a set of meaningful learning experiences that let students see academic concepts in action" (2003, 5–6).

Our service learning model encourages students to study missions and goals of organizations, primarily not-for-profit agencies and groups, to benefit individuals with very real needs. Our intent is to demonstrate to students that they can use their varied resources to change the lives of underserved populations in the community. They begin to move beyond thinking that technical communication is merely a set of skills, and they begin to see that a progress report, a letter of transmittal, or a report on options is not just a document that needs to be written in a certain style and be grammatically correct. By guiding students to write with and for the community, we help them, as Carolyn Miller notes, to "think of genres as forms of social action rather than simple formats" (quoted in Bowdon and Scott 2003, 36).

In the survey we also asked if organizations were interested in working with our students, and many indicated that they would. This response initiated many professional networks and relationships. Some of our early connections were made with the county juvenile justice center, the Chamber of Commerce, the Hispanic Chamber of Commerce, health clinics, the Boys and Girls Club, and the Westside Business Association. The Westside is the low-income section of our community, encompassing some of the poorest predominantly Hispanic and African American neighborhoods. The directors of the YWCA and the Boys and Girls Club became our first partners for student projects. They welcomed us with open arms since they operate with limited funds, limited staffs, and volunteers. These initial connections grew into many other dialogues with agency leaders, business owners, directors, and assistant managers.

Understanding Our Student Population

We are an HSI with 37 percent of our students self-identifying as Hispanic. Many of our students are first-generation university students, come from low-income homes, and were born and raised in the area[2] but may not be Spanish speakers[3]; transferred from the local community college; work in sales or other minimum wage part-time jobs more than twenty hours a week; are nontraditional students who hold management-level positions; are married and/or raising families; have strong family ties so they hope to remain in the area after graduation; and come from middle-class homes, enroll directly into the university as freshman students, and desire to go on to graduate school after graduation. The students come to our classes with many different levels of experience with professional writing and work experience in general, so their readiness for engaging with the community varies as well. For example, a police commander who has extensive experience writing various types of documents can take on the task of writing a grant in the introductory course. Other students have never written a memo or any type of report. Some students who entered the university following high school graduation have probably engaged in some community service because they know that is a factor in university admission decisions. Some of our transfer students, however, may have little experience and may be uncomfortable engaging with decision makers at the professional level. In high school they may not have even considered college in their futures, so their focus is different. They may need more nurturing and guidance to progress in their projects. Our program encourages all students to identify and make use of their backgrounds and areas of expertise. Also, because students bring to our courses a diversity of perspectives, experiences, and abilities, we guide them to undertake and manage projects that match and can build on their strengths and interests.

The Revisioned Technical/Professional Writing Program

The principal feature of each of the seven undergraduate courses in the revised program is flexibility, which allows students to engage in community needs according to their interests and abilities. We created broad parameters that allow students to determine how to apply the principles of effective writing, speaking, and visual design to solve problems or address needs in local contexts of their choosing. Joe, who has served for twenty-five years as buildings supervisor at the county mental health and mental retardation facility, chose for a class project the new task he recently received: to write a five-year plan to help maintain the existing buildings and anticipate future construction.

Flexibility also comes in independent choices that students make before they begin a project and in decisions of how engaged they want to be and how to proceed to complete the projects. Flexibility allows them to engage in problem solving individually or as part of a team. Students can even partner with other students in other technical and professional writing courses or collaborate with students in other disciplines.

Reorganizing the Class Approach

Ensuring successful and meaningful experiences for each student requires changes in how we might ordinarily organize our classes and how we assess student performance. The entire dynamics of the class must change. Because many of our students work and/or have families, as we pointed out earlier, class time has to be given to allow them to meet with their community contacts. Equally important, as some of our students do not have home computers, they need class time to use the resources on campus. Time has to be set aside for discussion and questions and problems that students encounter. In class we provide immediate feedback during the project and after its completion; students also receive feedback from the community contacts. And, because students are working on different stages of the invention, drafting, and revising processes, we must be very familiar with each project.

Our classes function as generative communities, emphasizing individual and collective achievement and accountability, respect, trust, cooperation, and interdependence. A workshop approach encourages students to discuss ideas, offer each other suggestions, write drafts together, and exchange them. Students use the skills and experiences they bring to the class, and they instruct peers. A computer programmer at one of the refineries, who is proficient with online Web sites and electronic data sources, uses his expertise to develop a Web site for the YMCA. In class he mentors students who have less understanding and ability in this area. Within this environment each student can feel valued and can be successful. Our classes mirror the kind of collaboration that characterizes actual workplaces.

Assessment of students' performances in community settings is ongoing. We look at students' work at various stages of the creation process. We ask students to e-mail progress reports that help us evaluate progress. Assessment is individual. Each student has different abilities, and each establishes the goals for his or her project. We study a student's completed portfolio, and we make comparisons between early work and finished products to determine the development of writing and changes in the perspectives of a student regarding his or her own writing. Students collaborate with their community contacts to create and revise documents, and that feedback becomes part of the assessment process as well. This approach is very important because, as we stated earlier, students come to our classes with varied backgrounds and experiences. By assessing their progress, they feel successful as writers.

The quality of the writing projects demonstrates that students develop an understanding of the importance of meeting the needs of readers and an increased awareness of the importance of effective writing. Two students who produced a volunteers' manual for a youth rehabilitation facility revised the document several times using feedback from county officials at various levels. Thus students begin to understand assessment as more than just what the teacher says about the writing as well as how many levels of assessment documents undergo in actual professional organizations and how the assessment of a project may extend beyond the community contact as well.

Preparing Organizations for Student Engagement

Preparing the organization for student engagement also is a key factor in the successful completion of a project. The most important act on our part is identifying company owners and directors of agencies who have a commitment to the students in our area and are willing to serve as mentors who guide them through this learning process. Many of these directors grew up in the area so they know what the students need to become successful and contribute to the community. For instance, the assistant executive director of the Nueces County Juvenile Justice Center, who has thirty-five years of experience trying to help juvenile offenders improve their lives, spends numerous hours providing information and guidance so our criminal justice majors can work on juvenile-related projects.

We are acquainted with many company leaders and directors of agencies, and we communicate with them at the beginning of each semester to determine whether they have projects that our students can undertake to apply and extend their abilities. These leaders help educate directors of other organizations about our service learning work. We meet with new community contact persons before we add the names of their organizations to our Community Partners Web site. As an example, the director of the county food bank approached us and another teacher in the program to seek help writing a grant proposal to obtain much-needed refrigeration equipment. We described what our students can do to help her achieve her objective and what she needs to do for our students, specifically setting aside time to devote to the students and providing information. We stressed that the purpose of these collaborations is to help students learn and grow as professional writers. Further, we stressed that the students will need mentoring at many different levels. Community partners, such as the director of the county food bank, may receive a finished project that they can immediately put to use, for example, a completed grant But, they are just as likely to see, at the semester's end, a product that shows student growth but may not be of use to the organization at that point. We make no guarantees about the end products. We have to work with community contacts and students alike to help them realize that the process of learning is just as important as the finished product. Even a student who spends an entire semester working on a project and presents only preliminary findings at the end of the semester has contributed to a community need. The student can still report on the findings and make recommendations for further work, a process that occurs quite often in the real world. We ask community leaders to serve on the Technical and Professional Writing Program Advisory Committee to gain insight into the expectations of the community partners and to help them better understand our program and our students' needs.

Enhancing Students' Experiences While Promoting the Coastal Bend Area As a Place for Opportunity

As students participate in these community engagement opportunities, they practice higher-order thinking, gain specialized knowledge, make decisions, and manage and meet challenges. Students integrate intellectual growth and applied experience. And, they experience the potential power of their discursive efforts. These gains are evident in the work of Sandra, reared in a middle-class Hispanic family, who entered our university as a freshman to study history and conduct research in social and political movements in South Texas. Sandra worked with the executive director and manager of a housing development that is home to more than 100 families, mostly Hispanic and African American. Motivated by her value of family, Sandra used her writing abilities to attempt to improve the quality of life for hundreds of children who live and thrive there. She secured information from the housing director and manager to write a grant for new roofs. As Sandra studied, planned, and managed the stages of the writing, she increased her knowledge base and expanded her abilities while examining, in a very personal manner, the social and economic realities of the Coastal Bend area. Along with the grant, Sandra created a brochure to send to parishioners of a local church as part of its Christmas fund drive to help support the children's programs. Her discursive actions resulted in a donation of $2,000 from the congregation, funds used for the Kids' Café, an after-school program that provides meals and mentoring to the children.

In the process of gathering information and interacting with the staff and the children of the housing development, Sandra became aware of the everyday lives of the residents. Her interventions helped her take on the identity of professional writer and what Bowdon and Scott (2003) refer to as an audience advocate (2003, 29).

Like Sandra, other students take pride in establishing or maintaining connections to the area. In a beginning technical and professional writing class, Fernando wrote a plan to help a youth center located in an underserved area of the community secure computers for the after-school tutorial program. He played basketball at this center during his teenage years, and he understands, in a very personal way, the significance of the center in the lives of young people in his neighborhood. Commander Walsh, a thirty-three-year veteran of the police department, wrote a grant proposal to secure funds to combat family violence that he has seen in the daily job. Students in an upper-level grant writing course wrote collaboratively to produce a grant for the director of the county food bank to obtain much-needed refrigeration equipment. They invested in the success of the grant, and they were thrilled to learn, even a semester after the class had ended, that the organization received the equipment. These kinds of student endeavors also plant the seed for future change. Students wrote a grant for the Boys and Girls Club to build a new facility, and although the initial grant was not funded, the impetus from that project resulted, five years later, in the realization of a new facility that engages youngsters in varied after-school and weekend activities.

Other contributors in this collection also point to the importance of preserving cultural roots and personal identity to promote achievement and success. In a community such as ours, where many needs and concerns affect so many lives, our students, from all social and economic backgrounds, come to understand how their individual, smaller, grassroots efforts can lead to larger social change. Having our technical writing students engage in service-learning endeavors to serve neighbors, to address pressing social problems, and to learn about the needs of the underserved produces many gains for them.

Conclusion

The academic, personal, and social benefits of service learning help promote the Coastal Bend area as a place for opportunities and successes. Young mothers need aid for their children, juvenile offenders require rehabilitation and direction, and the elderly need programs to help them thrive. That is the situation in our area, and we do not see a separate reality between the neighborhoods and our university. We see opportunity at many levels, not just disadvantages and problems. The activities, processes, and decisions that engage students represent the kind of active learning that is necessary to improve the academic environment and promote a mutual responsibility and an interconnectedness with our community—democratic values. For students, writing is an intervention, a seed that holds promise for individual lives and futures. Sandra articulates the significance of her engagement in the following passage:

> The volunteers with the Kid's Cafe used the money to improve the program and take several of the older children to a summer camp. They told me about how excited the kids were to go—none of them had ever left their neighborhood before. Those children really gained wonderful memories and personal experiences for the rest of their lives. They were able to interact with other children from different socioeconomic backgrounds, and I hope they are able to realize that they don't have to be limited by their socioeconomic status, but can accomplish all that they want to with determination and education. I was empowered by realizing that even though I was only a student, I made a difference in people's lives with my abilities.

Our program continues to grow because we listen to the needs of our students and our community, build on the diverse backgrounds and varying abilities and strengths of our students, and recognize the opportunities for community viability and student growth. Sandra capitalized on the melding of her classroom study of history and community work to apply for a summer internship at the Smithsonian Institute in Washington, D.C. Researching social and political movements in the South Texas area and creating resources for a teacher's program (her assignment) reinforced her identities as a student and community advocate.

This university-community partnership is essential to achieve the university's mission as an HSI. The identity that it has chosen and the central role it embraces promote positive perspectives within the community toward the university and to its future, creating a mutuality that is crucial to achieve economic and social advancement in the Coastal Bend area.

Notes

1. *Hispanic* is the term used in our geographic area.

2. For example, in one recent technical writing class of twenty-five students, only two students came to us from other areas of the state.

3. In this anthology, Araiza, Cárdenas, and Garza present survey results indicating that as many as 56 percent of Texas A&M University-Corpus Christi first-year students speak only English.

Works Cited

Adler-Kassner, Linda, Robert Crooks, and Ann Watters, eds. 1997. *Writing the Community: Concepts and Models for Service-Learning in Composition.* Washington, DC: American Association for Higher Education.

Bowdon, Melody, and J. Blake Scott. 2003. *Service-Learning in Technical and Professional Communication.* New York: Longman.

Deans, Thomas. 2000. *Writing Partnerships: Service-Learning in Composition.* Urbana, IL: National Council of Teachers of English.

"Institutional Vision and Mission." 2005. Undergraduate Catalog 2005–2006. Texas A&M University-Corpus Christi.

U.S. Census Bureau. 2003. State & County QuickFacts: Corpus Christi, Texas. http://www.quickfacts.census.gov/qfd/states/48/4817000.html (accessed May 26, 2006).

CHAPTER 8

IT IS ALL IN THE ATTITUDE— THE LANGUAGE ATTITUDE

Isabel Baca

Since I was a little girl, I knew I wanted to teach. Soon after I began my schooling in El Paso, Texas, I became convinced I would be an English teacher. I began learning English in the third grade. My native language is Spanish, and English became my second language. I learned French in high school and took two years of Latin. I even learned some sign language. Language fascinated me, and it became my destiny.

I was born in El Paso, Texas, lived in Juárez, Chihuahua, México, for the first four years of my life, and moved to and have lived in El Paso for thirty-four years. I am a product, a child, of the El Paso/Juárez border. I studied in Juárez the first four years of my academic life, completed grade school and high school in El Paso, received my bachelor's and master's degrees in English from the University of Texas at El Paso, and received my PhD in English from New Mexico State University in Las Cruces. I have taught students at all stages, from junior high to college seniors. I have taught in private schools, community college, and universities. I have been a technical writing consultant for companies and have conducted numerous workshops on different aspects of writing and language. And as a product of the El Paso/Juárez border myself, my primary concerns as an educator, learner, writer, and researcher have been constant throughout the years: How can writing instructors help Latino/a students whose first language is Spanish master the English language? How can writing instructors teach the academic discourse to help these minority students succeed in college and their professional lives? And as a Latina myself, whose first language is not English, how can I help other educators teach writing to minority students? How can my experience as learner and teacher contribute to the field of the teaching of writing? And thus my quest began.

The El Paso/Juárez Border

El Paso, Texas, and Ciudad Juárez (Chihuahua, México) are sister cities and provide a major point of entry for Mexicans into the United States. This is the northern border of Latin America. El Paso, the Sun City, as it is known, is located in the extreme west point of Texas. The Franklin Mountains, the southernmost portion of the Rocky Mountains, slice El Paso into Eastside, Westside, and Central areas with Ciudad Juárez, México, directly south across the Rio Grande. Ciudad Juárez is located in the semi-desert, north of the Mexican state of Chihuahua. It is the fourth largest city in México. El Paso and Juárez form the largest international border community in the world. In addition to their location, strong manufacturing base, and inseparable economies, cultures, and histories, these cities are a natural transition point between both countries (Greater El Paso Chamber of Commerce 1999, 24).

El Paso is suited for numerous industries, the most prominent being apparel and sewn products (especially denims and boots), copper refining, medical equipment processing, electrical component manufacturing, plastic injection molding, Southwestern food products, and natural gas pipeline operations. Its economy is based on the *Maquiladora*-related industries, and El Paso has attracted over seventy Fortune 500 companies (Greater El Paso Chamber of Commerce 1996). *Maquiladoras*, twin plants, have contributed to this area's industrial development. These twin plant industries pair manufacturing facilities on both sides of the El Paso/Juárez border. Components and parts are manufactured and prepared in the United States and shipped to México for assembly, since labor costs less there.

Another economic aspect of these border cities is the daily crossing of workers, students, and professionals. And though many borderland residents cross over for employment and educational purposes, many also cross over because they have family ties north and south of the border.

Characteristics of Basic Writers at a Hispanic-Serving Institution (HSI)

I teach at El Paso Community College (EPCC), which has five main campuses. In fall 2002, in terms of ethnicity, the student population consisted of 85 percent Hispanic, 9 percent white, .79 percent Asian, .35 percent Native American, 2.25 percent black, and 1.92 percent foreign. According to the fall 2002 credit demographics, the total student head count was 19,865, of which 12,392 were planning on academic transfer to a university, 5,500 were completing occupational/technical programs, and 1,973 were undeclared (EPCC 2003).

When I first began teaching Basic English Composition, English 0310, I soon discovered that at least half of the students in each class were students whose second language is English. Many of them are native Spanish speakers. These students share several of the following characteristics:

- They have done some or most of their schooling in México.
- They are ESL (English as a Second Language) students.
- They were placed in a regular English writing course because of their test scores on a national standardized test or a college placement exam.
- They completed high school in the United States after receiving only one or two years of intensive English (ESL programs) or bilingual education in high school.
- Their language at home is Spanish.
- Their social life primarily involves the use of Spanish.
- At work, they use English, but being on the El Paso/Juárez border allows or requires them to use Spanish as well.
- They believe they can express themselves better in Spanish.
- They believe English is the language of opportunity, the language that will help them succeed in their professional lives.
- They lack confidence in their English skills in writing, reading, and speaking, though many express more confidence in their reading abilities.
- They are repeating the Basic English Composition course either because they failed or withdrew from the course the first time.
- They lived or currently reside in Juárez and cross the border on a daily basis.
- They consider themselves bilingual to different degrees.

Based on my observations and concerns for students' perceptions of their own language abilities and their language attitudes, I began exploring ways of improving the teaching of writing so that Latino/a students would better learn and enjoy writing and academic discourse. In the summer of 2003, I was awarded a Faculty Development mini-grant to conduct a study of six Basic English Composition classes being taught at EPCC during the first summer session (lasting five weeks).

Conducting an Exploratory Study of a Basic Writing Course

The goal of the exploratory study was to evaluate the effectiveness and success of English 0310 Basic English Composition courses to better prepare basic writers for English 1301 (first freshman composition credit course) and to give them a better opportunity to succeed in writing courses and improve their writing skills. The official course syllabus, set up by the English department, outlines specific course objectives that must be met by the end of the semester (see Appendix A for a list of these course objectives).

With these objectives in mind, I examined English 0310 students' attitudes and perspectives of their writing skills, their confidence in writing, their confidence in the English language, and their learning process (level of improvement by the end of the semester). This study also focused on the effectiveness of the English Exit Essay Exam. (Assessed holistically, each essay is scored independently by three different faculty members. Students must pass it on one of two attempts to pass the course.) This exploratory study consisted of the following methods:

- Administering a pre- and post-survey to all English 0310 students in Summer I, 2003 (A total of 134 students completed the preliminary survey, and 118 students completed the final survey. See Appendixes B and C for a copy of both surveys.)
- Conducting random individual interviews with English 0310 students throughout the Summer I session to obtain input on their progress and attitudes in this remedial course
- Gathering all data, compiling, analyzing, and arriving at conclusions
- Offering recommendations on how English faculty can improve the English 0310 course to better meet the needs of these students

Assignments and Teaching Approach

To meet the course objectives and to evaluate the effectiveness of the course, I designed the following specific assignments and activities for students.

Four Persuasive Essays

The first essay was done in class and outside of class. Students began their writing process in class, produced their first draft in class, and did the rewriting outside of class; in other words, the final draft was produced outside of class. Two other essays were timed essays; a persuasive topic was given to them, and students had fifty minutes to complete the essay. However, the topic was given to students one day in advance so that they worked on the writing process at home, coming in ready to write their final draft of the essay in class in fifty minutes. For the fourth essay, a comparison/contrast essay, students selected their own topic and worked on the essay and writing process completely outside of class. They did a peer critique of the first draft of this essay in class.

A Writing Journal

In this journal, students did prewriting activities for each of their four assigned persuasive essays, activities such as freewriting, brainstorming, clustering, and outlining. Students also were given topics to freewrite either at the beginning or at the end of each class. Topics varied, such as:

How do you feel about writing and why? What has been the greatest gift you have ever received, and what makes this the greatest gift for you?

A Reading Journal
Students were assigned readings on a daily basis. For each assigned reading, students were to include an entry in their reading journal consisting of three main sections: Questions on the Reading, Questions on Writing, and a Reflection. The essays and questions were taken from their textbook, *Keys to Successful Writing*, second edition, by Marilyn Anderson. These questions promoted critical thinking not only in terms of reading comprehension but in understanding the writing style and approach of the essays' authors. The Reflection section asked students to relate the reading to their lives or to give their opinion about the essay.

Mini-Grammar Lessons and Exercises
Students worked on sentence and paragraph structure exercises. Handouts were given with exercises to complete for homework, and as a class, we reviewed these exercises on the blackboard. All students were required to go up to the board and explain their answers to the exercises.

I used different teaching methodologies: mini-lectures, collaborative activities, one-on-one conferencing with students, and lots of class participation. Students were asked to share their writing with the class; students read entries aloud to the class from their writing journal, and at times, they read drafts of their different essays. So students not only practiced their written English but their spoken English. In addition, students were not penalized if they used their home dialect (whether Spanish, a combination of English and Spanish, etc.) in their writing journal entries and/or at the prewriting stage of their essays. Students also could speak to me in Spanish, if need be, in class and more so in our conferences. By allowing students to use their first language or home dialect, I tried to demonstrate that I respected their language and valued their ideas, no matter from which language they originated.

Findings

I gathered and analyzed the data. The following list highlights key findings:

1. More students rated their skills (writing, reading, speaking, critical thinking, grammar, vocabulary, using different learning resources, and overall English language skills) as above average at the end of the semester, compared to their ratings at the beginning of the semester, when more students evaluated their skills as average or below average.
2. When asked how having taken English 0310 had affected them, 94 percent said it had improved their writing skills, 91 percent felt the course

had helped them recognize their writing weaknesses, 81 percent believed it had improved their grammar skills, 73 percent said it had improved their critical thinking skills, 68 percent believed it improved their reading skills, and about half of the students felt the course had improved their speaking skills, their self-esteem, and their language skills and helped them recognize their writing strengths and desire to continue writing.

3. On the final survey, most students evaluated the English 0310 course as being either helpful or extremely helpful.

Discussion

The aforementioned findings, survey results, and interviews provided the following helpful suggestions:

1. Students want more one-on-one conferences with the instructor, more time for in-class essays, and more narrative writing and less persuasive writing.
2. On surveys and in interviews, students cited ESL problems as being what they needed more help with in this course. When asked how the instructor could provide such help, students suggested more one-on-one time with the student and the removal of timed writing.
3. A task force—including English 0310 instructors, BASK 0303 (basic writing skills course taken before English 0310) instructors, counselors, course placement staff and advisors, and the division dean—should be established to provide more accurate course placement and a more effective transition between the remedial writing courses and the credit freshman composition course.
4. Placement of ESL students in regular English writing courses should be examined. Many students do not feel prepared and are not prepared to take a regular English writing course.

This exploratory study became the foundation for my future research and experimental teaching in my writing courses, and the redesign of my Basic English Composition course. In my teaching and research, I focus on students' perceptions of their ability to write, think, read, and communicate in English and academic discourse. I conference with students and make my classroom an open and a safe place for students to use their native language. By making these changes, I open the door for students to examine, practice, and improve their communication skills, both oral and written. Through informal conversations, one-on-one conferences, and journal writing, students share how and what their writing, reading, speaking, and overall communication skills are and what they hope they become.

Latino/a Students and Their Bilingualism

Teaching students at HSIs leads writing instructors to examine various aspects of their students' language use. Bilingualism is one of these elements, and this concept has led to much debate and research over the years.

Most people, even if they are bilingual, define bilingualism as the ability to speak two languages fluently. Grosjean states, "[F]ar too much weight has been put on fluency, to the detriment of other factors such as the regular use of two languages, their domains of use, and the bilingual's need to have certain skills (reading and writing, for instance) in one language but not in the other (1982, 231). Thus Grosjean provides a functional definition for bilingualism. He sees bilingualism as the regular use of two languages. I share his view on bilingualism when teaching writing to Latino/a students whose first language is not English. Furthermore, Grosjean differentiates between the monolingual (or fractional) view of bilingualism and the bilingual (or holistic) view of bilingualism. The monolingual view presents various problems for Grosjean, as he explains:

> I wish to argue that a monolingual (or fractional) view of bilingualism has played too great a role in our study of people who use two languages in their everyday lives. According to a strong version of this view, the bilingual has (or should have) two separate and isolable language competencies; these competencies are (or should be) similar to those of the two corresponding monolinguals; therefore, the bilingual is (or should be) two monolinguals in one person. (Grosjean 1985, 468)

Grosjean goes on to explain how the monolingual view of bilingualism has had a number of consequences, including the following:

- Bilinguals have been evaluated and described on the basis of the fluency and balance they have in their two languages.
- Monolingual standards are used to appraise language skills in bilinguals.
- Bilinguals themselves rarely see their language abilities as being adequate.
- Contact between a bilingual's two languages is seen as accidental, since the two languages should be autonomous.

Thus Grosjean contends that the monolingual view of bilingualism can be destructive, and that the bilingual view should be adopted. He says, "It is time, I believe, that we accept the fact that bilinguals are not two monolinguals in one person, but different, perfectly competent speaker-hearers in their own right" (1985, 471). The bilingual should not be seen as the sum of two complete or incomplete monolinguals; the bilingual is a unique and specific speaker-hearer because a bilingual's two languages coexist and are constantly interacting. This, in turn, produces a different but complete language system. Grosjean's analogy from biculturalism explains this view more effectively: "A bicultural individual, for example, a Mexican American, is not two monoculturals; the bicultural individual combines and blends the two cultures to produce a unique cultural configuration" (ibid. 471).

Many of these second-language students are what Guadalupe Valdés calls *incipient bilinguals.* These individuals are in the process of becoming bilingual, that is, learning English (cited in Hagemann 2003, 133). And using Lightbown and Spada (1999) as her sources, Hagemann explains that incipient bilinguals use their native language, Spanish in the case of Latino students on the border, to help them learn the linguistic rules of their second language, in this case, English. Thus I, as a writing instructor at an HSI, find myself telling students, "You're thinking in Spanish when writing in English." In other words, these students are borrowing rules and vocabulary from Spanish when they are writing in English, consciously and unconsciously. However, as Hagemann (2003) points out, these second-language speakers do not borrow as much from their first language as they become more proficient in the second language. These Spanish speakers now rely more on their knowledge of English (2003, 135). More proficiency in English (which comes from practice) blended in with positive language attitudes will contribute to improved writing performance and increased confidence in students as learners.

Language Attitudes and Their Influence on the Teaching and Learning of Written English

Baker and Jones (1998) define language attitudes as the beliefs and values expressed by people toward different languages in terms of favorability and unfavorability (1998, 702). These researchers explain the nature and types of language attitudes. They state:

> Unlike height and weight, attitudes cannot be directly observed nor perfectly measured. Attitudes are a disposition to respond favorably or unfavorably to something like a language, a person, an institution or an event. An attitude represents internal thoughts, feelings and tendencies in behavior across a variety of contexts.
>
> An attitude may be both a predisposing factor and also an outcome. As a predisposing factor, attitudes influence behavior. For example, if someone has a positive attitude to learning a second language, they may well succeed in becoming proficient in that language. Also, at the end of language learning, a desired outcome may be that students have a positive attitude towards that second language. Thus, attitudes are both an ingredient in language learning and also an important result. (1998, 174)

Baker and Jones then go on to list various types of language attitudes that include attitudes to specific minority or majority languages, attitudes to language variation (such as in the case of different accents when speaking English with a Spanish accent), attitudes to language lessons, and attitudes to learning a new language. I contend that language attitudes then include attitudes to not only learning a new language but more specifically attitudes to the different skills of writing, reading, and speaking the new language, English, as in the case of many students attending HSIs.

In terms of language attitudes, it is important to refer back to the monolingual (fractional) view of bilingualism. This view leads bilingual speakers to hold negative language attitudes about themselves and their competencies in language. These attitudes were reflected when various speakers, in an extensive case study of four English/Spanish bilingual families residing on the El Paso/Juárez border, criticized their own language competence. For example, one of the speakers, Mr. H., kept referring to his limited English vocabulary. Several of the participants expressed concern about their accent. Others viewed their mixing of the two languages as lack of proficiency in the language (Baca 2000, 239). The fractional view of bilingualism does affect these bilingual speakers' language attitudes.

I remember when I began my schooling in the United States. I was in the third grade, had only taken an intensive English summer course with a private English teacher, and was placed in a regular third-grade classroom with an English monolingual teacher. More than half of the time I had no idea what was being said in class, and when I wanted to ask questions, I was petrified of making a fool of myself by not making sense or, worse yet, by having the class laugh at my poor pronunciation of English. Embarrassment and fear dominated my learning experience when I first entered an American classroom. If I had realized then that everyone has an accent, and how no accent is right or wrong, then learning English would have been easier and more enjoyable.

Furthermore, Hagemann (2003) states that "good" or "right" English is a version of English appropriate to the audience and context, and I would include purpose as well. So "good" English is not necessarily standard English. Depending on who the writer's reader is, what the context is, and what purpose the writer has for writing, the student must have many languages, one being academic English. Thus learning academic English is not giving up one's self-identity (2003, 142). Academic English is more of an extension or a role that students must have or play, and they will use it depending on the situation at hand.

Writing instructors must value and acknowledge their students' ideas and voices. It is not enough to examine students' and instructors' points of view; it is crucial to value the way they express themselves and their language choice. When I first learned English I remember being slapped on the hand in school if I was caught speaking Spanish, and I was reprimanded at home for speaking English. I believe both my teacher and my parents wanted the best for me; they both wanted me to learn the power language, English, to get ahead in school and in my future. However, my parents feared I would lose my roots and forget my culture and native language, thus they insisted on using only Spanish at home. But these attitudes confused me, and in retrospect I see how easy it is to lose one's identity or not be able to find one when mixed messages are being sent to minority students about their home language and culture.

As a writing instructor, I catch myself telling students, "You're thinking in Spanish when writing in English." At first I saw this as the wrong way to learn how to write in English. But experience has taught me what Peter Elbow (2000) has discovered himself: inviting students' mother tongues into the writing classroom may be an effective way to help students express their ideas first, and then we can help them with Standard Written English. He says, "Full attention to thinking and rhetoric is not possible unless we can make the classroom a place that is safe for all forms of language considered wrong" (2000, 329).

Hearing Students' Voices

Students also share Elbow's and my belief. During the summer exploratory study students expressed the same concerns and offered similar suggestions in their writing journal. Lucia wrote:

> When I'm writing in english it is very difficult for me because my first language is spanish. I feel like I would be a better writer if the instructor give a topic in spanish. I think I could write more than 10 paragraphs. I feel that when I'm writing I don't know what I'm doing. I have many ideas in my head, but I don't know how to express myself. I think that these contribute that I don't know how to write in English. I think I need to read and write more to improve myself in writing. My greatest strength is that I need to write in english because I have a lot of thing that I can put in the paper. And my greates witness in writing is that I don't know how to put it in the paper. It is very difficult for me to express my ideas.

When Lucia and I talked about her concerns, and I told her that it would be all right for her to prewrite in Spanish, Lucia seemed relieved and began writing longer essays and having more to say in her essays. At the end of the semester she wrote the following in her journal:

> I feel more confident in writing. Freewriting helps us just write without thinking in spelling or punctuation. I believe that freewriting help us to improve and put our ideas in paper. I believe that my favorite part of writing is that right now I can put my ideas correctly in the paper. Before I took this class, I felt insecure, afraid to do an essay. What I don't like about writing is that some times you need to put attention in how to write a paragraph correctly. Sometimes you misspell words or even you forget how to say something. . . . One suggestion that I would give to students that are going to take this class is to practice and practice, so they can learn how to write an essay.

Lucia shows how being able to use her first language to generate ideas for her essay helped her improve the substance of her essays in English. She still recognizes that she needs help with Standard Written English, but she has gained more confidence in her language abilities and wants to write more in English so that she can improve. I, in turn, as a writing instructor, have shown Lucia that I value her ideas, in Spanish and English, and that her home language is not wrong. My response to Lucia is echoed by other writing instructors, such as Virginia Crisco (2004), who call for teachers to build "a cultural bridge where students' experiences are valued and necessary to the work of writing" (2004, 41).

Daniel Villa (2004), author of "*No nos dejaremos*: Writing in Spanish as an Act of Resistance," in *Latino/a Discourses,* also presents a similar argument. He states:

> The voices that express themselves in primary discourse, in either English or Spanish, must be valued. To fail to do so may well alienate the writer, resulting in her disengaging from working toward literacy. Students from Spanish-speaking backgrounds also come from diverse English-speaking backgrounds; accommodating this diversity presents a challenge to all those involved in developing literacy. (2004, 89–90)

I share Villa's belief that minority students need to understand, appreciate, and not forget the beauty of their first language, the language bequeathed to them by their families and community. They must make an effort to maintain it as part of their self-identity (2004, 94). The following excerpt illustrates the importance of conserving students' native language while learning a new language:

> As a child my life seemed strange and confusing. At home, which meant brothers, parents, an aunt and uncle (at different times) and grandparents, the language was mainly Spanish and the culture distinctly Mexican. At school, the language was only English, and the culture was a cold and distant way of being treated like the re-molding process of an Army boot

> camp. . . . When my parents first told me that I had to learn English in order to survive in this country, the impact of that statement had little immediate effect. But later, as a young person, I began to associate my feelings of alienation with the need to identify with a group, a cultural group. My capacity to use Spanish had dwindled to nothing. Identification with the dominant culture was no longer possible, but recreating my group sense seemed equally impossible without the help of Spanish, the language of my Chicano culture. I felt alone and lonely. . . . My parents were not at fault; from them English was a gift of love, a gift they had never received. They were sure that I would not endure the suffering that accompanies such labels as *foreigner* or, in my case, *wetback* and *spic*. . . . My years without Spanish now appear tragic. How can I ever make up that loss? I barely communicated with my own grandparents! They died . . . before I relearned Spanish. (Castro 1976, 4–8)

Understanding students' language use outside of the classroom may help writing instructors better prepare students for academic discourse and writing beyond the classroom. And just like code switching can be a learned behavior, so can language attitudes. According to Baetens Beardsmore, parents must convey positive attitudes to both languages and cultures (cited in Baker and Jones 1998, 26). Thus not only parents but teachers need to be positive in their views on language and culture. Growing up bilingually and biculturally should be seen as empowering, and as parents, educators, and members of a community we should instill and promote positive attitudes toward diversity, biculturalism, and bilingualism.

English and Spanish should be recognized as equally valuable languages. Additionally, code switching on the border should be viewed as a linguistic strategy that empowers speakers. The complexity of languages and codes leads to the complexity of identity for the speakers. If viewed in a positive light, code switching can enhance speakers' identities. Bilingual speakers should not be forced to choose one language or the other, or one culture or the other. Both coexist, and both are equally valuable, as their third code (code switching) should be.

So What Should Writing Instructors at Hispanic-Serving Institutions Do?

From my experience, as both a learner and teacher of writing, I have discovered several key factors and activities that have been effective in helping students improve their writing when English is not their first language. Several of these suggestions also are offered by other researchers in the field and are supported by students' comments in conferences with me and/or in their writing journal entries. These suggestions include the following:

1. Establish an open, student-centered learning environment. The writing classroom should be established as a setting where collaborative learning takes place, where the instructor serves as a facilitator of learning, and students are not afraid to ask questions and make mistakes. The writing classroom should invite in all mother tongues and respect all accents. Belanger and Panozzo (2003), quoting John Dewey, stress the importance of creating an environment to which students and teachers can bring all of their experiences and cultures, their knowledge and understanding, their hopes, their fears, their lack of awareness, and their questions so that a bridge can be constructed between these known cultures and the new culture of the academy (2003, 96).
2. Give students informal writing assignments for which formal grades are not given but credit and acknowledgment are. This act gives students practice in writing without pressure, so they may enjoy the act of writing. Students themselves believe in the benefits and positive outcomes of practice. Students will write more if they enjoy it more; informal writing assignments allow students to do this. Informal writing assignments may include prewriting activities for assigned essays and journal writing.
3. Give students credit for their entire writing process: prewriting, writing, and rewriting. All ideas are valuable, and how these come about should be valued as well.
4. Have students practice their spoken English in the classroom. This expression will help them in their writing. Many researchers have shown the connection between oral and written fluency and how the negative beliefs of students about their pronunciation or their accents make them poor communicators and affect their writing abilities.
5. Teach grammar mini-lessons on Standard Written English. These brief lessons will help students work on surface propriety in their essays. Lessons should be based on students' needs.
6. Hold one-on-one conferences with students. Students believe this helps them improve, targets their specific weaknesses, and builds their self-confidence as writers of English.
7. Allow students to use their home language, whether Spanish, code switching, and so on in the classroom. In terms of writing essays, allow students to use whatever language they need or prefer to come up with ideas, create substance in their writing, and build their rhetoric.
8. Promote reading. Show students the connection between reading and writing, and have them practice both skills on a daily basis. Reading should be in everyday language, such as in newspapers and magazines, in addition to students' academic school reading. A writing journal and a reading journal are helpful in improving students' language skills and critical thinking. Students themselves believe that practice does not make a perfect but a better performance.
9. Hold and express positive language attitudes. In doing this, Elbow's (2000) suggestions on how instructors can get students to write without resentment and to write more than the minimal required amount can

> demonstrate positive language attitudes. He suggests that instructors show respect and acceptance of their students' dialects as "full, complete, sophisticated languages" (2000, 327). Elbow also suggests that writing instructors recognize and show that students whose first language is not English are smart, that they are linguistically sophisticated because they can use and switch multiple dialects (2000, 327–28).

By applying these guidelines, writing instructors can more easily and effectively facilitate learning and build more confidence in students as writers of English and of academic discourse. This confidence helps students concentrate more on their efforts, find personal significance in writing, and make the required writing course a lifelong learning experience that does not die with the end of the semester. I share Elbow's short-term and long-term goals as a writing instructor: I too want to help minority students, particularly students on the El Paso/Juárez border, to quickly and easily learn to write essays in correct Standard Written English, and I too want to demonstrate my respect and show the value of students' home dialects by legitimizing their use in students' writing processes. I wish to make my classroom a safe haven where students feel free to use their language, whatever that may be, to learn to write successfully in Standard Written English.

More importantly, I want students to stop fearing writing and speaking in English. My goal is to make them feel comfortable with their language abilities and to want to write and speak in English. Students themselves see the importance of being able to feel this way at the end of a writing course. Lucia underscores this desire:

> The objectives of a college writing course should be, that at the end of the course the student should feel more comfortable with writing. If students leave the classroom, wanting to and actually writing without being required to do so, much has been accomplished and the course has indeed been successful.

I continue researching, reading, writing, and teaching. I hope that my efforts, trials, and errors will make a difference in the learning and teaching experiences of others at HSIs. I find myself in the midst of English departments in higher education. How did I get here? It took years of practice, challenges, frustrations, failures, and accomplishments for me to finally get it. "*Yo tambien pensaba en español* when I wrote in English." (I too thought in Spanish when I wrote in English.) Once in a while, I still catch myself worrying about my accent, especially when I am presenting work at professional conferences or speaking to scholars and colleagues in the field. But then I smile to myself and think: I am a product of the El Paso/Juárez border and am proud of it. In order to help Latino/a students improve their writing and academic discourse, the instructor's, students', and society's language attitudes matter. After all, it is all in the attitude, *the language attitude.*

Works Cited

Baca, Isabel. 2000. "English, Spanish, or los dos? Examining Language Behavior among Four English/Spanish Bilingual Families Residing on the El Paso, Texas/Juárez, México Border." PhD dissertation, New Mexico State University.

Baetens Beardsmore, Hugo. 1986. *Bilingualism: Basic Principles.* Clevedon, Great Britain: Multilingual Matters.

Baker, Colin, and Sylvia Prys Jones. 1998. *Encyclopedia of Bilingualism and Bilingual Education.* Philadelphia, PA: Multilingual Matters.

Belanger, Kelly, and Diane Panozzo. 2003. "Challenging but Safe Environments: Helping Students Succeed in College Writing." In *Academic Literacy in the English Classroom: Helping Underprepared and Working Class Students Succeed in College,* ed. Carolyn R. Boiarsky, 95–105. Portsmouth, NH: Boynton/Cook.

Castro, R. 1976. "Shifting the Burden of Bilingualism: The Case for Monolingual Communities." *The Bilingual Review* 3: 3–28.

Crisco, Virginia. 2004. "Rethinking Language and Culture on the Institutional Border." *Journal of Basic Writing* 23:1: 39–63.

Elbow, Peter. 2000. *Everyone Can Write: Essays toward a Hopeful Theory of Writing and Teaching Writing.* New York: Oxford University Press.

El Paso Community College (EPCC). 2003. *EPCC Today: Fiscal Year 2002–2003.* El Paso, TX: Author.

Greater El Paso Chamber of Commerce. 1996. "El Paso: Community Profile." El Paso, TX: Author.

———. 1999. "El Paso: Deep in the Heart of NAFTA." El Paso, TX: Author.

Grosjean, Francois. 1982. *Life with Two Languages: An Introduction to Bilingualism.* Cambridge, MA: Harvard University Press.

———. 1985. "The Bilingual as a Competent but Specific Speaker-Hearer." *Journal of Multilingual and Multicultural Development* 6: 467–77.

Hagemann, Julie. 2003. "A Metalinguistic Approach: Helping Students Acquire the Language of the Academy." In *Academic Literacy in the English Classroom: Helping Underprepared and Working Class Students Succeed in College,* ed. Carolyn R. Boiarsky, 131–44. Portsmouth, NH: Boynton/Cook.

Lightbown, Patsy M., and Nina Spada. 1999. *How Languages Are Learned.* Rev. ed. Oxford: Oxford University Press.

Valdés, Guadalupe. 1999. "Incipient Bilingualism and the Development of English Language Writing Abilities in the Secondary School." In *So Much to Say: Adolescents, Bilingualism and ESL in the Secondary School,* ed. Christian J. Faltis and Paula Wolfe, 138–75. New York: Columbia University Teachers College Press.

Villa, Daniel. 2004. "*No nos dejaremos*: Writing in Spanish as an Act of Resistance." In *Latino/a Discourses: On Language, Identity & Literacy Education,* ed. Michelle Hall Kells, Valerie Balester, and Victor Villanueva, 85–95. Portsmouth, NH: Boynton/Cook.

APPENDIX A

English 0310 Course Objectives
El Paso Community College

The official course syllabus, created by the English discipline at El Paso Community College, outlines the following course objectives for English 0310, Basic English Composition:

1. Develop effective personal writing processes that are appropriate for time and untimed situations, which include prewriting, writing, and revising strategies.
2. Write well-structured short essays of 400–600 words each that are unified, coherent, and adequately developed and that contain an introduction, body paragraphs, and a conclusion.
3. Develop various types of short essays that are rhetorically appropriate for a variety of subjects and audiences and that meet the following purposes: relating personal experiences, informing, and persuading.
4. Manage self-referenced writing topics as well as subject-referenced topics by the end of the course.
5. Compose and edit sentences so that they are correct in grammar, punctuation, and mechanics.
6. Improve and vary sentence structure by using subordination and coordination.
7. Use the dictionary as an aid in improving vocabulary and word choice.
8. Analyze model essays or other types of writing to enhance critical thinking, improve vocabulary, stimulate ideas for writing, and appreciate the power and the pleasure of the written word.

APPENDIX B

Preliminary Student Survey

BASIC ENGLISH COMPOSITION
English 0310 Summer I, 2003

The following data will help the EPCC English faculty better meet students' needs in this basic writing course. Your input is important. English faculty will be provided with the findings in fall 2003. Please complete the following questions by being honest, thorough, specific, and clear. If need be, you may be asked to be interviewed by Dr. Isabel Baca, English instructor and researcher. Thank you.

Student's Name ____

Instructor's Name ______________________ Section ________

Time of Class ________________________ Room # ________

COURSE PLACEMENT

How were you placed in English 0310?

A. EPCC Placement Exam E. TASP Scores

B. Passed BASK Writing Course D. Other ______________

C. SAT/ACT Scores

I belong in English 0310 based on my writing skills.

A. Strongly Agree C. Unsure E. Strongly Disagree

B. Agree D. Disagree

ASSESSING ONE'S SKILLS

My English writing skills are best described as:

A. Excellent C. Satisfactory E. Poor

B. Above Average D. Below Average

My English reading skills are best described as:

A. Excellent C. Satisfactory E. Poor

B. Above Average D. Below Average

My English speaking skills are best described as:

A. Excellent C. Satisfactory E. Poor

B. Above Average D. Below Average

My critical thinking skills are best described as:

A. Excellent C. Satisfactory E. Poor

B. Above Average D. Below Average

My English grammar skills are best described as:

A. Excellent C. Satisfactory E. Poor

B. Above Average D. Below Average

My English vocabulary is best described as:

A. Excellent C. Satisfactory E. Poor

B. Above Average D. Below Average

My ability to use learning resources (library, Internet, tutoring, etc.) is best described as:

A. Excellent C. Satisfactory E. Poor

B. Above Average D. Below Average

My overall English language skills can best be described as:

A. Excellent C. Satisfactory E. Poor

B. Above Average D. Below Average

My confidence level with the English language can best be described as:

A. High C. Average E. Very Low

B. Somewhat High D. Low

How do you feel you will do in this course?

A. Excellent C. Average E. Very Poor

B. Above Average D. Poor

EVALUATION

English 0310 should be a Pass/No Pass course. No letter grades should be given.

A. Strongly Agree
B. Agree
C. Unsure
D. Disagree
E. Strongly Disagree

The exit essay exam (and passing it) should be required to pass the course.

A. Strongly Agree
B. Agree
C. Unsure
D. Disagree
E. Strongly Disagree

Students should be given the opportunity to revise their writing assignments.

A. Strongly Agree
B. Agree
C. Unsure
D. Disagree
E. Strongly Disagree

Timed writing (50 minutes for a final draft of an essay) should be a primary focus in this course.

A. Strongly Agree
B. Agree
C. Unsure
D. Disagree
E. Strongly Disagree

SHORT-ANSWER QUESTIONS

What are your expectations of this course? What do you expect to learn? Be specific.

What are your strengths in this course?

What are your weaknesses in this course?

With what do you want or need more help in this course?

Can and how can the instructor provide this help?

At this point in the semester, how do feel about taking English 0310?

APPENDIX C

Final Student Survey

BASIC ENGLISH COMPOSITION
English 0310 Summer I, 2003

This survey completes the study on the course English 0310, Basic English Composition. Your input will help the English faculty better assess and better meet students' needs in this basic writing course. Please complete the following questions by being honest, thorough, specific, and clear. If need be, you may be contacted by Dr. Isabel Baca, English instructor and researcher, during the next month for a brief telephone interview. No names will be used in the findings of the study. Thank you for your participation.

Student's Name ______________________ Telephone # __________

Instructor's Name ______________________ Section __________

COURSE EVALUATION

English 0310 was the appropriate writing course for me.

A. Strongly Agree C. Unsure E. Strongly Disagree

B. Agree D. Disagree

I met all of the course's objectives, as stated in the course syllabus.

A. Strongly Agree C. Unsure E. Strongly Disagree

B. Agree D. Disagree

The textbooks were helpful in assisting me in my writing.

A. Strongly Agree C. Unsure E. Strongly Disagree

B. Agree D. Disagree

The instructor helped me improve my writing skills.

A. Strongly Agree C. Unsure E. Strongly Disagree

B. Agree D. Disagree

The instructor made me aware of what my weaknesses and strengths are in my writing early on in the semester.

A. Strongly Agree C. Unsure E. Strongly Disagree

B. Agree D. Disagree

The instructor offered proper guidance in showing me what I had to do to improve/succeed in this course.

A. Strongly Agree C. Unsure E. Strongly Disagree

B. Agree D. Disagree

English 0310 should be a Pass/No Pass Course. No letter grades should be given.

A. Strongly Agree C. Unsure E. Strongly Disagree

B. Agree D. Disagree

The exit essay exam (and passing it) should be required to pass the course.

A. Strongly Agree C. Unsure E. Strongly Disagree

B. Agree D. Disagree

Being given two opportunities to pass the exit essay exam is fair enough.

A. Strongly Agree C. Unsure E. Strongly Disagree

B. Agree D. Disagree

Students should be given the opportunity to revise their writing assignments.

A. Strongly Agree C. Unsure E. Strongly Disagree

B. Agree D. Disagree

The amount of timed-writing assignments given in this course is best described as:

A. Too Many C. Unsure E. None

B. Just Right D. Not Enough

The total amount of writing assignments (in class, outside of class, paragraphs, essays, journal, etc.) given in this course is best described as:

A. Too Many C. Unsure E. None

B. Just Right D. Not Enough

The amount of reading assignments in this course is best described as:

A. Too Many C. Unsure E. None

B. Just Right D. Not Enough

The time spent on grammar and mechanics in this course is best described as:

A. Too Much C. Unsure E. None

B. Just Right D. Not Enough

This course, English 0310, is best described as:

A. Extremely Helpful C. Average E. Useless

B. Helpful D. Not Very Helpful

ASSESSING ONE'S SKILLS

After completing this course, my English writing skills are best described as:

A. Excellent C. Satisfactory E. Poor

B. Above Average D. Below Average

After completing this course, my English reading skills are best described as:

A. Excellent C. Satisfactory E. Poor

B. Above Average D. Below Average

After completing this course, my English speaking skills are best described as:

A. Excellent C. Satisfactory E. Poor

B. Above Average D. Below Average

After completing this course, my critical thinking skills are best described as:

A. Excellent
B. Above Average
C. Satisfactory
D. Below Average
E. Poor

After completing this course, my English grammar skills are best described as:

A. Excellent
B. Above Average
C. Satisfactory
D. Below Average
E. Poor

After completing this course, my English vocabulary is best described as:

A. Excellent
B. Above Average
C. Satisfactory
D. Below Average
E. Poor

After completing this course, my ability to use learning resources (library, Internet, tutoring, etc.) is best described as:

A. Excellent
B. Above Average
C. Satisfactory
D. Below Average
E. Poor

After completing this course, my overall English language skills can best be described as:

A. Excellent
B. Above Average
C. Satisfactory
D. Below Average
E. Poor

After completing this course, my confidence level with the English language can best be described as:

A. High
B. Somewhat High
C. Average
D. Low
E. Very Low

Having taken English 0310 this semester did the following for me (mark all that apply):

_______ Improved my writing skills

_______ Improved my reading skills

_______ Improved my critical thinking

_______ Improved my language skills

_______ Improved my speaking skills

_______ Improved my grammar skills

_______ Improved my self-esteem

_______ Improved other skills (please list)

_______ Fear writing

_______ Recognize my writing strengths

_______ Doubt my writing ability

_______ Recognize my writing weaknesses

_______ Want to continue writing

_______ Made no difference

SHORT-ANSWER QUESTIONS

What did you enjoy the most about this course?

What did you enjoy the least about this course?

What gave you the most difficult time in this course?

How can this course be improved? What could be omitted? Added? Revised?

How do you feel about the exit essay exam? Do you have any suggestions for this exam? Explain.

Please feel free to comment on any aspect of this course.

Chapter 9

Changing Perceptions, and Ultimately Practices, of Basic Writing Instructors through the *Familia* Approach

Barbara Jaffe

> *Academia has for far too long encouraged us to lead fragmented and inauthentic lives, where we act either as if we are not spiritual beings, or as if our spiritual side is irrelevant to our vocation or work. Under these conditions, our work becomes divorced from our most deeply felt values, and we hesitate to discuss issues of meaning, purpose, authenticity, wholeness, and fragmentation with our colleagues. At the same time, we likewise discourage our students from engaging in these same issues among themselves and with us.* (Astin and Astin 1999, 2).

For thirteen years, I had the honor of teaching in California's acclaimed *Puente* Project at El Camino Community College, a Hispanic-Serving Institution (HSI), in Torrance, California. My perception of basic writing students, and the ways in which I teach my basic writing courses, has completely changed as a result of my work as the *Puente* writing coordinator and instructor for my campus. I attribute my success in teaching to the countless hours of training in which I participated through the state *Puente* Project, as well as my own "experimentation" within my basic writing classrooms. I have literally "'revisioned' the borders" of my own teaching, and in this metamorphosis I have become a different writing instructor, and, frankly, a much better one.

My life-changing teaching experiences ultimately led me to my research on teacher training at the postsecondary level, primarily in HSIs. I have been fascinated with the areas of basic writing, basic writing pedagogy, and retention theories, with the ultimate goal of creating a more holistic approach to teaching basic writing. My hope was that the research would reinforce and support what I have intuitively "felt" as an instructor of basic writing for over two decades. I have seen countless students drop out of college despite their keen intelligence and desire to succeed. Specifically, extensive studies on student attrition in higher education validate what I have seen firsthand—the majority of postsecondary students are unsuccessful, especially in basic education courses, due to *nonacademic* reasons, ranging from family problems to financial limitations (Rendon 2002a; Tinto 1987). Thus for the purposes of this chapter, concurrent with references to seminal-related research, I will highlight some of the results of my own research with a teacher-training program, emphasizing both cognitive and affective skills within a basic writing curriculum. My research underscores two critical concerns in postsecondary education: a more holistic approach in our writing classes—one that supports connecting social and personal skills as a way to address student success, satisfaction, and, ultimately, higher transfer rates in basic writing—and an emphasis on the importance of more research concerning teacher training at postsecondary HSIs.

First, it is essential to present an overview of the California *Puente* Project, which has been used as a model for various state programs as well as First-Year Experience Programs, all of which include key elements of intensive basic writing instruction. *Puente*, which means "bridge" in Spanish, was cofounded in 1981 at Chabot College in Hayward, California, by an English instructor, Patricia McGrath, and a counselor, Felix Galaviz. At that time, the program was created to address the low rate of academic success among Mexican American and Latino community college students. Galaviz and McGrath reviewed over 2,000 community college student transcripts and inferred that students were not seeking academic counseling; they were not enrolling in college-level writing courses, and they also were the first in their families to attend college.

Their research led to the *Puente* Project Model, consisting of three key elements: counseling, writing, and mentoring. *Puente*'s mission remains "to increase the number of educationally underserved students who enroll in four-year colleges and universities, earn degrees, and return to the community as leaders and mentors to future generations" (*Puente* Project 2002). Each of the sixty-five participating California community colleges has one to two designated *Puente* classes, a cohort of about thirty students taught by *Puente* cocoordinators: an English instructor, a counselor, and a community mentor. Students begin the program with a developmental writing course, one semester below freshman composition, and they complete the year with freshman composition. Specifically, the goal of the first semester's writing course is to provide students with an opportunity to explore their writers' voices through

Latino literature and numerous writing assignments to develop the connection between themselves and the literature.

While the *Puente* Project is currently established only in the state of California, political and social challenges continue to threaten financial support for programs, such as the *Puente* Project, both in California and in other states. Resistance stems from the belief that programs such as these are "isolating" and "restrictive" and "for some" and "not for others," when in reality what all effective educators do is teach the "whole" student, regardless of background. I have experienced firsthand the ability to replicate one of the program's most successful and critical components—the writing component—for all of our institutions, serving all students. Clearly, with little more than institutional staff development support, a metamorphosis can occur in our teaching and our students' learning—one that requires only a willingness to help our students find their innate writers' voices.

Research over a five-year period, from 1996 to 2001, shows that, statewide, *Puente* students averaged a success rate of 80 percent in their prefreshman composition courses, compared to a 56 percent success rate for non-*Puente* students. In addition, statewide, *Puente* students completed their second-semester writing course at a rate close to 70 percent, while only 57 percent of non-*Puente* students successfully completed their freshman composition courses. Statistics at El Camino College are even more promising, with 86.5 percent of the *Puente* students successfully completing their basic writing courses, and 87 percent successfully completing their freshman composition writing courses.

Increasingly, studies indicate that all students, and especially those considered at risk, benefit from strong and competitive writing skills along with counseling in personal and academic issues. In addition, when students are given the opportunity to reflect on their values and choices, success and retention are positively affected (Downing 1996; Weiner 1974). Unfortunately, research on teacher training in postsecondary institutions is minimal, at best, and does not indicate how teachers can be trained to enhance their academic curricula to address the personal and social reasons for student attrition in their courses and ultimately college.

In responding to this problem, I began my research during the fall semester of 2003. I provided training workshops designed to help instructors experience firsthand the logic and practical application of integrating academic and personal skills, such as accountability[1] and interdependence,[2] into their courses. At each training session, I introduced different techniques extracted from research and my own teaching practices that could reinforce student success (see Appendix A for an overview of the training sessions). After my semester-long training with six community college basic writing instructors, I assessed how they perceived changes in their instruction when incorporating academic and personal skills within a writing classroom. I also examined their respective students' perceptions of the changes in their own behaviors and attitudes after their writing classes.

In the workshops, I introduced writing instructors to two key elements of my own basic writing instruction: the *Familia* Writing Process and accountability concepts and activities, which integrate the foundations of basic writing with personal skills of responsibility and interdependence.

The *Familia* (Spanish for "family") Writing Process is more than a traditional peer-group approach within a writing class. Groups of four to five students are formed by the instructor to be part of their *familias* for the entire semester. The students participate in various writing activities designed to encourage not only stronger academic writing but also accountability and interdependence. Through the *familia*'s frequent, shared personal and academic writing activities, a foundation of trust grows (Healy 1990).

The *familia* also serves as the main support system in the Strong Line and Question Asking Activities. Soon after students are introduced to their *familias*, they learn more about each other by reading aloud their short, reflective narratives to their group members. During their readings, their peers are instructed to listen for "strong lines." The instructor defines "strong lines" only as sentences that are "powerful" for the listener. After the reading is completed, listeners state, "A strong line for me is . . . ," and writers underline these sentences. No explanation is given as to why a particular line is chosen by listeners, and nothing more is said other than "thank you" by both the reader and the listener. The activity is completed when everyone finishes reading the essays aloud. The instructor then asks the students for feedback regarding this process. Students discuss how they felt reading their essays aloud, what they learned from doing so, and what they perceived as strengths and weaknesses of this format. Furthermore, the Strong Line Activity provides students with additional validation of their compositions. Two of the teachers in my study reported that several of their students expanded their strong lines in subsequent drafts to include even more details without being told to do so. When one instructor asked a student why he chose to develop his sentence, the student replied, "If someone thought it was strong enough to comment on, then I figured that it was worth writing more on." The instructor recognized that the student felt empowered by his essay's strong line, and his decision to expand this phrase was based on his group members' support rather than on the teacher's recommendations.

Once the students are accustomed to the Strong Line Activity (usually after two class sessions), the second step in the *Familia* Writing Process is introduced—the Question Asking Activity (see Appendix B for an explanation of this process). Again, writers read their essays aloud, and instead of discussing Strong Lines, each student in the *familia* is responsible for generating at least three questions for the reader. These students then read their questions aloud, and the reader of the essay writes them down on a question sheet. Students learn early in this process that they are responsible for generating questions for each other and using the responses to the questions as details in their essays. Students are graded by both the questions they ask and the way in which they answer them within their essays in subsequent drafts. Thus the *familia*s function as interdependent academic and personal support teams, while simultaneously reinforcing writing as well as accountability skills.

Often through the *familia* members' constant connection and the sharing of their guided writing assignments, they learn to trust and assist each other in their course work and other areas of their lives. The students in their *familias* create their family norms, such as their rules for attendance, tardiness, and work ethic, and they present them to the class. They learn to listen to each other's writing and ask questions of the writer/reader. This process helps the *familia* members take responsibility for listening and providing thought-provoking questions, which in turn helps writers strengthen their essays. While group work has been a main focus of writing courses for over two decades, the *familia* approach allows for more consistency in sharing beyond writing since the students work together on far more than their essays.

Overall, after the series of workshops, the most significant finding was the teachers' reports that they had modified the workshop materials and ideas to correspond to their own classroom structures and teaching styles. To various degrees, they adapted the *Familia* Writing Process, which included the Strong Line and Question Asking Activities as well as the *Familia* model. They also modified student accountability concepts and exercises introduced in the workshops while adjusting the materials for use in their respective classes. Also noteworthy is that some of the teachers felt that they had adapted a different perspective of personal responsibility, affecting their views of themselves as well as their students. Finally, the teachers acknowledged that the integration of academic and personal skills within their writing courses was an enriching experience for their students. The students also recognized that the integration of academic and personal skills within their writing courses enhanced their classroom experiences (see Appendix C).

I was amazed that in my attempt to assist basic writing students to become more successful in their education, my study guided me to the critical need for research on teacher training at the postsecondary level, and especially at HSIs, in which the Latino/a population is rapidly growing. Amazingly, as of 1990, while 39,000 documents dealt with teacher training, 26,000 argued the deficits in teacher training. Only thirty-five of these materials covered teacher preparation for basic writing, with almost 100 percent representing the K–12 grade levels (Moran and Jacobi 1990). Studies on teacher training for college-level basic writing instructors remain greatly deficient. Baiocco and DeWaters (1998) emphasize that research and training at this level are also at least a "decade behind the best practices in primary and secondary education" (1998, 41). Teacher training for postsecondary HSIs is virtually nonexistent, with the exception of my recent study.

One reason for the lack of training is that institutions cannot easily correlate effective teaching with increased productivity (financial benefits from student enrollment). Also, teachers in postsecondary education often are hesitant to take the necessary risks fundamental in teaching transformations. Such risks call upon instructors to devote additional training hours, preparation, and experimentation with new classroom teaching techniques at a time when their classroom sizes are increasing and students' academic placement levels are decreasing.

Within my research, and related to teacher training, an essential question arose as to why the participants agreed to first adopt the new materials and concepts and then adapt them. Clearly, both processes required additional preparation and energy in an ongoing hectic semester comprised of a demanding teaching load of four composition classes, addressing the needs of roughly 120 basic writing students. In exploring answers to this important question, I analyzed the teachers' adaptation process:

Process of Teacher Adaptation of New Materials and Ideas

1. Participants are introduced to materials/ideas in workshops.
2. Participants practice exercises together in their "*familia*" in the workshop.
3. Participants return to their classrooms, and some employ modified elements of the concepts and/or activities.
4. Participants reflect in journals about their experimentation in their classrooms and any hesitancies in employing the new concepts.
5. Participants return to the subsequent workshop and share their classroom experiences and ask each other questions about what did and did not work with their students.

6. Participants return to their classrooms and may implement the exercises, often with additional modifications from the first time, making the materials "their own."
7. Participants discuss their "new" lessons in their journals and in the workshops, sharing more specific information from their additional classroom experiences.
8. Participants continue to assess their modifications and what works best for them in their incorporation of the new materials and ideas (both internally reflective and externally with colleagues).

I realized that without significant time to reflect and share both academically and personally, adaptation could not occur. The instructors' success in adapting the elements of the *Familia* Writing Process occurred only after they had weeks to reflect on the process and on how they planned to implement the activities in their classrooms. Their decisions to implement the new classroom format took place only after they had the opportunity to write their thoughts in their journals and, most important, talk about their concerns and hesitancies with the other participants at three prior workshops.

The participants' changes in their teaching practices over the semester provided a glimpse into the processes of both adoption and adaptation. Seminal research on these processes emphasizes that for acceptance and modification to occur in teaching practices, several elements must be in place, all of which were inherent in my study's training workshops (Elmore and McLaughlin 1988). First, the teachers must obtain a degree of confidence in the new practices, perceiving that the additional activities and concepts can assist them more effectively in communicating the subject matter. Second, sharing and obtaining feedback about these new teaching processes are instrumental elements in any adaptation. Finally, instructors need regular opportunities to reflect on their experiences with each other.

Intrinsic in the *familia* format during five workshops was a trust that built over time among members. In the workshops, the teachers' relaxed conversations provided a natural means for sharing and reflection to occur. They also had the opportunity to express their thoughts through their writing in the workshops and journals. Furthermore, the participants reported that they often continued their conversations regarding classes, lessons, and students outside of the workshops.

While I had never labeled the participant group as a *familia,* soon after the second workshop, one of the instructors referred to the group as our "*familia.*" From then on, the other participants began using this term to refer to the workshops. The internalization of acceptance of the *familia* unit was significant because it provided a glimpse into what students feel in their own classrooms and showed that the *Familia* Writing Process provides a level of emotional support that may be lacking in the traditional peer review format.

Moreover, the emotional component connected to a *familia* unit is significant in teacher training, especially in postsecondary education, where instructors lead increasingly hectic and fragmented professional lives. The personal or emotional element of the *familia* underscores the importance of an intrinsic dimension of trust and mutual respect that occurs over time. The *familia* dynamic enabled the teachers to come together in a group that they named and recognized as their own. The *familia* also helped the participants establish the connection between their own learning processes and their community of teachers. Research supports the establishments of these bonds among participants in order for transformation in teaching practices to occur. Showers (1985) found that teaching skills and ideas discussed in trainings often are transferred to the classroom when there is a type of peer-coaching model that promotes the "development of norms of collegiality and experimentation of teaching issues" (1985, 45). Essentially, the *familia* workshop could be viewed as a type of peer-coaching model in which no one is the "guru of knowledge." The nonthreatening environment enabled participants to comfortably practice and share the new exercises and ideas with each other.

Interestingly, after our first training session, several of the participants brought in their own materials to share. Elmore and McLaughlin (1988) suggest that teachers participate in meaningful changes when they view the benefits to their students and when they are actively collaborating in the process: "Teachers not only must see a proposed change as relevant to their classrooms, they also must have a measure of confidence about its consequences for their students" (1988, 42). The format of the workshops provided the participants with a "safety net" in which they could share their frustrations, try the new activities, and discuss whether they would feel comfortable implementing them in their teaching, an essential process in adaptation. Gillespie (2002) further validates the concept of a *familia* model of training when he states that like their students the ways in which teachers learn are "personal, experiential, emotional, intellectual, ethical, and practical" (2002, 225).

Also inherent in the process of adaptation is the risk factor, which was experienced by each of the participants who introduced the new materials and experimented with the accountability techniques in their classrooms. One of the instructors' final journals provided a glimpse into the process of taking risks. She believed that it was a necessary part of the changes she made during the semester:

> Another important change that I have experienced this semester is to take risks. I have created new activities and assignments; some did not work as well as I had expected while others worked out better than I had planned. I found that I had been using the same assignments even if they were not very effective. In essence, I was stuck in a rut! This semester I tried some new activities and assignments in both my English A [basic writing] classes and in my English 1A [freshman composition] class. . . . I have also learned that change is healthy and good! This ties in with learning to take risks, but it is an essential lesson that I have learned. It also ties in with letting go of some of the control. By allowing myself to let go of the reins, I have opened myself up to change. I had not revised some of my assignments because it was much easier to keep things as they were or because I did not have time to change things. I made small changes so that the task would not be so overwhelming!

Studies on changes in teaching practices underscore the importance of teachers recognizing that along with change there is a period of chaos and uncertainty. They can adjust when there is a "degree of psychological and professional safety associated with the change effort" (Shein, quoted in Elmore and McLaughlin 1988, 43). The safety created in the *familia* workshop approach reinforces the theory that "no change will occur unless members of the system feel it is safe to give up the old responses and learn something new'" (1988, 44).

Based on the results of my data, it is evident that the addition and implementation of the affective elements within a basic writing classroom reflect an internal process for the instructors. The list in the next section provides an overview of the processes of integration that I observed the participants employ over the course of the semester. It is interesting to note that this process is similar in its construction to my findings on adaptation.

Process of Integration

1. Introduce concepts of personal skills (accountability concepts and materials) in the workshop.
2. Teachers practiced personal skills together in pairs within their participant *familia.*
3. Teachers wrote based on a prompt and shared their writings using the *Familia* Writing Process, which emphasizes interdependence.
4. Teachers returned to their classrooms; some participants integrated the actual personal responsibility materials in written form, and some integrated the concepts in their oral interactions with students.
5. All of the participants reflected on the process in their journals, writing about the concept of accountability in their classrooms and in their lives.

6. In the subsequent workshops, teachers discussed how they incorporated the exercises in their writing assignments or in the group work.
7. Several of the participants reflected on how the integration of these skills impacted their teaching and their "outside" lives.
8. For these teachers, the integration process appeared to be ongoing throughout the semester. The integration of personal skills in a basic writing class created a paradigm shift, as they slowly felt more comfortable with the concept of integrating cognitive and affective skills in an academic discipline.

According to the teachers, the adoption and modifications of the workshop materials and ideas appeared to provide the foundation for the integration of the academic and personal skills in their basic writing classes. Clearly, in order for the teachers to feel comfortable in introducing and integrating personal skills within their writing courses, they have to first feel a level of comfort in experiencing this process themselves. The workshops provided the participants with a nonthreatening environment in which they could experience academic and personal connections. In fact, research on holistic teaching supports my findings. The studies emphasize the importance of validating the inner life of the students and the teachers, connecting life experiences and the classroom for both the educators and the learners (Broomfield 1997; Palmer 1998; Rendon 2000a). Rendon (2002b) suggests that teachers should create a curriculum that integrates academic with social, emotional, and even spiritual elements to address the total student, especially underrepresented populations. In her observation of a *Puente* classroom, she noted that the instructors, as well as the guest speakers, all shared some personal elements of themselves with the students (Rendon 2002a).

The way in which I constructed the five training workshops enabled the teachers to experience being the students so that they could feel the results of the integration of personal skills within an academic context. The participants wrote during the workshops, emulating what their students would do in their own classes. The reflective writing prompts and exercises provided the teachers with an opportunity to learn about each other while creating an academic writing environment, a concept, supported by Freire's (2001) work, that teachers who also could view themselves as students could enhance the educational process in their classrooms.

I also wanted the participants to feel firsthand that the integration of personal skills, such as responsibility and interdependence, would not diminish the academic rigors of their courses. Studies that focus on adult learning further support such connections. Cross's (1981) research emphasizes that adults who are successful learners often utilize self-reflection in their learning processes, a practice that reinforces their self-confidence and positive feelings about themselves.

At every workshop I provided time for reflection in both writing and discussion. Furthermore, participants had an additional opportunity to reflect in their journals, exploring frustrations, concerns, and triumphs regarding their teaching and their own learning. This time to reflect was absolutely essential in their own understanding of the process of integration of personal skills, such as accountability and interdependence, within their writing courses. That this contemplation was necessary for teachers to change is substantiated in research on transformations in teaching methods. Paulsen and Feldman (1995) underscore the importance for teachers to become "reflective practitioners" in order for any training to result in teaching adaptations (1995, vii).

Classroom reform initiatives that have led to minimal or no changes in teaching practices often are blamed on teachers who are labeled "resistant" and "uninterested" in new ideas and unwilling to change their current practices. I had none of these experiences over the course of my research, but such an analysis of the failures in classroom teaching misrepresents the real problem: professional development has not included personal development. According to Watts and Hammons (2002), "To improve a person's performance, there is a need to focus on the whole individual, not just that part that relates to the job" (5). It is critical to explore the meaning of "personal" in this context, for just as we cannot separate the implications of the learning process from students, we cannot isolate teachers from their feelings about teaching and how they view themselves in the classroom.

It is ironic that while teaching is a profession that requires daily, personal exchanges of knowledge and ideas with both students and colleagues, there is often little emphasis on teachers' feelings in most teacher training. The personal component in this sense refers to the reflective process of teaching, which was clearly evident in the workshops but has only recently been addressed in the literature (Astin and Astin 1999; Rendon 2002b) and is virtually nonexistent in traditional teacher training in higher education. The participants explored how they felt when they had specific classroom interactions with students as well as when a lesson was particularly effective or disappointing. Rarely do we have the opportunity to hear from our colleagues that they too had a "rough day" in the classroom for perhaps the very same reasons we experienced. And seldom, if ever, can we express such feelings within the institution itself. However, these shared challenges help create the bond that defines both the *familia* as well as the personal connection.

Typically at conferences and staff development activities, new educational theories based on research are introduced, some of which can be applied directly to the classroom. Forums to discuss personal development issues related to our lives and our classrooms are rarely provided.

For quite a while, the business sector has offered programs for the personal development of employees, but to date, few colleges offer such support (Watts and Hammons 2002).

Current research on teacher training provides further insight as to the possible reasons the participants in my study chose to utilize and adapt the workshop materials in a basic writing curriculum. The workshops incorporated a formalized sharing component that naturally evolved into both an informal mentoring component and "peer coaching." Paulsen and Feldman (1995) suggest that successful teacher training often incorporates "collegial coaching" or the "peer-coaching" models, essential forms of collaboration. Such models not only emphasize a professional camaraderie but also a developing sense of empathy that facilitates both personal and professional growth. In fact, they believe that this collaboration among colleagues must occur for teachers to change their beliefs and implement innovative teaching methods.

This idea of collaboration in a low-keyed workshop environment, where the participants become a *familia* over time, bears significance on the field of teacher training, especially at the community college level, where such a format is virtually nonexistent. Traditionally, the primary focus of many teacher training programs has been on establishing professional relationships among participants (the coach and the teacher). In this case, the teachers are observed and told what they could improve. In contrast, the peer-coaching model follows the main principles of "collegiality, trust, nonevaluative assistance, nonjudgmental assistance, and reflective dialogue" (Thoman 2003, 4). My workshop format reflects this same model taken a step farther, as the participants create their own sense of family, resulting from frequent and regularly planned meetings during which participants are valued for their expertise.

In addition, built into the foundation of the workshops are elements of "testing and retesting." New ideas are both explored and discussed before and after they are tried out in the classrooms. The continual reflection, experimentation, and dialogue enable participants to further practice with the new materials and lessons that they might not feel comfortable doing on their own. Having colleagues to discuss the challenges and the feelings about implementing new lessons provides yet another "safety net" conducive to the adaptation and implementation of teaching practices.

I modeled my training workshops on the elements that I found most invaluable as a trainee. Many of the most inspirational and helpful trainings I have attended have been workshops that introduced professional and personal themes and allowed me to work within a group, experimenting with, sharing, and discussing the new techniques introduced by facilitators who also participate in the learning process. In my own study, I observed that the environment created in the trainings provided a forum for both the training's success and the participants' involvement and learning. Gladwell's (2002) theory holds much relevance for my own training model:

> If you want to bring about a fundamental change in people's belief and behavior, a change that would persist and serve as an example to others, you need to create a community around them, where those new beliefs could be practiced and expressed and nurtured. (2002, 173)

The community, or *familia* approach, also enables teachers to freely experiment with and discuss new teaching methods and materials that they might be reluctant to approach with colleagues with whom they have not established a prior close connection. My training, without formal presentations, allowed the teachers to become the students and to learn from each other in a nurturing yet academic environment.

To ensure both the success and retention of our basic writing students, especially at HSIs, we as teachers must be provided the optimum training experiences that can immediately translate to our classrooms. The *familia* approach to teacher training provides us with a holistic foundation, enabling us to learn the way our own students learn best.

Notes

1. Becoming responsible for oneself.
2. Learning to depend on and learn from each other during much of the class session.

Works Cited

Astin, Alexander, and Helen Astin. 1999. *Meaning and Spirituality in the Lives of College Faculty: A Study of Values, Authenticity, and Stress.* Los Angeles: University of California-Los Angeles Press.

Baiocco, Sharon, and Jamie DeWaters. 1998. *Successful College Teaching: Problem-Solving Strategies of Distinguished Professors.* Boston: Allyn and Bacon.

Broomfield, John. 1997. *Other Ways of Knowing.* Rochester, VT: Inner Traditions International.

Cross, Patricia. 1981. *Adults as Learners.* San Francisco: Jossey-Bass.

Downing, Skip. 1996. *On Course: Strategies for Creating Success in College and in Life.* Boston: Houghton Mifflin.

Elmore, Richard, and Milbrey McLaughlin. 1988. *Steady Work: Policy, Practice, and the Reform of American Education.* Santa Monica, CA: Rand.

Freire, Paulo. 2001. *Pedagogy of the Oppressed.* 30th anniversary ed. Translated by M. B. Ramos. New York: Continuum.

Gillespie, Kay Herr, ed. 2002. *A Guide to Faculty Development: Practical Advice, Examples, and Resources.* Bolton, MA: Anker.

Gladwell, Malcolm. 2002. *The Tipping Point: How Little Things Can Make a Big Difference.* New York: Little Brown and Company.

Healy, Mary Kay. 1990. "Effecting Change in Schools: A Personal Account." Paper presented at the International Federation for the Teaching of English, New Zealand.

Moran, Michael, and Martin Jacobi, eds. 1990. *Research in Basic Writing: A Bibliographic Sourcebook.* Westport, CT: Greenwood Press.

Oakes, Jeanie. 1980. "208 English Teachers: (Technical Report 11)." Los Angeles: UCLA.

Palmer, Parker J. 1998. *The Courage To Teach: Exploring the Inner Landscape of a Teacher's Life.* San Francisco: Jossey-Bass.

Paulsen, Michael, and Kenneth Feldman. 1995. *Taking Teaching Seriously: Meeting the Challenge of Instructional Improvement* (ASHE-ERIC Higher Education Report 2). Washington, DC: John Wiley and Sons Press.

Puente Project. 2002. "Community College Program Implementation Guidelines." Oakland: University of California, Office of the President.

Rendon, Laura. 1994. "Validating Culturally Diverse Students: Toward a New Model of Learning and Student Development." *Innovative Higher Education* 19:1: 33–52.

———. 2002a. "Community College *Puente*: A Validating Model of Education." *The Puente Project.* Special issue of *Educational Policy: An Interdisciplinary Journal of Policy and Practice* 16:4: 642–67.

———. 2002b. *Engaging the Intellect and the Heart in Learning Communities.* Unpublished essay.

Showers, Beverly. 1985. "Teachers Coaching Teachers." *Educational Leadership* 42:7: 43–48.

Thoman, K. 2003. "Introduction to Peer Coaching." Paper presented at the SMMUSD Literacy Teacher Coaches, Santa Monica, California.

Tinto, Vincent. 1987. *Leaving College: Rethinking the Causes and Cures of Student Attrition.* Chicago: University of Chicago Press.

Watts, Gordon E., and James O. Hammons. 2002. "Professional Development: Setting the Context." *Enhancing Community Colleges through Professional Development* (Winter): 1–5. San Francisco: Jossey-Bass.

Weiner, Bernard. 1974. *Achievement Motivation and Attribution Theory.* Morristown, NJ: General Learning Press.

APPENDIX A

Overview and Outline of the Teacher Training Curriculum

The teacher training schedule and curriculum for the fall 2003 semester, upon which I based the workshop agendas, follow:

Session One: Developing a Vocabulary of Responsibility

1. Participants are introduced to the concepts of Sleeper and Achiever. Achievers are people who assume responsibility for themselves and for all of their actions, both positive and negative. Sleepers *do not* take responsibility for their actions, both positive and negative. Generally, Sleepers see outcomes as a result of "someone or something else" and often see positive elements as a result of "luck." Sleepers make excuses, blame, complain, repeat ineffective behavior, "have to do things," pretend their problems belong to others, and say they will "try" rather than make a commitment to do something. They often give up.
2. Teachers are given handouts and role-playing activities related to Sleeper versus Achiever. For example, they receive a list of Sleeper statements and transfer each into an Achiever statement:
   - The teacher gave me a D on my last essay. ➔ I earned a D because I did not study.
   - I was late to class because the bus came late. ➔ I was late to class because I overslept and got to the bus stop later than usual.
3. Participants self-reflect as they journal about this experience of turning Sleeper language into Achiever language. They share their writings and discuss the qualities of Sleepers and Achievers within their "families" (groups).

Session Two: Integrating Personal Responsibility Vocabulary into the Writing Classroom

1. Participants receive a handout that lists Sleeper words that limit a student's personal responsibility and then are given ways to change these phrases into Achiever "talk" by omitting the use of "tentative" helping verbs of possibility/probability (may, might, should, could have, if):
   - *If* (*If* I get the chance) ➔ *When* (*When* I go); *Think* (I *think* I can ➔ I will; I *might* ➔ I *will*; I *should* ➔ I *will*.

2. Teachers are introduced to the importance of students using the word *choose.* For example, if a student says, "I came late because I missed my bus," the teacher reflects on this comment and says, "Oh, you *chose* to miss your bus." At first, students are taken aback and will say "no," that they had no control over the fact that the bus was late, but upon reflection, they eventually admit that they did get up late and missed their regular bus. The participants receive scenarios (e.g., papers not ready to submit; having to miss a class due to a doctor's appointment). These activities will enable their students to understand that they *do* have a choice in their actions.

Session Three: Modeling Interdependence and Responsibility in the Writing Classroom

1. Participants hear an explanation of the organization of class groups, which are called families/*familias*. Each group has four to five students, maximum, with a balanced mix of gender and abilities. The students stay together all semester and meet together at each class session. During the first class meeting students exchange phone numbers so they can call group members to get the work if they are absent. If members are missing, then they are to call them and find out why they are absent and report back to the teacher at the next class meeting. If students have problems with group members, then they have to work out the obstacles as one element of accountability. Participants can tell their students to meet in groups and to come up with a list of norms (rules) and present it to the class. The groups are responsible for typing a list of these norms for each family to present the rules to the class. The participants experience these groups firsthand. The philosophy behind these groups is explained, with a focus on empowering students to be accountable for themselves and in their group work and interactions.
2. Writing groups (small clusters of four to five students) are quite common in today's process-oriented writing courses. Teachers are encouraged to establish these groups, yet the groups will take on a far more specific role than peer editing. A theme of responsibility, both individual and shared among the group members, is created within these clusters of students. Once the groups are established, the participants are introduced to the writing/reading role of the group members. Students learn to be responsible for reading their own essays to the other

members of their groups. If they are not prepared, then they must call group members to read their essays over the phone. Participants become familiar with helpful questions that they can instruct their own students to use. These are questions that will allow students to receive helpful feedback in the next draft of their essays. This process also puts responsibility on students to ensure that they listen attentively because they will be helping others with their writing. Everyone is responsible for generating questions that will help group members with their grades.

Session Four: Critical Thinking and Case Studies and Prompts Using the Language of Responsibility

In this session teachers practice using case studies of responsibility, such as "Who is most responsible in a given situation?" Students can direct their writing toward an analysis on a critical thinking level. One element that is stressed with these teachers is that this is not an aside from writing but a direction of the writing about a specific topic that relates to critical thinking.

1. Case studies emphasizing student accountability are introduced. These case studies encourage critical and reflective writing while focusing on the stories' characters "who are the most responsible" (see sample in Appendix B).

Teachers practice using these quotations as prompts to engage them in critical thinking about issues of responsibility.

1. Specific quotations are used as prompts to engage participants in issues of critical thinking. Specific quotations that refer to responsibility are introduced. Participants practice responding to these quotes so they will be familiar with what they will ask their own students to do with the quotes:

   "I am the master of my fate; I am the captain of my soul." (William E. Henley)

   "I believe that we are solely responsible for our choices, and we have to accept the consequences of every deed, word, and thought throughout our lifetime." (Elisabeth Kübler-Ross)

   "A person defines and redefines who they are by the choices they make, minute to minute." (Joyce Chapman)

Session Five: Personal Writing Using Terms and Concepts of Responsibility

1. Participants are given instructions on how to respond to students who come unprepared for their class reading assignments. They practice what they will have their students ultimately do, which is to write a note (while the other students are doing the course work) to the teacher addressing the issue of why they chose not to do the reading. This short exercise allows students to reflect on the choices that ultimately led to being unprepared for class. Students do not always realize that they make choices that stop them from doing their homework. For example, a student has written that she realized that the time she spent talking to her boyfriend on the phone was one of the major reasons she came to class unprepared. Before the exercise, she blamed her lack of work on her job. This ten-minute writing exercise allows students the time to take responsibility for their educational choices.
2. Participants practice the six-step Wise-Decision Process. These steps can easily be duplicated in their classrooms in group work or through their writing. The Wise-Decision Process follows:

    A. Student describes his or her circumstances as objectively as possible (e.g., I am not passing my math class).
    B. Student explains how he or she wants the situation to be (e.g., I want to pass my math class with at least a C).
    C. Student decides if he or she has a choice in the situation (the answer is always "yes"). Students need to realize that they always have a choice, and not making a choice *is* a choice as well.
    D. Student lists his or her possible choices (e.g., (1) drop the class; (2) go to the professor for help; (3) get tutoring; (4) ask for any extra credit).
    E. Student tries to predict the outcomes of each option (e.g., If I drop the class, I won't graduate on time; If I go to the professor for help, she will be able to tell me more effective ways to study; If I get tutored, I will understand the material better; If I ask for extra-credit work, the professor might not offer it, but it won't hurt to ask).
    F. Student will choose one or more choices (from Step D) and take action (e.g., the student chooses choices 2 and 3: go to the professor for help and get tutoring).

APPENDIX B

The Evolution of the *Familia* Question Process

1. In the beginning of the semester (or the process), introduce the idea of strong lines. Have students write in class (freewriting) and pair off. This works best if first the teacher models this in front of the classroom with two students sitting and facing each other at their desks. Each student sits with his or her essay and a pen or pencil. The first reader will read, and the listener will "listen" for a strong line. The student will have the pen to write down the sentence. After the reader is finished, the listener will say "thank-you" and "A strong line for me is . . ." The reader says "thank you" also, and then students switch roles. We do not go into details about the strong lines, and so on.
2. After doing Step 1 for a week or so, spend about one hour on the following: discuss the two types of questions we have in English: WH Questions, or Information Questions (who, what, where, when, why, how, who, whose) and Yes-No Questions (answers are always yes/no). I usually draw a T Diagram on the board with the two types of questions. I ask students to generate questions, and we decide which types of questions they are.
3. Within the same day as Step 2, I use the overhead projector to show a large paragraph with a story that is missing many details. All I tell students is that it is a story. First I read it aloud without putting it on the overhead projector. Then I put it on the overhead projector and read it aloud again. Last, I keep it on so everyone can see, and I have the students, as a *familia*, generate questions based on the paragraph (five to ten minutes).
4. To continue this exercise, I ask students from each *familia* to write their questions on the boards in the class. Once the questions are on the boards, we review them to make sure they are all Information Questions. Invariably, there are a lot of Yes/No Questions that show up, so I ask students to "translate" these questions into WH Questions (question words that begin with "wh," such as who, what, where). They can do it with a little practice and help. Most of the help comes from other students, not me. There are always those who catch on quickly and understand the difference between the two types of questions.
5. Once Step 4 is complete, I ask students to take out one of their quick writes that they have completed (either that day or another). Each *familia* member reads a paper aloud and waits to be given

questions from the other members (as we did in Workshop 3). I remind the students that when they are listening, they should take notes when they hear information about which they have a question. If they just sit and listen without *actively listening* (with a pen in hand), then invariably, they will forget what was read. When students do not listen, they really do waste time. Since this quick write with questions is informal (a practice for students' essays), I will not see these papers, but I still give students the Question Sheet so they can become accustomed to filling it out with their own name and the names of their *familia* members. (Note: Students often get confused in the beginning as to whether they write down the questions and give them to others or answer their own. Because I have seen this confusion, I reiterate the following: Students need to get used to hearing the questions and writing them down on their own question sheet. They should not ask other students to write down their questions and then submit them to the reader/student. This is a different process. By reading the questions aloud, the other *familia* members hear the questions. This is helpful and important and can generate even more questions. It also is good practice for the reader/writer to write down on paper these questions, changing pronouns, and so on, for example, How long have *you* lived in LA? → How long have *I* lived in LA?) *Note to Instructor:* Yes, it does take time to practice this, but the time you devote to it will decrease the time it takes to get it right as well as to correct it since you will read so many more details and see stronger content. Also, these steps give students yet another chance for several other ears to hear the work before *you* do. When students are reading, I go around to each *familia*, and I also listen and take notes. I will ask questions to the reader/writer only after everyone in the *familia* has asked questions. Depending on the length of the essays (what part of the semester it is), reading essays with five *familia* members could take one hour. If you have fewer members, of course it will take less time, but they also will have fewer questions to bring home.

6. Finally, everyone has read and received questions (in the beginning, some *familias* may not take this process seriously or will not be listening carefully, but when the students see that the work in their *familias* has a direct correlation to their essay grades, the process becomes fine-tuned and productive). As a class we then reflect on the process and what the experience was like for students. We discuss what they will do with these questions. A few students always see the connection and state that they will

add the information (answers to the questions) to their essays. We discuss *where* they will put the answers to the questions. While this might be obvious to instructors and some of the students, it must be discussed since once I had a student who spent a lot of time answering each question on a separate piece of paper (not in his essay!).

7. When students submit their next draft, they must turn in the question sheet (when I copy it on colored paper, it is easy to see that it is there), the "new" draft (the one with the answered questions), and the draft they read in their *familias* (pre-questions). They are graded on each section. I usually find that I will read the essay first and then look at the list of questions to see what they understood and how their essays improved.
8. Occasionally, students will not bother to rewrite essays from the *familia* work, even though they received the questions. Of course, it is very clear that they *chose* not to do a rewrite, and they will receive low grades as a result of their lack of effort. Students learn quickly that the questions are essential for their grades and improvement.
9. There are no evaluative comments other than the initial questions. Of course, by the time I read the drafts, they have been written and rewritten, so I do add my comments and suggestions. Most of my suggestions are in the form of questions, except for grammatical remarks.

*Also, if students miss the reading day and do not have questions, they can call their *familia* members on the telephone to get questions. They also can come to my office, and I can give them the questions. A student may say, "My *familia* didn't give me hardly any questions." Most of the time, it is because the other *familia* members have not really listened. In this case, I will offer to read the paper and write some questions. If there is time, I will have the student read a paper again to the *familia*. The whole activity is a process and involves the following levels:

- reading aloud
- learning to listen attentively and with a pen
- asking productive questions
- finding a way to answer the questions at home while rewriting

APPENDIX C

Findings

Finding One	Finding Two	Finding Three	Finding Four
The teachers perceived that they adapted the concepts and activities from the *Familia* Writing Process, introduced in the workshops, to fit within their own classroom structures and styles. (The Process of Adaptation in Teaching Practices)	The teachers perceived that they adapted the accountability concepts introduced in the workshops to fit within their own classroom structures and styles. (The Process of Adaptation in Teaching Practices)	The teachers perceived that the integration of academic and personal skills enriched their basic writing students' classroom experience. (Integration of Academic and Personal Skills)	Students perceived that the integration of academic and personal skills enriched their basic writing classroom experiences. (Integration of Academic and Personal Skills)

Part 4

The Personal Narrative: Exploring Our Cultures as Hispanic-Serving Institution Students and Teachers

Chapter 10

The Politics of Space and Narrative in the Multicultural Classroom

Robert J. Affeldt

Space, Composition, and Teaching in the Multicultural Classroom

Space has come to occupy a central role in theories of meaning. Space connects us to a frame of reference, our experience in the world, and thus, in contrast language-based models, it provides us with new ways of thinking about reading, writing, invention, and discourse. But what is a theory of space, and does it have practical implications for the politics of teaching composition to Latino/a and other minority students? As Kristie Fleckenstein (2002) observes, our experience of space is complex and multilayered, joining us to the world through an array of mental, visual, and verbal imagery (2002, 7). In this chapter, I focus on a specific kind of psychological space, or embodied imagery, that operates at a point in consciousness where the mind and body intersect in the personal narrative. This space, I argue, possesses a unique cognitive status, for it is here, at the intersection of mind and body, that meanings emerge in ways that challenge conventional views of the self and how the self is written into culture. At this intersection of meaning and bodily space, we can, perhaps, best engage minority students (Latino/a and others) who may have different experiences of the body and how it is shaped by culture.

In what follows I return to some still unanswered questions about the role of space and narrative in composition studies and then use this discussion to frame my experience teaching a summer bridge course to Latino/a and Native American students at the University of New Mexico (UNM). Throughout the semester, these students experimented with components of the personal essay by using their experience as a way of thinking through and resolving conceptually complex issues. Within their personal narratives, they use their sense of space to open up, occupy, and complicate dominant images of success and learning. In so doing, they demonstrate that narratives are more than rigid artifacts to be reflected upon and analyzed, but ways of engaging and negotiating culture at the site where meanings emerge from our most private sense of the body.

Perspectives on Narrative Time and Space

The personal narrative continues to be a controversial subject in composition studies. This is largely because it raises questions about the epistemological status of intuited, primary experience, that is, our immediate perception of past, present, and future occurrences from our present moment in time. As Paul Ricoeur (1984) observes, narratives are intimately connected to our sense of becoming in the world. According to Ricoeur, narratives become meaningful because they are constructed in time, and time becomes human to the extent that it is constructed in narrative (1984, 52).

Narratives, however, are closely connected to our perceptions not only of time but space. Within any given moment, we employ our sense of orientation to construct representational images that model our experience of the world and the way it works (Johnson-Laird 1983, 8). Years ago, Kenneth Craik defined a representational model as any "physical or chemical system which has a similar relation-structure to that of the processes it imitates." Our thoughts, writes Craik, represent reality, because they imitate or "parallel" the way events operate in the world (quoted in Johnson-Laird 1983, 3). Unlike linguistic signs and signifiers, representational models or images have dimension and shape that reproduce our embodied experience of the world. They possess what Aristotle called *energeia*, the energy and motion of living events and actions. For Aristotle, metaphorical images possess *energeia* when they evoke not the idea of something but the experience, bringing "before the eyes . . . things engaged in activity" (Aristotle 1991, 248). More recently, Jerome Bruner (1986) has investigated how we narrate in order to construct possible worlds that reflect our real-life surroundings. For Bruner, and others such as Gregory Bateson, such worlds cannot be confined to the rigid and hierarchical categories of analytic logic but are organized like perceptual images with radiating webs of interdependent relationships.[1]

In the field of composition, two questions are central to current discussions of the pedagogical value of the personal narrative. One is a matter of epistemology, the other, politics and personal agency. First, given that we often use narratives to make sense of experience, how is narrating like reasoning? Second, how can narrating help our students challenge stereotypes that may limit their ability to negotiate cultural space? As Bruner (1986) remarks, despite our "vast knowledge of how science and logical reasoning proceed," we know very little about "how" people make stories (1986, 14).

The traditional view of narratives is that they are intellectually less rigorous than analytic arguments and critical reflection. Teachers of writing, for instance, frequently ask their students to write personal stories because they provide a starting point or "warm-up" for generating interest and ideas about topics that, ultimately, may be converted into more complex academic essays. The personal narrative, in many ways, has become the focus of debates between expressivist and constructionist views of writing pedagogy. Since the social turn in writing theory, many have spoken of the death of the personal narrative because of its, supposedly, naïve focus on self-absorbed, personal self-expression and self-discovery (Harris 2000).

Today, the personal narrative remains a controversial subject as is evident in two issues of *College English* devoted to exploring the value of writing stories about oneself (Hindemann 2001, 2003). In her essay that calls for a new approach to narrative, "It's Time for Class: Toward a More Complex Pedagogy of Narrative," Amy E. Robillard (2003) attributes a democratic quality to narratives because of the way narratives orient students in time. She asks us to take advantage of all students' "relative comfort" with narrative in order to help them analyze and interpret events that are constructed in different experiences of time and, thus, are often excluded from academic discourse. Quoting the work of Linda Brodkey, Lynn Z. Bloom, and Shirley Brice Heath, Robillard (2003) explains that working-class students often construct their lives around their immediate struggle to fulfill such pressing economic needs as paying rent and supporting families. Such concerns, however, run counter to an academic life that emphasizes the abstract, self-reflection, and the delayed fulfillment associated with pursuing a degree.

Robillard (2003) expresses a need felt among both students and academics alike to bridge a division between the institutional priority given to argumentative discourse and our more personal and everyday lived experience. In recent years, feminist critics and academics of color have criticized the political implications of valuing one kind of experience over another, pointing out that abstract reason is never neutral but culturally constructed (Villanueva 1993, 88) and that, in subscribing to such impersonal modes of discourse, we may be "complicit in our own subjugation" (Fleckenstein 1999, 285). Robillard (2003) argues, and I agree, that we should encourage students to bridge their personal experiences and analysis of this experience by demonstrating how narrative and argument are not separate modes of thinking but rather "interanimate each other," dialectically (2003, 82).

Some Deeply Entrenched Views of Narrative

Unfortunately, it remains unclear how narratives and argument interact. In an effort to shed light on this, Robillard (2003) emphasizes the thoroughly interpretive nature of narrative. Although she does well to point out its generative qualities, some of the most compelling portions of her essay consist of those features she has difficulty explaining, such as how we use narrative to think abstractly and the semantic value of concrete human experience or space. I explore these issues in order to identify the point at which hermeneutical approaches fall short and need to be shored up by a more materially informed view of narrative.

In seeking to bridge narrative and analytic modes, Robillard (2003) observes that we rarely separate the two in our everyday, practical experience:

> Every experience I've had with narrative—both writing and reading—leads me to believe that we cannot distinguish between narrative and analysis, between narrative and argument. (Robillard 2003, 82)

Quoting Candace Spigelman, she points out that our narratives often have an "argument-based role" (see Spigelmen 2001, 64) when we use them as evidence or as rhetorical frames to interpret our past experience to others. Robillard's (2003) comments about the interpretive quality of narrative are reminiscent of Paul Ricoeur's phenomenological study of narrative and time, in which he argues that narratives (i.e., the dynamics of emplotment) do not progress linearly but engage us in a process of negotiating, cyclically, among meanings prefigured in our past and refigured for future audiences. According to Ricoeur, as we move in and out of these mediating moments, we simultaneously construct and are constructed by our experience of time (Ricoeur 1984, 53). Relying on the work of Martha Marinara, Robillard similarly argues that personal narratives provide us with the unique opportunity to help students negotiate among their own temporal experiences, "between work and school, past and present, self and other" (2003, 76). By teaching narrative, we may promote a "new sort of class consciousness," in which students have the freedom to make sense of their own unique experiences of time (2003, 79).

Although Robillard emphasizes the liberating effects of telling personal stories, she tends to diminish the interpretive value of concrete, embodied experience. She asks, "What happens to the concrete when we narrate it?" Citing James Moffett, she replies that the concrete plays an important role in abstract reasoning because stories provide the material phenomenon that we reflect upon—the "stuff from which research papers and reports abstract," the material from which we "develop theories" (2003, 81). "[W]ithout the stories, without the concrete," she asks, "from what might one abstract? From what would theories be developed?" (ibid.).

In relying on Moffett, Robillard makes a significant theoretical move, one that portrays narrative's concrete properties as the material surface upon which reason operates. This creates a rift between what is uniquely narrative (i.e., its imagelike representation of embodied experience) and higher-order processes. Although Moffett recognizes the abstract, organizing properties of narrative, he does so at the expense of concrete experience. For Moffett, narratives take on the properties of reason only to the extent that they become more analytic, hierarchical, and detached—less like narrative.

In his still-much-quoted *Teaching the Universe of Discourse*, Moffett advances a theory of abstract reasoning that separates mind and body, time and space. In a section entitled "Abstraction," he reflects on how we are able to categorize or reason from concrete tokens to more abstract classes, from such items as "bartering" to the more inclusive class "international trade" or, similarly, from "dogs" to "mammals." Moffett (1986) speculates that our ability to move back and forth from things to classes of things is cohered by the "extension in time and space of the referent" (1986, 19). We are able to categorize and gather things into common categories and thus reason and draw inferences about them, because our minds have the ability to detach from concrete things in the world in gradually more abstract and inclusive moments of time and space. In an effort to account for the link between narrative and analytic modes of discourse, Moffett classifies narratives along an increasingly more abstract and impersonal spectrum of time and space in which

> (1) speaker, listener, and subject become gradually more diffused in time and space—more generalized; (2) each technique subsumes the previous ones and is built up out of them; in the same way classes include subclasses by an increasing summary of primary moments of experience. (Moffett 1986, 122)

Moffett defines narrative in terms of a hierarchy of reflective processes that invests it with the properties of classical logic. He encourages us to view narrative as a matter of gathering together experience and generalizing about it in a series of more general and inclusive sets of character, action, and event types. The problem is that in seeking to demonstrate how narratives resemble classical reasoning, we are likely to overlook how we reason, uniquely, through concrete, embodied experience.

The Body in Narrative

In order to understand how narrating can be a type of reasoning, we need to move beyond models that portray consciousness as a series of self-referring and increasingly abstract moments of interpretive reflection. Such models are constructed upon a metaphor of circular engagement and detachment that prevents us from seeing how, in reality, our reasoning is grounded in embodied experience. According to recent findings in the cognitive sciences, when we think, we (1) employ easily intuited concrete images that radiate outward among many simultaneous meanings (Lakoff 1987), and (2) map these images onto abstract concepts in order to give them meaning (Lakoff and Johnson 1980). As a result, our narratives employ concrete experience, metaphorically, to structure images that guide our imaginative constructions of the world. These embodied systems are not merely "operated upon" by reason but remain actively embedded within abstract concepts, shaping how we imaginatively structure categories that constrain reason. In this respect, the concrete and abstract are not opposed terms but operate as components of a larger ecology of simultaneous relationships that interact with each other. We rely on the concrete, and our personal connection to it, to access crucial source structure that we use to generate and extend meaning. Ultimately, our bodies provide us with a way of realizing and shaping meaning—a way into language, thinking, and social discourse.

What Ricoeur leaves unexplored is how we use metaphor to build narratives from the ground up, at that point where consciousness arises from our bodily attachment to the world. Although Kristie Fleckenstein has discussed the connections between narrative and metaphor (1996, 924; 2003, 184, fn. 12), and Nathan Crick has spoken of the need to consider how the body is mapped onto the mind (2003, 268), little has been written about how these processes work and how we employ them while reading and writing. For insight into this dynamic, I turn to cognitive science.

In the past twenty years, cognitive science has focused on how we use sentence-level conceptual metaphors to build category structure for abstract concepts (Lakoff and Johnson 1980; Lakoff and Turner 1989). Such metaphors include the familiar sentence-level expressions "Life is a journey," "Time is money," and "Argument is war." More recently, however, cognitivists have been exploring how we think within and across multiple metaphorical systems that exist at different levels of sensory, visual, and enacted experience (Turner 1991; Kövecses 2002). At a higher level of generality exists a species of highly generic, spatial, or orientational metaphors that will structure the narrative embedded in the source structure of more specific metaphors (Turner 1991, 161). These highly generic, spatial metaphors organize the way more specific conceptual metaphors work. They include such expressions as the "Self is a projectile on a path," which structures the notion of "Journey in Life is a journey" and "Value is mass that can be weighed," which structures the concept of money in "Time is money" and "Conflict is an opposing force," which structures war in "Argument is war." These spatial metaphors are linguistically unique in that, in contrast to sentence-level expressions, we encounter them subtly at work across large passages of discourse, dramatized within an unfolding narrative. For example, while reading, we may experience a character as moving along a path, weighing values, or fighting opposing forces. In terms of their cognitive properties, these metaphors are unique in that they operate as open-ended source structures that we use to search for and complicate additional metaphors and narratives.[2]

While reading, we imaginatively probe the spatial contours that shape the action of the text and use this structure to generate metaphors in order to fill in, extend, and complicate narrative models of self, action, and event. Reading and writing compel us, creatively, to construct patterns of reasoning that allow us to fill in missing causal inferences that cohere texts. I wish to argue that constructing such patterns requires us to access space in order to invoke, simultaneously, our culture's perception of the ordinary while carving out our own place within it. Narratives and metaphors draw us into complex aesthetic experiences that invite us to inhabit the embodied space of another in order to search for more adequate representations of personhood. In a sense, every act of reading, the experience of textuality itself, is a sensual act of inhabiting the skin of another through the experience of our own body. It is this complicating and mixing of bodies, of crossing private borders, that make reading and writing both real to us, a living experience, and potentially disruptive.

It is at this site of the body and cultural narrative where concepts open up, where we inhabit and reposition ourselves within commonplaces, that we can perhaps most deeply and effectively recover our sense of agency (Fleckenstein 2003, 1–9; 1996, 928–29; 1999, 281–82). At this site between body and concept resides what Susan Miller (1998) calls the "power of ordinary writing" (1998, 17). In order to help our students discover this power, particularly in a multicultural classroom, we need to be alert to the subtleties of space at work in their narratives as they seek to build up and recast metaphors of self. We need to be careful to avoid misrecognizing these dynamics and constituting what may depart from our own idealized narratives as reading and writing errors.

The University of New Mexico's Summer Bridge Program

In what follows I narrate my experience of teaching portions of a summer bridge class on writing at the University of New Mexico and focus on how two of my students, one Latina, the other Native American, used personal narratives to reflect on and reason about their sense of personhood in popular culture. These students were asked to use their writing to enter into conversation with the texts we were reading. One was Barbara Ehrenreich's (2001) "Cultural Baggage" and the other Roger von Oech's (2001) "To Err Is Wrong." These students use their personal narratives to explore questions raised in the readings about how one becomes independent, develops a sense of self, and learns from failure. In their writings, we can see how these students invoke commonplace narratives that address these issues, inhabit the author's subject position, her or his sense of space, and then, at a critical turning point, shift the audience of their essay to their own personal, cultural community. In doing so, something interesting happens. They begin to complicate and extend a shared sense of cultural space, giving expression to their own unique experience of culture within conventional commonplace forms.

The UNM Summer Bridge Program serves as both an introduction to academic writing and a sort of probationary makeup class in which students who have not done well in high school are given the chance to demonstrate that they are capable of reading and writing at the college level. As part of taking the class, they must attend a series of lectures and workshops on study skills and college life. If they can pass the writing class, they are permitted to take freshman composition the following semester. The class I taught was comprised of eighteen-year-old students, the majority of whom are Latino/a, and some Native American. Most of these individuals, who would be first-generation college students, were coming from troubled backgrounds that included drugs, divorce, and teenage pregnancies. They were holding down jobs and highly aware that by coming to the university they were changing themselves in fundamental ways.

My own place in the story, as both storyteller and an Anglo male teacher, is problematic and reflects my own bias and discomfort as I seek to understand, without reducing or romanticizing, my students' efforts to enter a new language in both body and mind.[3] As a person who grew up in the Midwest and attended a predominantly white high school and college, as someone whose father was a civil rights attorney, specializing in sex and race discrimination law, I, nevertheless, never really associated with people of color. There were formative events, like the day when a

Dodge Rambler rumbled into our middle-class neighborhood and a number of African American factory workers stepped out and rang our doorbell to talk with my father about assembling a class action lawsuit. Still it was our neighborhood and not theirs. And, to this day, I realize that I do not really understand my students and they do not understand me. That day on our block people stopped to look, much as I look at my students (and they, at me), but we never really see one another, never really connect, for we inhabit different places, both physical and psychological, which we guard dearly and, I think, desire to move beyond.

The struggle of representation, as Gregory Jay (1994) calls it, is for me a struggle both to understand my students and respond responsibly to their desire to participate in mainstream culture without failing to see and respond to their unique identities. On some level my students were, themselves, conscious of the politics of representing who they are, as they enacted in the classroom their own efforts to gain control of their bodies, their writings (their right to revise or not revise), and choices about how to inhabit the stories and concepts of others. These negotiations of self and culture, I discovered, were neither private nor public but blended the two, for they involved personalizing the highly general and politically biased meanings that we all inherit. To write personally, in this sense, as Victor Villanueva (1993) observes, is a thoroughly political act that dramatizes how we seek to find our way into popular discourse without losing a sense of self (1993 xviii).

Journeys of Faith

Dani is an attractive, Latina woman who sits with two of her female friends in the front row. All three have tinted hair, are dressed in slacks and summer blouses that expose midriffs, revealing navel rings and miniature tattoos on their lower torsos. For one of her essays, Dani reflects on Barbara Ehrenreich's "Cultural Baggage," in which Ehrenreich subtly invokes a distinctly Americanized version of the journey motif, explaining that rather than finding identity and security in her heritage, she has developed a better sense of who she is by tossing aside cultural encumbrances. Reflecting on her Anglo-Scottish heritage, Ehrenreich (2001) playfully comments that her culture is the culture of "none":

> [W]e are the kind of people, . . . whatever our distant ancestors' religions—who do not believe, who do not carry on traditions, who do not do things just because someone has done them before, . . . What better philosophy, for a race of migrants, than "Think for yourself . . . Try new things"? (2001, 191)

Subtly at work in Ehrenreich's language is a narrative constructed upon the notion of a traveler moving through space. In her rough draft, Dani summarizes Ehrenreich's position and then moves on to contemplate the difficulties of truly finding one's self in the world. Instead of addressing the mainstream public, as does Ehrenreich, she directs her comments more specifically to those of her own generation. Dani picks up the traveler motif, but rather than merely portraying herself as a solitary traveler of paths, she refigures herself as a sort of precarious edifice in need of support and sees life as a risky venture that threatens to topple her over. Inscribed within the imagery of her language is a different experience of physical and conceptual space. For Dani, the prospect of traveling is filled not with adventure and liberation but anxiety and a desperate need for "help" and cohering "answers." For this reason, she explains, she has chosen to "follow" the guidance of her parents and her religion.

> Everyone in life needs someone to share ideas to *fall back on*, and we depend on that person to give us help or answers. My religious background is Catholic. Because I was raised to be a Catholic, I *follow* the beliefs of my parents as well as myself. Having a Catholic background has *made me* the person who I am today. As a Catholic *I have become* more responsible, respectful, aware of my culture, and I have learned to understand it more. (emphasis added)

Dani's restructuring of Ehrenreich's authorial space illustrates that she has not merely rejected Ehrenreich's argument in rigid, analytic terms. This rejection would leave her with the assertion that Ehrenreich's story somehow does not work and with little to propose in its place.[4] Rather, she inhabits the embodied contours of the author's subject position and inserts it into a larger narrative of spiritual journeys, a journey that, for her, is deeply connected to discovering her Hispanic-Catholic roots.[5] She uses the generic image of self as traveler to reason her way into a discourse whose underlying metaphors she extends and complicates. Traveling, for her, means "falling back on" and "following" others, being "made" into and "becoming" more responsible.

Dani turns the trope of "following others" against those who might object that she has surrendered her independence, for she follows not only her parents and her religion but her own beliefs—she is her own guide. "I follow," she writes, "the beliefs of my parents as well as myself." Similarly, in the next passage, she fuses this complex image of following and guiding with Ehrenreich's solitary traveler, who shrugs off pressures to conform. Here she redirects her discourse about independence to her Hispanic classmates, suggesting that many "people" who pretend to be self-reliant, perhaps by imitating popular depictions of selfhood, may themselves be participating in a type of "raceless" conformity (see Villanueva 1993, 39) because they are ashamed of their cultural identity.

> I have *found* that people need to express who they are by having a cultural background and not being ashamed of it. People shouldn't worry about what society thinks and [she crosses out] ~~believe in their own beliefs~~ . . . use their culture to *explore* answers to their problems they are currently *facing* today. (emphasis added)

Dani's crossing out portions of her last sentence indicates that she continues to struggle with articulating how one can discover herself through culture, for she is drawn between two experiences of space and time. On the one hand, she sees herself as someone who expresses her independence by ignoring what others think ("believing in [her] own beliefs") and, on the other hand, she seeks to find a way to avoid getting stuck in the past, to "use" her culture to live her own life. In what follows, she investigates how religion and culture can be not "baggage" but a resource for making personal choices.

> Being a young teenager, I have *faced* many stages in my life to try a variety of drugs from friends. Every time it came down to this I had a decision to make, and from my religious *background* I knew it was very inappropriate. I had to do what I thought was right and what I believed in. . . . I turned down all these offers and by having a Catholic *background* that has helped me get *through* my everyday temptations I *face* in life. (emphasis added)

For Dani, religion and culture provide the support or "background" to steer her to the right decisions. She does not seek simple solutions, to hide or "just say no" to temptations. Rather, she knows that she must "face" and "get through" these adversities by finding her own reasons. She responds to the challenge by inhabiting the competing stories and images that constitute her complex experience of culture and using them to reason through her unique place in the world. Her use of space and narrative allows her to invest in religious imagery, such as journeying, temptation, falling, and getting through, with personal meanings that evoke pressures to succumb to a life of drugs, conformity, and a type of cultureless self-denial and self-loathing. She suggests that she has discovered a way to "use" her cultural background to connect her to her past and the person she is yet to be.

Learning from Mistakes

Mary is from the Pueblo of Zia, one of the many reservations near Albuquerque, New Mexico. Unlike other students in the class, she refuses to revise her papers, which reminds me of similar experiences I have had teaching Native Americans in a nearby community college. One of my friends, a linguist who is Choctaw and raised her son Navajo, writes to me that "individuality" is highly valued among many who live on the Pueblo, to the point that children are allowed to make decisions about "whether they go to school on a particular day and always about their property."[6]

I wish to observe that Mary's experience of culture is complex and may have influenced her reading of Roger von Oech's (2001) essay, "To Err is Wrong." Error, of course, is a sensitive topic in the writing classroom. Students often judge themselves in terms of error, and yet their progress, Shaughnessy (1977) reminds us, is connected to their ability to work through error. Like Ehrenreich, von Oech employs a popularized version of the journey motif, arguing that rather than avoiding failure we can use it as a "stepping-stone" for finding new approaches to solving problems.

Although most people see success and failure as opposites, von Oech views error as an opportunity for invention and enterprise, for discovering new ways of controlling and shaping one's environment. His emphasis on individualistic and capitalistic values is evident in the examples he selects from manufacturing, technology, and the banking industry and his celebration of such American icons as baseball legend Carl Yastrzemski and Thomas Edison. Both of these cultural figures embody the qualities of endurance and industry necessary to solving problems and accomplishing goals. Yastrzemski reached the 3,000 hit mark despite being called out over 7,000 times, and Edison discovered "1,800 ways *not* to build a lightbulb" (von Oech 2001, 86).

In responding to von Oech's essay, Mary is sensitive to the concept of error. Drawn to the "stepping-stone" image, she uses it to position herself in relation to what she has discovered about learning from mistakes. She writes:

> Like von Oech says failure is only a stepping stone and it is because you learn from your mistakes. . . . I have found that it is okay to make mistakes because you can create a positive *outcome* from it [*sic*]. You can always learn from your mistakes because you can *retrace* what you did wrong, so *next time* you do it again you will be successful at it. I can relate to this whole situation because in my high school English class I was always afraid about doing my assignments the *wrong way*. (emphasis added)

Mary goes on to explain that she figured out what she was doing wrong in her papers and then received the "highest score in the class."

> So what I'm trying to say is that there can be a positive *outcome* to [wrong] answers, you can learn from your mistakes and later on success. Failing can never be too bad unless you make it bad. You just have to

> step up to the plate and take responsibility in your own hand by trying *to look back* on what we needed to work on, then try to make our failure *turn into* success. (emphasis added)

Mary's language is filled with images that portray experience as a matter of "retracing" one's steps, "looking back" on past choices, and the possibility of "turning" or refashioning events into something new. Although she agrees that one can learn from failures, she restructures the spatial dimensions that define this learning experience. Rather than viewing the self as moving through individual moments of trial and error, she writes of a self that is spread out over time, the product of integrated actions and choices that may remain embedded in one's history, may have lasting effects, and may be "retraced" and corrected.

As a result, Mary's perception of error takes on different dimensions and overtones as well. Rather than viewing error as an instrument of learning and process as using and discarding resources that no longer work, Mary is personally invested in the entire process, product, and byproduct of learning. She does not seek merely to get beyond or use error to resolve a problem. In many respects, she sees error as the object of the destination itself, character flaws that linger in one's personal history and that must be remedied before moving on. Reenvisioning von Oech's portrait of the enterprising capitalist and innovator, she suggests that learning from failure requires more than controlling one's surroundings and solving problems but perfecting and fulfilling one's nature.

It would be easy to overlook these subtleties of language and reduce Mary's response to series of fractured idioms and failures to understand the text. A close reading of her response, however, reveals that these departures in meaning occur at a point where the author's text unravels, where meaning relies on our diverging experience of space and cultural narrative. Mary inhabits and redirects the contours of von Oech's story to her own community and thus complicates conventional portraits of discovery, learning, and error. Her imagery reveals her sensitivity to the stigma of not performing well, which for her means making "mistakes" that have disrupted her relationship with others and her surroundings. She concludes by expressing her need to cleanse and construct herself on her own terms or, as she puts it, to take "responsibility in [her] own hand."

Mary's concern for managing her place in a complex network of relationships is a value that anthropologists have identified as central norm of Southwest Pueblo culture. In their award-winning ethnographic fieldwork on the connection between Native American customs and tribal law, Robert D. Cooter and Wolfgang Fikentscher (1998) hypothesize that despite the loss of many customs and traditions, the Native American "way of life" has survived "embedded" in their concept of "justice and fairness" and the way they implement these concepts into their daily life and legal proceedings (1998, 313). The authors propose that despite the influence of the American legal system, which tends to associate the person with specific, behavioral acts and judge the person in terms of a codified set of laws, tribal culture defines discord against the background of the obligations and duties that people owe to each other within the context of relationships. In their study, they observe:

> Tribal people live their lives among kin, so a dispute indicates a rupture in these relationships. Dispute resolution in the tribe typically aims to repair relationships. To repair relationships, adjudicators examine the *character* of the parties and the history of their interaction, not just the particular event in the legal complaint. Compared to other American courts, . . . tribal courts . . . attend to relationships more than rules. (1998, 314, emphasis added)

From interviews, the authors discover that tribal officials value developing character through relationships with others, a concept they have difficulty translating into English. They explain, "Whites fear the law. Indians live it" (1998, 312). Further, Cooter and Fikentscher state, "In a culture in which so much rests on oral tradition, a given word weighs much more," and judicial rulings (especially those involving juvenile offenders) are "not only about justice, [but] . . . education" (1998, fn. 105, 313).

In her reading of von Oech, Mary tries to come to terms with making mistakes in a highly individualistic, industrial society that seeks to regulate an individual's behavior through written codes and contracts. Although she appreciates the need to manage her behavior and use error as a resource, for her the value of making mistakes is connected less to securing autonomy and control of one's environment than building character and preserving harmony within the community. Although her use of language is subtle, Mary's experiences of space and time, and subsequent mixing of images, illustrate her profound attempt to find a point of contact among competing portraits of living responsibly in relation to others.

The Politics of Space, Narrative, and Error

Recently, scholars have focused on the way personal narratives engage us in the politics of space. In her book *Relocating the Personal*, Barbara Kamler (2001) comments that personal experience is, itself, a narrative production in which "space is as crucial a component of that production as time" (2001, 5). Quoting postmodern geographer Edward Soja, she reflects that the "apparently innocent spatiality of social life" is filled with "politics and ideology" (2001, 2). Seeking to foreground these politics, Kamler makes two important theoretical moves. She draws attention to the spatial constructions within the conventional narrative and interprets personal writing in terms of its "social and cultural landscape" (2001, 2). Most significantly, in her research on writing and aging, Kamler examines how her female participants use the embodied space of their narratives to produce "new metaphors," "new ways of speaking about aging," and "new forms of subjectivity" (2001, 59).

Similarly, in her book *Traversing the Democratic Borders of the Essay,* Cristina Kirklighter (2002) traces the evolution of the essay in terms of various defining features, such as using personal narratives to communicate authenticity and challenge the status quo. Kirklighter explains that many Latin American and Latino(a) scholars in particular, such as Paulo Freire, Ruth Behar, and Victor Villanueva, employ personal narratives to raise consciousness about alternative experiences and, when combined with self-reflexivity, to construct a sense of cultural identity, a sort of "essaying to be" (2002, 79). In his book *Bootstraps: From an American Academic of Color,* Victor Villanueva (1993) expresses the need to create a dialogue between "official ideologies" and "lived experience" (1993, 136), which he demonstrates by weaving together academic critical theory and his more personal reflections about moving to the projects ("a step up") in Bed Stuy: "No graffiti. No urine. Elevators. An incinerator chute on every floor" (1993, 1). Villanueva narrates detail about his past not just to provide testimony but to generate the critical space needed to reorganize common perceptions about what it means to be an academic and a person of color.

I have attempted to illustrate how two student writers, when asked to enter into conversation with a text, occupy space in the underlying narrative cohering the text's argument. These students are doing more than using narratives to provide evidence. Much like contemporary essayists and scholars, they are narrating as a way of "becoming" in order to generate category structure about personhood so that they can reason about what it means to be Latino/a or Native American in popular culture. Narratives allow us to reason, to abstract and generalize because they compel us in our everyday discourse to reorganize and reinterpret such features as space, time, action, and character. They are political to the extent that they allow us to access concepts at that point where meanings emerge from our personal sense of embodied space.

My students are not just composing self-absorbed, subjective stories or turning specialized literary tropes. Rather, they are complicating common cultural narratives about the self as a solitary traveler or capitalist manager. Such popular narratives are constructed upon assumptions about what it means to move or orient oneself in the world. These students inhabited these idealized portraits in order to construct meanings that were more specific and relevant to their own communities. Dani extends popular portraits of journeying to include the possibility of using her cultural heritage as a resource rather than viewing it as an encumbrance, and Mary complicates individualistic and opportunistic assumptions about living successfully in order to consider how to live responsibly within a close-knit community. Although we may at first be inclined to read their writings as subtle miscues or variations upon the readings, as they developed their ideas it became clear to me that they were attempting to do more than merely reproduce dominant ideologies. Rather, they were seeking to move beyond cultural divisions and connect. They were expressing their need to read themselves into the text, filling in its missing experience, and making it fit their own felt experience of the world.

My students risked expressing the familiar in unfamiliar places. On some sensory level, I am reminded of that puffing and choking Dodge Rambler that wandered into my neighborhood years ago. I am revisited by the image of the car, its disruptive backfiring (the neighbors looking) and the challenge it posed to ordinary, idealistic ways of thinking about identity, language, and the teaching of writing. Such challenges are similarly invoked for me by students who articulate their sense of body, their experience of language and culture, in everything they write, from tattoos exposed on midriffs to a student's efforts to share her sense of movement through conflicting portraits of environment and community.

Personal narratives emerge on the borders between the ideal and real, the personal and public, and thus are always potentially disruptive. I wish to suggest that for this reason they may serve as important sites for cultural critique. As Patricia A. Sullivan (2003) remarks, rather than asking students to come to terms with the overdetermined theories of instructors, students may use personal narratives to explore their own lived experience of the dominant in their "own vernacular," in the "materially oppressive content of [their] everyday life" (2003, 44). As teachers, we need to be aware, however, that our students are often building narratives from the ground up from the way they experience themselves as bodies in the world. As a result, what may look like a fracture of idiom or misreading may in fact be a subconscious attempt to fill in the story beneath a concept by redirecting it to those who matter most to us, to those with whom we share our most intimate and personal sense of space.

Notes

1. As I explain later, the notion of categories structured like radiating webs, consisting of a system of mutually interdependent relationships, helps explain how the embodied space, inherent in narratives, structures our more abstract concepts, making them more fluid and open to adjustments in everyday discourse.

2. In his book *Reading Minds: The Study of English in the Age of Cognitive Science,* Mark Turner (1991) observes that these highly generic metaphors have no fixed target domain, for they serve to structure the mappings of other, more specific metaphors at various levels of experience (1991, 284, fn. 7).

3. I wish to thank my students, who granted permission to use their work in this essay and were enthusiastic about helping me understand their efforts to make meaning. Dani writes, "I feel that [the] part on culture does give justice to me because it expresses my strong beliefs as a Catholic." Mary responds, "I am okay that you pointed out that Native Americans are independent minded because I am . . . I feel that you have made my thoughts clear about the stepping stone. We all learn differently and I appreciate how you are trying to put out an understanding of how we learn and comprehend things even when we come from different backgrounds."

4. See Lakoff's and Johnson's (1980) critique of analytic versus metaphorical truth claims: "This Is a Fake Gun" (1980, 120).

5. Hispanic is used here and below in keeping with the way students self-identify in this region of the country.

6. Quoted from personal correspondence with Dr. George Ann Gregory of the University of New Mexico, March 20, 2004.

Works Cited

Aristotle. 1991. *Aristotle on Rhetoric: A Theory of Civic Discourse.* Translated by George A. Kennedy. New York: Oxford University Press.

Bruner, Jerome. 1986. *Actual Minds, Possible Worlds.* Cambridge, MA: Harvard University Press.

Cooter, Robert D., and Wolfgang Fikentscher. 1998. "Indian Common Law: The Role of Custom in American Indian Tribal Courts (Part I of II). *The American Journal of Comparative Law* 46:2: 287–337.

Crick, Nathan. 2003. "Composition As Experience: John Dewey on Creative Expression and the Origins of 'Mind.'" *CCC* 55:2: 254–75.

Crowley, Sharon. 1990. *The Methodical Memory: Invention in Current-Traditional Rhetoric.* Carbondale and Edwardsville: Southern Illinois University Press.

Ehrenreich, Barbara. 2001. "Cultural Baggage." In *Viewpoints: Readings Worth Thinking About,* ed. Royce Adams. 189–92. Boston: Houghton Mifflin.

Fleckenstein, Kristie. 1996. "Image, Words, and Narrative Epistemology." *College English* 58:8: 914–35.

———. 1999. "Writing Bodies: Somatic Mind in Composition Studies." *College English* 61: 281–306.

———. 2002. "Inviting Imagery into Our Classrooms." In *Language and Image in the Reading-Writing Classroom: Teaching Vision,* ed. Kristie S. Fleckenstein, Linda T. Calendrillo, and Demetrice A. Worley, 3–26. Mahwah, NJ: Lawrence Erlbaum Associates.

———. 2003. *Embodied Literacies: Imageword and a Poetics of Teaching.* Carbondale: Southern Illinois University Press.

Harris, Joseph. 1997. "Person, Position Style." In *Publishing in Rhetoric and Composition,* ed. Gary A. Olson and Todd W. Taylor, 45–56. Albany: State University of New York Press.

———. 2000. "Meet the New Boss, Same as the Old Boss: Class Consciousness in Composition." *CCC* 52: 43–68.

Hindemann, Jane E. 2001. "Personal Writing." Special focus of *College English* 64:1: 34–108.

———. 2003. "The Personal in Academic Writing." Special issue of *College English* 66:1: 9–104.

Jay, Gregory. 1994. "Knowledge, Power, and the Struggle for Representation." *College English* 56:1: 9–29.

Johnson-Laird, Philip. 1983. *Mental Models: Towards a Cognitive Science of Language, Inference, and Consciousness.* Cambridge, MA: Harvard University Press.

Kamler, Barbara. 2001. *Relocating the Personal: A Critical Writing Pedagogy.* Albany: State University of New York Press.

Kirklighter, Cristina. 2002. *Traversing the Democratic Borders of the Essay.* Albany: State University of New York Press.

Kövecses, Zoltán. 2002. *Metaphor: A Practical Introduction.* New York: Oxford University Press.

Lakoff, George. 1987. *Women, Fire, and Dangerous Things: What Categories Reveal about the Mind.* Chicago: University of Chicago Press.

Lakoff, George, and Mark Johnson. 1980. *Metaphors We Live By.* Chicago: University of Chicago Press.

Lakoff, George, and Mark Turner. 1989. *More Than Cool Reason: A Field Guide to Poetic Metaphor.* Chicago: University of Chicago Press.

Miller, Susan. 1998. *Assuming the Positions: Cultural Pedagogy and the Politics of Commonplace Writing.* Pittsburgh, PA: University of Pittsburgh Press.

Moffett, James. 1986. *Teaching the Universe of Discourse.* Boston: Houghton Mifflin.

Ricoeur, Paul. 1979. "The Metaphorical Process as Cognition, Imagination, and Feeling." In *On Metaphor*, ed. Sheldon Sacks, 141–57. Chicago: University of Chicago Press.

———. 1984. *Time and Narrative, Volume 1.* Translated by Kathleen McLaughlin and David Pellauer. Chicago: University of Chicago Press.

Robillard, Amy E. 2003. "It's Time for Class: Toward a More Complex Pedagogy of Narrative." *College English* 66:1: 74–92.

Shaughnessy, Mina. 1977. *Errors and Expectations: A Guide for the Teacher of Basic Writing.* New York: Oxford University Press.

Spigelman, Candace. 2001. "Argument and Evidence in the Case of the Personal." *College English* 64:1: 63–87.

Sullivan, Patricia A. 2003. "Composing Culture: A Place for the Personal." *College English* 66:1: 41–54.

Turner, Mark. 1991. *Reading Minds: The Study of English in the Age of Cognitive Science.* Princeton, NJ: Princeton University Press.

Villanueva, Victor. 1993. *Bootstraps: From an American Academic of Color.* Urbana, IL: National Council of Teachers of English.

von Oech, Roger. 2001. "To Err Is Wrong." In *Viewpoints: Readings Worth Thinking About*, ed. Royce Adams, 83–89. Boston: Houghton Mifflin.

Chapter 11

Collaboratively Mentoring Our Identities as Readers, Writers, and Teachers

A Black Cuban, Black American's Impact on a South Texas Community

Cathy Freeze, Dundee Lackey, Cristina Kirklighter, Jennifer Anderson, Peter Cavazos, Rachel Eatmon-Hall, Misty Lynn Garcia, Jennifer Nelson Reynolds, Sandra Valerio, Billy D. Watson, Elizabeth Worden, and Stacy Wyatt

Dr. Cristina Kirklighter's Preamble

Often when I read journal articles or anthologies, I receive snippets here and there of student voices selected and contextualized by their teachers or other academics. I would like to see these submerged voices come to the surface. Sometimes teachers need to step back and let their students take the reins in researching, interpreting, and recording what they experience in the classroom and beyond. This shift in authority is especially significant when students play a key role in helping to fulfill the mission of an English department in regard to community engagement. The English Department at Texas A&M University-Corpus Christi (TAMU-CC) actively promotes community literacy. One important event is the annual University Author's Day, which focuses on Latino/a authors whose experiences may have relevance for the local population. In this chapter, my students describe the event and their efforts to collaborate among themselves and with local secondary school teachers and students to celebrate the writings and visit of Evelio Grillo, a black Cuban American writer and civil rights activist.

Since this anthology focuses on writing at Hispanic-Serving Institutions (HSIs), I shudder as a coeditor at the enormous responsibilities that come with ethically representing and depicting these institutions so as not to feed into stereotypical notions. One way to accomplish this ethical representation is to allow graduate student voices to be heard and validated since they have much to teach us about their experiences at HSIs. Many Latino/a academics in composition and literature, such as Victor Villanueva, Cecilia Rodríguez Milanés, and I, know how our *cuentos*, or personal stories, can serve to establish a place for us in academia as we search for ways to belong under our own terms. We teach our students to find ways of belonging by encouraging them to write their *cuentos* as they engage with texts, authors, and other students. This need for belonging may be particularly poignant for HSI graduate students who may experience difference as teachers, researchers, and students in minority institutions situated in predominantly minority communities. What and how they write might be considered by others nontraditional, experimental, and multivoiced. However, writing differently in academia may lead to understanding, as we see in Villanueva's (1993) *Bootstraps*. Such difference serves to enrich our perspectives of what HSI graduate students bring to the teaching of writing and literature.

In spring 2003, my students spent weeks preparing a series of activities on campus to engage students, faculty, and minority high school students for Author's Day and the celebration of the author. I now step back and let you read their narratives of this community literacy engagement event.

Introduction

In keeping with South Texas culture's friendly and personal introductions, we open this chapter by sharing with readers who we are as a community and the event that we participated in. Corpus Christi is almost 60 percent Hispanic, with a minority population of (4.4%) African Americans, (0.6%) Native Americans, and other ethnicities. Anglos make up around 35 percent of the population (U.S. Census Bureau 2003). Our community is located in the Coastal Bend area of South Texas. As part of an HSI located three hours from the Mexican border, TAMU-CC's English Department frequently seeks projects that best serve our predominantly Latino/a community population. The University Author's Day, held since 1994, focuses on engaging young writers from the community.

History of University Author's Day

In building the idea of University Author's Day, Dr. Robb Jackson, a professor at TAMU-CC and founder of this event, felt that it was important for students to realize that they "know who [they] are." He notes, "If you give [them] voice, you can participate and celebrate." He actively participates in service learning and community literacy in Corpus Christi.

When he headed the event's program, he called it "Creating Writing in Community Service," and he offered grad students independent study credit to work with him. He envisioned University Author's Day as a way to give underprivileged students a window into the college experience.

University Author's Day Today

University Author's Day has evolved into a departmental event that invites an author who can speak to the experiences of the local population. The invited author participates in a two-day literary and writing event that involves the community and predominantly Latino/a high school students, as well as university staff, faculty, and students. Day one is reserved for an author's reading, followed by a question-and-answer session; on day two, students from area high schools attend writing workshops instructed by faculty, graduate students, and the author. University Author's Day helps the Latino/a students understand college writing classrooms, and it encourages them to explore their cultural identities through their personal writing processes. In this chapter, we describe how our participation created collaborative and transformative experiences not only for us but for those with whom we interacted in our community.

In the spring of 2003, we enrolled in an Academic Writing and Publishing capstone class. As a way of helping us in our professional development as MA students, our professor included a service component that required us to actively participate in University Author's Day. In our community vision of this writing event, we expanded University Author's Day to a week of planned and facilitated activities, on and off campus, involving members of civic and academic communities. We facilitated a reading circle at a local coffeehouse, gave a public panel presentation, conducted an interview with the author, facilitated high school class sessions for University Author's Day, and met with the author in a lunch setting to further understand his experiences. The explorations of our lives in relation to the author and his work and the impact we made on community learning and writing led us to the conclusion that publishing a description and analysis of this project will serve HSI graduate programs and the greater academic community.

We enhanced our knowledge and participation in community-based learning and writing through the selection of Evelio Grillo, a black Cuban, black American civil rights leader and national community activist for forty years. His writing was provocative, his personality engaging. Inspired by our interactions with him and with the local community members, we had a rich story to tell of our endeavors and discoveries, of our individual growth and identity as individuals, classmates, students, and members of our South Texas community.

Although the early setting of Grillo's (2000) *Black Cuban, Black American: A Memoir* is in a small Cuban, Spanish, and Italian community outside of Tampa, called Ybor City, his struggles resonated with the working-class and Latino/a communities and HSI students of South Texas.[1] As he matured, Grillo realized that his black Cuban, black American identities could serve as an asset instead of a liability. He learned to take pride in his dual identities and to use his biculturalism to reach out to many communities of various ethnicities.

This respectful, caring, empathetic man also reached out to us during his week's stay in Corpus Christi. He nurtured us to take pride in our identities and enhanced this pride in the predominantly Latino/a high school students as well. Grillo's unabashed joy as a participant in activities—especially with students from area high schools and TAMU-CC—revealed to us that the love we as teachers and students see as the province of the classroom was Grillo's defining quality for his social work and teaching. His sharing of his community identities, knowledge, involvement, and writing exceeded our expectations and helped us appreciate the art of collaborative learning and writing based on community. What follows are collaborative descriptions, reflections, dialogues, and analyses of three University Author's Day events that we led as readers, writers, and teachers: a panel presentation, a reading circle, and a creative writing introductory class for predominantly Latino/a high school students.

Panel Presentations

Introduction

Grillo's *Black Cuban, Black American: A Memoir* opened a window into the life of the author as well as the lives of those who attended our panel presentation, the second event in a week-long series of interactions between Grillo and our South Texas community. The panel presentation allowed us to exhibit our scholarly engagement with Grillo's memoir and helped us better prepare some of our peers to teach high school students about Grillo. A sense of community literacy developed as Grillo answered questions about his life and views on society in response to our presentations. Our collective identities became the subject, and Grillo, an active and energetic octogenarian, was up for the challenge.

As readers of his memoir, we were captured by the author's sonorous narrative voice. Grillo speaks with authority and emotion about his bicultural life. As panel presenters, we wanted to showcase this book in the best light by exploring the content and adding to our knowledge gleaned from the book through individual experiences and research. In this way, a dialogue and discourse of community literacy was fostered and developed.

Reflections

Liz: Like Florida, Texas represents a melting pot for many cultures and ethnicities—Spanish, Mexican, German, Polish, Czech, Irish, and so on. I grew up in a Texas community made up of mostly Mexican and German immigrants. Many of the kids I went to school with had grandparents who spoke either Spanish or German exclusively and did not understand English. These families formed tight-knit, exclusive communities that did not accept newcomers to such a small-town society. Moving to town at age eight, I was an outsider because my grandparents were not born there. Thus I made a social connection with Grillo's experiences of trying to fit in as a black Cuban, black American, based on my own small-town, working-class life. That is why I chose to research the topic of Grillo's hometown of Ybor City for the panel presentation. Ybor City, like my town, has a very interesting history of multiculturism as well, an epic story of immigrants, one that reaches out to today's audience and the Corpus Christi community. Like Grillo's family, I shared a heritage of ancestors who immigrated to a new nation full of promise. Grillo's look at the American dream is honest and at times raw. He calls attention to the hypocrisy of an age that considered skin color above all else and lived to achieve in a society that slowly changed its views on race due in large part to social activists such as himself.

Sandra: Within every triumph lies the question of how Grillo came to achieve the state of "self" that represents his success. This line of questioning may be traced to the formation of one's identity and to the contributors of that identity—namely, family. I chose family because I instantly connected with Grillo's familial experiences with matriarchal influences and with memories of "home." Matriarchal influences can stand as a bridge between how we come to know and feel about ourselves, and how we come to know and feel our sense of "home."

Grillo begins his memoir with the sights and sounds of Ybor City as he opens the door of his home and invites us to experience his family. In the same way, I reflect on the sights and sounds of my Molina—a barrio on Corpus Christi's west side, where poor, working-class Mexican Americans and African Americans are separated only by a street, and where a ditch separates us from everybody else. Grillo demonstrates, in spite of any geographical context, side of town, or town in itself, that a home becomes its own entity, somewhat separate, behind closed doors, private, intimate, sacred, and small.

Grillo's recollection of his family begins with a supposed look at something that did in fact happen but the details of which are blurred by the passage of time. He writes, "It had to be a Saturday afternoon because of the way the house smelled, the way it felt, and the way that it sounded" (2000, 3). Grillo helps us envision what a day used to mean to us as children—being home with our family. He shares the smells of cleanliness, of good food, and the feelings that accompany the awakening of these senses. The specific feeling that he shares is the feeling of being home with *la familia.*

And what about our mothers? How much influence can our mothers claim over the formation of our identity? For Grillo, as for most of us who had a working mother, the role of the mother goes beyond the woman who birthed us. It extends to the other women in our lives who helped make us who we are and who we became. To say that we benefited (or not) from only one maternal influence could not be true in a world where a woman, for whatever reason, had to work to support, or to help support, her family. Grillo benefited from the maternal influence of his primary caretaker and neighbor, Mrs. Byrna, from his mother, and from his older sister as well. While a precise measurement of exactly how much each contributed to Grillo's identity probably cannot be calculated, we can gather that the influence of each female was instrumental in Grillo identifying himself as a black Cuban, black American. Like most of us, he chose to gather and use the characteristics from each maternal figure that could make him a better and stronger person. And this is something that many of us do—we gather from the familial community around us to make us who we are, who make us who we want to be, and to become more than they could with those same characteristics. With various caregivers over the years, I cannot, try as I may, find my own Mrs. Byrna. Instead, I find myself creating a mother whose affection gave me enough wisdom to know that a mother's love is almost never enough. That mother, of course, is me. As I raise my nine-year-old son, I find myself attempting to be both a mother and Mrs. Byrna. I find myself realizing that there is a reason Grillo's mother needed a Mrs. Byrna. There simply are not enough hours in the day to be everything for a child. The feeling that Grillo reaches in each of is maturity—something we gain from our mothers only after we lose them.

Jennifer A.: Grillo's reflections on his education inspired me to consider my own educational experiences. His experiences directly reflect the historical events of recent years. As we learned from Grillo, despite the Supreme Court ruling, segregation and discrimination continued to exist. The majority of students today have not had the opportunity to experience segregation firsthand—it simply does not exist as it did before. It is only through recounts and memories of people such as Grillo that we vicariously experience the effects of racial discrimination—particularly in the classroom. When reading Grillo's narrative of discrimination in schools, I found myself wondering why. As one of the many who did not experience segregation firsthand, I could not understand the true definition of discrimination. I found, through personal research and Grillo's reflections, that the effects of discrimination represented more than just laws and boundaries. Grillo's disadvantages allowed him to ultimately value the education I took for granted.

When asked how he felt about hyphenation (black-Cuban, black-American) dividing and at the same time defining us, Grillo replied that this question "puts me in the posture of being you, and I don't feel that at all." Within his book, Grillo takes us along his journey through the school system in hopes of completing an education. But the real tests he speaks of are not about algebra, chemistry, or English. The ultimate test is of life and reality—a test of humanity in the midst of inhumanity. Grillo shows us how to pass this test and move beyond social restraints to discover the importance of individual identity. He embraced this new-found freedom, the freedom to learn, and he has applied his curiosity to his education. His educational journey is one of great inspiration. I too have had influential instructors, all of whom are the voices and the faces behind mine.

Billy: As a naturally thoughtful person, I could not help but ponder the idea of memoir: "What is a memoir? What operational definition can we develop for this literary device?" I must ask these questions before proceeding with my portion of the presentation, which was devoted to Grillo's experiences in a segregated military during World War II.

I would offer the following interpretation. If one examines the first four books of the New Testament, the reader discovers the works of the Apostles Matthew, Mark, Luke, and John. All alleged to have been witnesses to the crucifixion of Christ, but in recounting this event, they offer such wide interpretations as to bring into question their authenticity. And yet these widely different viewpoints stand as Gospel. Do we discount them, or do we accept them as being the true accounts as told to us by eyewitnesses? Were the Apostles writing an autobiography or a memoir? It is rather obvious to me that these are memoirs because we as readers allow for the emotionally charged interpretation of these individuals to be different. Each of our eyewitness accounts differs based on our situated perspective of the event and the emotional impact that the event has upon us as observers.

Thus I would define memoir as personal reflections of an event situational to the observer/participant. Such reflections are emotional responses rather than attempts to examine the recollection objectively. As I read Grillo's memoir of his service in World War II, I realized that we did not share the same emotional responses to the jungles of Indochina. For Grillo, the jungle was to be conquered, to be bulldozed, to be tamed, plowed into submission. The Ledo road that he and other black soldiers built to link India with the Burma roads was an engineering marvel. For each mile of road constructed, 100,000 cubic feet of earth had to be moved. But for Grillo and the men who worked with him, it was the place that began at the edge of their encampment—it was their enemy along with the discriminatory U.S. Army. It was the mind and mindless forces that killed so many of their numbers. To this day, the road runs like a great gray scar through those lush tropical jungles. As a member of the armed forces of the 1960s, I have a different memory. I embraced the jungle not as something to be feared, not as a thing to be conquered, but as a place to be understood and cherished. My fellow Marines and I were the "Forest Ghosts" that the superstitious Indo-Chinese feared and in some cases worshipped. We became part of the forest, and it protected us as its children. The majority of our enemies were city dwellers unused to the demanding ways of the jungles and unprepared for its eccentricities. It was a dangerous place that did not long abide fools. In many ways it pleases me that we became part of their mythology. We are the modern-day bogeymen that Indo-Chinese mothers tell their children to be wary of if they wander too far into the jungle alone.

So my own military experiences and impressions of service differ somewhat with Grillo's. Yet we both served our country in a time of war—a country that we both wanted to claim and needed to claim us. Every man has to fight his own battle in his own time. We both did. To that extent, we were successful soldiers, each in our own way.

Peter: As the moderator of this panel presentation, I want to follow the notion that Grillo's book is based on a man's search for his true identity. Not so much in the sense of not "knowing" who I am but wondering why my life took certain roads. Did my upbringing contribute to my failures or successes in my life and career? Why am I, who am I, and how did I get here? I based my moderator approach on this basic human need to search for identity—our own and Grillo's.

As I see it, an identity can be created with dreams and goals that will help us make a difference and find our place in an ever-changing world. Each panelist and the moderator tried not only to present Grillo and interpret his work but also to find a personal connection to his identity as a black Cuban, black American. Each presenter helped create Grillo's identity with each part of our panel presentation, while our own efforts to affirm Grillo's identity through respect created an affirmation of our own identities that night of the presentation. After visiting with Grillo, I know that his personal "discovered" identity explains the fact that at this octogenarian point in his life, he is a happy, well-rounded individual with good memories and continued plans for the future.

We enjoyed this communal panel experience, and all worked well as a group, each one tackling a section that held the most promise for personal growth and reflection. The presence of the author helped clarify misconceptions about his writing, so we could better understand his literacy in his many communities. We misconceived that he was an unhappy child, painfully aware of racial issues. Grillo says that he was not—that he was a happy, normal child who was loved by family and friends alike.

Grillo's *Black Cuban, Black American* strikes a blow at segregated America. It tells the story of a man who battled prejudices that unfortunately still haunt America today. Despite all of the adversity, he triumphed and contributed to making his country a better place for all. His black Cuban, black American upbringing gave him the best of both worlds, one foot in the old world and one foot in the new land of promise. Through courage and tenacity, Grillo found his place as we hope others will in our predominantly Hispanic community for years to come.

Reading Circles

Rachel, Dundee, Jennifer N.: The English Department traditionally held reading circles on campus to prepare community members for University Author's Day. We tried to do something different here by moving beyond the university to embrace the community at large. To involve as many community members as possible, we held the event off campus, made lists of community organizations, made note of contact persons, and sent out invitations to the reading circle in the weeks leading up to the event. We also posted announcements in various local bookstores, as well as at some local churches. This served not only as a springboard for other events planned in honor of University Author's Day but also the exploration of the various identities within our community to foster connections between persons of diverse backgrounds.

In his interview, Grillo said, "There is nothing terminal about learning . . . [and] I will learn how to be who I am until the day I die." To us, this was the crux, the pinnacle, the enticement of the memoir—the lifetime, evolving process and complexities of owning self.

So for this reading circle we did not just want to inform but rather to plea, entice, invite, challenge, demand, command, negotiate, and position ourselves for others to hear and respond, think, act, do, and be, in recognition and opposition of who we are and what we represented, even as we questioned our own moves to define what we knew, thought, and believed. It is a dance, you see, a dance for recognition that is not smooth or equalizing.

The Preparation

Rachel: The genesis of this reading circle revolved around a book, a simple memoir, of no consequence, it would seem initially, except that the author's life breathed, melded, disjointed, revealed, and disconnected the complexities of living, of moving, and of being in this world.

Dundee: We each collected information according to our own interests and pooled these resources to compile a primitive but functional Web site and a notebook of essays, photos, and historical information to the text. We made these available to the university community. We left copies of the notebook and of Grillo's book, as well as a stack of flyers about the reading circle and Grillo's reading, in the coffee shop as advertising.

Rachel: So, in the forefront, we educated ourselves through the power of naming. We pulled snapshots of faces, places, and ideas that represented the realities and revolutions that defined eras of Grillo's life—even as, I think, we began to realize and reconcile these same kinds of realities and the revolutions that defined the eras of Grillo's life.

Dundee and Rachel: In the background, we had to reconcile what we internalized as the fractured pieces of Grillo's identity (black Cuban, black American) with our own experiences and multifaceted identities.

Jennifer N.: In preparing for the reading, we considered questions that would help circle participants make connections between their own self/identity constructions and Grillo's recorded identity construction. He spent time telling his own story. We asked ourselves, "How can we each define our own stories and borderland experiences?" We straddle multiple worlds, even if we are not from backgrounds such as Grillo's.

Rachel: In the background, we discussed and struggled with what it meant to be an American. What is an American? As the only African American in the class, let alone a whole department, I understood what Grillo meant in being unambiguously black. He stated it better than I ever could, in our interview with him: ". . . a complete sense of joy and freedom to be just another black boy . . . not struggling with being black Cuban or American or anything other than finding a group that would have me." It meant that he had the privilege of choice, not afforded to most African Americans. He could be, as he often called himself, "a little black boy," or not. What made this identity and code switching more possible was his skin color, which blurred the boundaries, allowing for the escalation of status in the black culture. With this internalized dialogue, I concentrated on how the success of Grillo's life journey depended on traversing and transgressing boundaries. At every turn, Grillo challenged notions of race through assimilation into a race historically, culturally, politically, economically, and socially oppressed.

Dundee: I chose to focus on the idea of hybridization, blended identities, and "American" identity, as this is something I meditated on after reading his book. America is a country peopled by immigrants and the descendents of immigrants. Labels such as "black American," "Mexican American," and "Irish American," for example, mark our heritages, but sometimes they are adopted or thrust upon us. Sometimes they represent marks of culture and sometimes of race, and, sadly, differences are not yet equal in the United States. At what point do hyphenations become markers of otherness? Is there such a thing as an "American"? Are some hyphenations more divisive than others? Grillo's life shows us that some hyphenations meant separations.

Jennifer N.: When I read this book a few weeks ago, I was struck by the idea of the segregation of troops during World War II. My friend, a veteran, came to share his experiences with my high school classes. He was shot down over Germany and held in a POW camp for seven months. The officers resided in large bunk rooms. At one point, they received word of a captured African American pilot being assigned to their room. One soldier voiced racist comments and refused to stay in a room with the new prisoner. The other eighteen men loudly put the dissenter in his place and said they would protect the new man: "He fought and sacrificed for all Americans; he can stay with us." Since this was the only story I had heard about race and soldiers during World War II, I was surprised to read of Grillo's experiences of segregation and sometimes humiliating incidents. But as he commented, it really does depend on the attitude of the officers in charge.

At the time of the reading circle, we were on the brink of another international conflict; it seemed appropriate to consider the military's historical role at the forefront of racial integration and if strides toward ethnic appreciation and harmony still occur today.

The Event

Jennifer N.: Allowing graduate students free rein to design and implement a community reading circle gave us an opportunity to practice service learning. We have experience planning classes for first-year college students; this proved to be excellent practice for teaching assistants to plan an event geared to and targeted for the city community.

Dundee: We intended to explore identity formation, and many participants helped this happen by sharing their life experiences. In retrospect, this is interesting because of Grillo's comment in an interview several weeks later: "I recommend to everybody that they write a book—especially if they are concerned with just telling a story. . . . Don't write it for a Great American Novel, or to make you famous or rich—write it because you have to know yourself."

Most participants were either class members or TAMU-CC faculty, but we did succeed in enticing a few members from the larger community to join us, and a few students brought along family members they felt would be interested in the book. Though we did not have the expected turnout, those who did attend were interested and engaged. Those persons did attend Grillo's reading, so our plan to have a reading circle to support the author's reading did successfully work out.

The Future

Jennifer N.: This event was affirming to me as a student, a community member, and an educator. I loved the intimacy and safety of the small discussion setting. As a high school and first-year college teacher, this event helped me practice discussion facilitation.

Dundee: This event was important for community literacy because it showed people engaging with the written word and trying to find connections to that word, and to each other. It became a transformative experience—helping us develop a richer understanding of our multicultural community in South Texas. We began to understand that we all possess layers to our identities, most of them invisible. This realization helped us see others more truly by helping remove preconceived expectations; this cannot help but carry over to the ways our communities act, react, and interact.

Though planning and participating in the reading circle created a successful service-learning experience for us, we discussed ways to extend this experience outside of the academy. For example, the Moody and Miller students who would soon arrive on campus for the Creative Writing Introductory classes were not part of the panel presentations or reading circle.

Jennifer N.: High school students have so much to add to reading circles, especially if the book appeals to their sense of self-discovery and self-definition. They also learn a lot about themselves and the text.

Dundee: By extending our plans to include these students, this experience could go from a liberatory learning experience for us to an ongoing event that encourages us to make connections between the academy and community at large; it would also begin a more involved service learning program, from which both our department and Corpus Christi could benefit. Without some kind of follow-up, this is not really a true service learning or community literacy project but the seeds of one.

Dundee and Jennifer N.: The chance for high school students to sit in a discussion group with more mature academics who don't strive to elicit any predetermined response from them would be invaluable. This safe environment would affirm and encourage their thoughts.

Rachel: The integrity of Author's Day events depends on the university investing time and publicity. The greatest benefit of the proposed extension outside of the university campus and sustained dialogues among embraced communities would crystallize through the processes of examining and negotiating underlying assumptions, values, biases, and judgments connected to and ingrained in texts. I mean texts in a greater sense—human lives, roles, and experiences in this world. What academics bring is no greater than what high school students would bring to the table, if we respect these experiences and stories.

Dundee: We propose to continue making these events more interrelated, and to encourage participation from the community as a whole (including students and teachers at all levels and community members outside of the academy). The adjustments required would be slight (such as changing the time or venue of certain events to allow for high school students to attend) but would have profound benefits. University Author's Day could evolve into a Community Author's Day, providing a rich service learning activity for the university community and literacy activities for the community as a whole.

Introductory Creative Writing Classes: Promoting the Voices of High School Students

> *I am from Mexico, and I have experienced a lot of discrimination because I did not know any English. But now here I am speaking Spanish and English and now I'm taking French. I'm glad of having met someone who truly remembers his background and talks about it with so much passion.* Qué Dios lo bendiga! (Monica Espericueta, Roy Miller High School)

> *I was moved by what they wrote to me. They are all very fortunate, for they all had the capacity to express what they believe clearly (and correctly!). More importantly, they were able to give voice to their innermost feelings.* (Evelio Grillo)

> *In this class, we were able to learn that how we perceive others and how others perceive us may differ significantly from time to time, but we should still be ourselves.* (Alilehi Berrios, Foy Moody High School)

In response to Grillo's participation in University Author's Day, students such as Monica Espericueta showed their appreciation by writing Grillo letters that expressed their enjoyment of this day and his inspirational words of encouragement. Students such as Alilehi Berrios responded positively to the classes we taught to prepare them for their creative writing session taught by Dr. Jackson. For years, Dr. Jackson worked with underprivileged Latino/a students in Corpus Christi to help them write about their experiences and find their voice as Latino/a young writers.

Background and Goals for Class Sessions

When we started planning for the 2003 University Author's Day, we wanted to walk in Dr. Jackson's shoes, assuaging student fears of entering college. We took on the task of creating informative and fun introductory creative writing classes.

We invited two groups of students from local high schools, Miller High School (http://www.corpuschristiisd.org/miller/website/) and Moody

High School (http://www.caller2.com/educate/moody/moody.htm), to participate in the writing events. The enrollment of Moody High School is 96.5 percent Hispanic/black, and approximately 48.3 percent are economically disadvantaged. Miller High School has a similar student population.

We deemed it important that the students receive background information prior to coming to campus, so we sent them packets of information, including a synopsis of Grillo's memoir with quotes, information about Jim Crow practices in the South, and information about Ybor City. We also asked students to create and bring in two lists. One list consisted of their own character traits from their perspective; the other list consisted of traits ascribed to them by others.

We designed our classes to be student centered, with a focus on identity building and the value of individual creativity—the worthiness of a single voice as an affirmation of self and as a window of social revelation. The activities provided an excellent prelude to Robb Jackson's creative writing class, where he stressed the importance of writing about one's self and expressing experience.

Student Engagement with the Class

When the students arrived, we split them into two groups. An object, tossed from one person to another, designated the speaker in each group.

First Class Session

One of the high school groups came to class prepared as we had asked, reading certain chapters from Grillo's book and their lists related to identity questions about themselves; the other had not done any preparation. When the class began, and we discovered that the author was unknown to the majority of students, we decided to give a brief introduction about Grillo—some of the events of his life, what it was like living in the Jim Crow South—and then we gave students time to make their lists.

Students used most of the remaining class time reading, one item per turn, from their lists. They primarily focused on emotional characteristics related to their identities, not the physical (which was as we had hoped); they also gave some details about the traits as they read them. The student teachers also participated in reading items from their lists. As class drew to a close, we had time only to briefly summarize the activity as one of identity examination and how that would relate to our author. Grillo became part of our group about midway through the hour, receiving and tossing our stuffed animal and making his own character insights. His participation in this informal class introduced him to the students for the question-and-answer session later that morning.

The students' reading lists seemed honest and uninhibited. Tossing an object, the small stuffed tiger, from one student to another as a participation initiator made for easy transitions and a relaxed atmosphere. Some throws fell short, some were not caught, and laughter became part of the unpretentious air. Also, reading one item at a time removed the students from the pressure of occupying the stage for an extended time. We gave no instructions for the students to elaborate on their traits, but we were satisfied when they did so. Unfortunately, we ran short of time. We could only summarize the value of individual expression and relate it to the value inherent in autobiographical works. We wanted more time for student participation on this topic. The high school teachers sat in on our class but remained on the sidelines. They seemed surprised by some of the students' evaluations, and we hoped that they gained additional insights about their students.

Second Class Session

As with the first class, we wanted students to come into the classroom having read excerpts from Grillo's book, and we contemplated how their lives resembled the author's—how their search for identity mirrored his and how it differed. Also, students were to have composed two lists. We started with a round-robin—students formed a circle into which I, my fellow teacher Misty, and their high school teachers randomly joined in. We threw a nerf ball around, and each person verbally expressed, first, how other people saw them and, second, how they saw themselves. We explored the reasons for these differences, bringing in Grillo's problems with finding his identity in a place and time that shackled him with Jim Crow. Students engaged in the exploration of themes and issues represented in Grillo's book. They eagerly defined issues of prejudice—what causes it, who feels its sting, who participates, however unwittingly, in its proliferation, and what that says about the human condition. Students explored the differences between Grillo's time and place and their own and discussed whether racism declined or simply became redefined. They also discussed other forms of discrimination—class, social groups (skaters/preps/goths), and so on—which, to them, seemed rampant in their schools—and what they should do about it. Unfortunately, we only had a short time at the end to give the students an opportunity to explore the importance of hearing Grillo's story—what that did for him and for those of his time and what listening to his story does for those of the present generation. The students seemed to agree that people need to hear each other's stories to understand and accept cultural differences. They embraced the idea that people find themselves through writing, admitting that they often wrote for that reason, and that teachers in high school encouraged them to write for that purpose.

We wanted to ask students if they thought writing their own stories, stories they felt were ordinary, was important—who could benefit from the telling of their stories. Unfortunately, we did not get there completely, but we did touch upon the value of their personal stories—an important prerequisite for Dr. Jackson's class later that day. Dr. Jackson attended our class and heard our discussions, and so had fodder for enabling students to understand the uses for personal writing once they came to his class.

Reflections

Stacy: I am amazed how a piece of writing can inspire people. From the memoir of a man much older than I am, written about a time several decades before my birth, I saw similar struggles that I endured, the struggle for an identity, for a place to belong, and for a bond. From this connection, I met with others to share the same connections and to create a syllabus of sorts to help high school students take a crucial step in battling the struggles they are about to face.

Misty: Whether we realized it or not, this event went beyond what the world was like in the past; it linked that world to today. Students realized that issues, such as identity and perception, remain immediate and pertinent. This realization will never change. We must realize that each person is unique and not always seen or appreciated for whom he or she is. We must continue to tell our stories to the world, as Grillo did, to make a positive impact on society. I hope the students walked away with a stronger sense of the importance concerning their identities and extend Grillo's example to their own lives.

Cathy: Emancipatory learning, service learning. Having read Lisa Delpit and Mike Rose, I became fascinated at how Grillo lived the ideas advanced by these social expressivists—telling his life in an open, joyous way to show the world his world. By telling his story, he validates Cuban Americans, the black men living in Jim Crow South, the poor, the fatherless, and children of hard-working mothers who immigrate to this country and try to fit in. His story is universal and intensely personal and, because of that very engaging. His book was the perfect way to show students that they are important, that their stories have merit.

Conclusion

In keeping with South Texas culture's appreciative farewells, we thought that we would end our descriptions, reflections, dialogue, and analyses with a young community writer and future mentor who writes about his inspirations from this black Cuban, black American's visit to our community:

> I just wanted to thank you and show my gratitude from my entire being. You have taught me more in one day than all my years combined have. Your voice inspires me to continue writing and to always believe that what I think cannot be wrong. I truly hope to continue this journey so that I may be able to help others continue or start theirs as you have helped me with mine. Thank you. (Rudy Rubio, Miller High School)

Dr. Cristina Kirklighter's Conclusion

As I bid my farewell, I want to explain the significance of involving HSI graduate students in community literacy endeavors that reach out to their Latino/a communities. Some of the students who wrote this chapter are now teaching or working at HSI four-year and community college institutions. Others have gone on to PhD programs and may return to HSIs as faculty members. A few teach high school or are administrators at schools with significant Latino/a student populations. I am sure that what we described is indicative of what takes place at many HSI English graduate programs.

Professors at HSIs have a responsibility to prepare graduate students for possible future endeavors with Latino/a students. However, as many contributors to this book point out, some composition faculty entering HSIs are unprepared to teach their Latino/a students. We must change that. As Representative Pat Tiberi, chairman of the Select Education Subcommittee, recently pointed out, "There is no doubt that HSIs improve access to higher education for Hispanic and disadvantaged students, and are committed to providing academic excellence. HSIs enroll and graduate thousands of students each year, and enrollments at these institutions are climbing" (U.S House Education & Workforce Committee 2005). With our government's commitment in the last ten years to support excellence in education for Latino/a students at HSIs, we as compositionists must address and fulfill this national commitment within and beyond our classrooms.

Note

1. The memoir focuses on the first twenty-six years of his life, where he lived on the boundaries of black Cuban and black American societies. Like many from black immigrant families living in Jim Crow South, he joined the black American community to attain an education and to escape poverty. Ybor City, a predominantly socialist and Marxist Cuban immigrant community in the 1920s and 1930s, laid the groundwork for Grillo's radical ideas for social justice and equality. During his high school years in both Tampa and Washington, D.C., where he attended the prestigious Dunbar High School, Grillo learned about the black

American experiences related to a history of slavery, discrimination, and prejudice. As a "poor black boy from the South" who became immersed in the elite black intelligentsia at both Dunbar and Howard University, Grillo gained further confidence in his ability to be a black American, black Cuban leader. Black American community leaders would one day follow in their footsteps and mentor others. In his memoir, Grillo describes the mentors throughout his early years, from his family mentors in Ybor to his military mentors and comrades during World War II, who helped shape his growing commitment to community organization. Because of Grillo's love and respect for others who helped him, these community mentors not only served as a force of positive advice and direction, they represented models for his future work as a local and national community activist. In later years, he worked side by side with Chicano leaders such as César Chávez and Herman Gallegos, as well as African Amerian leaders such as Lionel Wilson and William Byron Rumford.

Works Cited

Grillo, Evelio. 2000. *Black Cuban, Black American: A Memoir.* Houston, TX: Arte Publico Press.

U.S. Census Bureau. 2003. State & County Quick Facts: Corpus Christi, Texas. http://www.quickfacts.census.gov/qfd/states/48/4817000.html (accessed April 20 2006).

U.S. House Education & Workforce Committee. 2005. "Hispanic-Serving Institutions of Higher Education Expand College Access, Field Hearing Shows." *U.S. House Education & Workforce Committee News Update.* (May 2).

Villanueva, Victor. 1993. *Bootstraps: From an American Academic of Color.* Urbana, IL: National Council of Teachers of English.

CONTRIBUTORS

Robert J. Affeldt is an assistant professor of rhetoric and composition at the University of Texas-Pan American. He teaches courses in first-year and advanced composition, personal and autobiographical narrative, and a graduate seminar on the rhetoric of metaphor. His research focuses on metaphor, narrative, and the personal essay as ways of reasoning, inventing, and negotiating cultural discourse.

Jennifer Anderson received her BA from the University of Houston-Victoria and her MA from Texas A&M University-Corpus Christi. Currently she teaches for the University of Houston, grades for the SAT, and also tutors as an online e-instructor.

Isabel Araiza, assistant professor of sociology at Texas A&M University-Corpus Christi, teaches Sociology of Education, Sociology of Aging, Sociology of Family, and Social Class and Inequality. She received her PhD in May 2004 and is collaborating on a project addressing literacy practices in the classroom at Texas A&M University-Corpus Christi.

Isis Artze-Vega, a full-time lecturer in the University of Miami's Composition Department, is one of the cowriters of the text *Composing Inquiry,* an inquiry-based composition textbook written by members of the UM program (forthcoming with Pearson). A graduate of Duke University (BA) and the University of Miami (MA), she worked as a journalist for publications including *People en Español, The Hispanic Outlook in Higher Education,* and *Hispanic Magazine* prior to teaching.

Isabel Baca is an assistant professor of English at the University of Texas-El Paso, and she received her PhD from New Mexico State University. For ten years, she taught writing courses at El Paso Community College, where she also served as an English Discipline coordinator and a Service Learning Program coordinator. Her teaching and research focus on workplace communication, basic writing, bilingualism, intercultural communication, community writing, and discourse analysis.

Diana Cárdenas, associate professor of English at Texas A&M University-Corpus Christi, teaches undergraduate and graduate courses in advanced composition, technical writing, and teacher preparation. Her areas of specialization include service learning, intercultural communication, and the interconnectedness of literacy, race, gender, and identity. Her article, "Creating an Identity: Personal, Academic, and Civic Literacies," appears in *Latino/a Discourses: On Language, Identity, and Literacy Education* by Kells, Balester, and Villanueva (Heinemann, 2004). She has published articles in *Technical Communication Quarterly* and *Language and Learning across the Disciplines.* Her service on community boards allows her to incorporate local needs into her curriculum.

Humberto (Tito) Cárdenas Jr. holds an MA in rhetoric and composition from Texas A&M University-Corpus Christi. He was a public schoolteacher in Laredo, Texas, for three years and a composition instructor at Texas A&M University-Corpus Christi. An English instructor at Laredo Community College-South, he is involved in literacy, intercultural rhetoric, border rhetoric, writing center issues, computer-based writing instruction, and basic writing. He is collaborating on an article with Isabel Araiza, Susan Wolff Murphy, and Susan Loudermilk Garza.

Peter Cavazos, a native of Corpus Christi, Texas, received his MA in English at Texas A&M University-Corpus Christi and was an intervention specialist from 2001 to 2004 with this university's Title V grant program. He works at the university as an academic advisor for the College of Education.

Elizabeth I. Doud, a Seattle native, spent eight years working with a refugee education program serving new entrants from Cuba, Colombia, and Haiti at Miami Dade College, where she taught and worked on curriculum development for non-native English speakers. She received her MFA in creative writing from the University of Miami, and she teaches English composition and ESL. She has published works in *The Miami SunPost's Arts Journal, Mad Love, Mangrove,* and *The Madera Tribune.*

Rachel Eatmon-Hall resides in Corpus Christi, Texas, taught first-year writing, and received her MA in rhetoric and composition at Texas A&M University-Corpus Christi.

Cathy Freeze is an English instructor for the First-Year Writing Program at Texas A&M University-Corpus Christi, where she received her MA in English. A horror editor of *Ideomancer,* a semi-pro speculative e-zine, she has published horror and dark fantasy short stories that include "Duck

Plucker" in the *e-zine Fortean Bureau* and "Cold Blood, Warm Heart" in *Gothic.net.* She is currently writing a novel.

Misty Lynn García received her BS in biology from the University of Texas-San Antonio and her MA in English from Texas A&M University-Corpus Christi. Music, medicine, and composition are her three passions in life. She plans to attend medical school and to eventually have her own practice in family medicine.

Susan Loudermilk Garza is an associate professor of English and Faculty Partner in Writing to the Writing Center at Texas A&M University-Corpus Christi. She serves as director of faculty development activities for the university's Title V grant program. Most recently she published a teaching guide, *Teaching Visual Rhetoric,* with Prentice Hall, and a textbook, *Every Audience Has a Different Purpose: New Approaches to Learning Technical and Professional Writing,* with Fountainhead Press.

Barbara Jaffe holds a BA, MA, and EdD from the University of California-Los Angeles. She is a professor at El Camino College in California, where she has been the Puente English coordinator since 1993. She recently held the position of California's coordinator in charge of teacher training for the Puente Project, which is a one-year intensive writing, counseling, and mentoring program with a focus on transferring "at-risk" students to four-year institutions. Most recently, her own research has focused on teacher training and basic writing instruction.

Rebecca Jones, assistant professor of rhetoric and composition at the University of Tennessee-Chattanooga, teaches courses in rhetorical theory and composition studies. Her current projects include studies of the intersections between American pragmatism and protest discourse and the place of activism and academic prose in the academy. Her article is forthcoming in a collection titled *Image Events: From Theory to Action,* edited by Joe Wilferth and Kevin DeLuca.

Michelle Hall Kells, assistant professor in the rhetoric and writing program at the University of New Mexico, has ten years of college teaching experience. Kells teaches courses in rhetoric, composition, and sociolinguistics. Her areas of specialization (civil rights rhetoric, sociolinguistics, and composition and literacy studies) coalesce around problems related to ethnolinguistic stratification and intercultural communication. She coedited *Attending to the Margins: Writing, Researching, and Teaching on the Front Lines* (Heinemann Boynton Cook, 1999), with Valerie Balester, and

Latino/a Discourses: On Language, Identity, and Literacy Education, with Victor Villanueva and Valerie Balester (Heinemann Boynton Cook, 2004).

Cristina Kirklighter is an associate professor of rhetoric and composition at Texas A&M University-Corpus Christi, where she teaches graduate and undergraduate courses in composition theory, the personal essay, autobiography, technical writing, and ethnic literature. She has published *Voices and Visions: Refiguring Ethnography in Composition* (Boynton-Cook, 1997), coedited with Cloe Vincent and Joe Moxley, and she authored *Traversing the Democratic Borders of the Essay* (State University of New York Press, 2002). She served as a member on the CCCC's Executive Committee and the Ad Hoc Committee Guidelines for the Ethical Conduct of Research in Composition Studies.

Dundee Lackey is a PhD student in the Rhetoric and Writing Program at Michigan State University and is working on a dual concentration in cultural rhetorics and digital rhetoric/professional writing as a graduate teaching assistant in MSU's Tier One Writing Program, which gives her the opportunity to teach a variety of first-year writing courses such as American Women and the Media.

Jody Millward, former TYCA chair, CCCC's Executive Committee, and current chair, TYCA Research Initiative Committee, cofounded Santa Barbara City College's Multicultural English Transfer (MET) program. The program received state and national awards for academic excellence and increased success rates of underrepresented students. Millward cofounded SBCC's College Achievement Program (a collaboration of English and mathematics, with 80 percent to 90 percent enrollment of students of color).

Susan Wolff Murphy is an assistant professor of English at Texas A&M University-Corpus Christi. For the third year, she is inhabiting the "dual citizenship" role as director of the First-Year Learning Communities Program and coordinator of the First-Year Writing Program. Previously she served as coordinator of the Writing Center. Her current research projects focus on the literate and language practices of Latino/a students, teaching civic engagement as part of the first-year experience, and writing attitudes and practices of undergraduate students.

Beatrice Méndez Newman, professor of English at the University of Texas-Pan American, has been Writing Center director and coordinator of Freshman English, and Developmental English, and English Teacher Certification. Her articles have appeared in *The Writing Center Journal, The Writing Lab Newsletter, The Journal of College Reading and Learning, English in*

Texas, and *Perspectives on Practice in Developmental Education*. Her book, *English Teacher Certification in Texas*, was published by Allyn and Bacon.

Marianne Pita, associate professor of English at Bronx Community College, holds a PhD from New York University. Her publications on the Dominican community, coauthored with Sharon Utakis, include "An Educational Policy for Negotiating Transnationalism," in *Reclaiming the Local in Language Policy and Practice*, "Educational Policy for the Transnational Dominican Community," in *Journal of Language, Identity, and Education*, and "Placing Our Students at the Center of the Curriculum: Literature for Dominican Americans," in *Community College Humanities Review*.

Dora Ramírez-Dhoore is an assistant professor of American literature at Boise State University. Her forthcoming publication, *Reworlding Composition with Studies in Writing and Rhetoric* (coauthored with Damian Baca and Patricia Trujillo), focuses on Latina/o rhetorical theory specific to teaching and writing. Her work, "The Cyberborderland: Surfing the Web for Xicanidad," published in *Chicana/Latina Studies*, examines Chicana identity through a rhetorical lens, listening for the way alternative discourses find shape in the public sphere.

Jennifer Nelson Reynolds received her MA in 2003 from Texas A&M University-Corpus Christi. She is an adjunct instructor for Embry-Riddle University.

David Starkey is editor of *Teaching Writing Creatively* (Boynton Cook, 1998) and *Genre By Example: Writing What We Teach* (Boynton Cook, 2001). He cowrote, with Wendy Bishop, *Keywords in Creative Writing* (Utah State University Press, 2006). He and Bishop also coedited *In Praise of Pedagogy* (Boynton Cook, 2000).

Sandra Starkey, former director of the MET program and director of composition, recently completed a sabbatical project on Generation1.5. She has presented locally, statewide, and nationally on the pedagogy of teaching in a multicultural classroom.

Belkys Torres is a graduate student in the Department of English at the University of Notre Dame. Her interests lie in the areas of U.S. Latina/o literatures and cultures, postmodernism, popular culture, radical Third World feminism, and bilingual education. She currently teaches the first-year composition course Language, Cultural Hybridity, and U.S. Popular Culture, which practices and expands upon the methodology addressed in her coauthored piece in this anthology.

Sharon Utakis, assistant professor of English, holds a PhD in linguistics from City University of New York. She is currently the ESL coordinator at Bronx Community College. Her publications on the Dominican community, coauthored with Dr. Marianne Pita, include "An Educational Policy for Negotiating Transnationalism," in *Reclaiming the Local in Language Policy and Practice*, "Educational Policy for the Transnational Dominican Community," in *Journal of Language, Identity, and Education*, and "Placing Our Students at the Center of the Curriculum: Literature for Dominican Americans," in *Community College Humanities Review*.

Sandra Valerio received her MA from Texas A&M University-Corpus Christi. She is an adjunct instructor of English at Del Mar Community College. In addition, she works as an independent writing consultant for small businesses.

Billy D. Watson completed his MEd in teaching at the University of Texas-Arlington in 1994. He is currently an assistant principal at Memorial Middle School in Kingsville, Texas. He has presented papers at the American Association of Colleges for Teacher Education and has facilitated a number of district-level workshops. He also is a grant reviewer for Texas Education Agency programs.

Elizabeth Worden received an MA in English from Texas A&M-Corpus Christi and is currently enrolled in the PhD program of the Department of Mass Communication and Journalism at the University of Southern Mississippi. She was named Collegiate All-American Scholar in 2003 and taught composition at Del Mar Community College. She has presented papers at regional and national conferences.

Stacy Wyatt received an MA from Texas A&M University-Corpus Christi and is currently teaching online at Tomball College and DeVry Institute. She also tutors online at SmartThinking.com. At the 2004 CCCC conference, she presented a paper based on the "Collaboratively Mentoring" chapter in this book.

INDEX